THE RESEARCH EVENT

How can we research the not-as-yet? *The Research Event* is concerned with enabling and nurturing an empirical and analytic sensibility that can address – that is speculate on – the emergent and the prospective in social life.

A distinctive and novel contribution, this book introduces and expands on the notion of the 'research event', equipping the researcher with the speculative means to connect with the changing landscape of social scientific research. As such the research event is understood as a fluid, unfolding process that encompasses a multitude of heterogeneous ingredients, ranging from the formulation of research questions, through the vagaries of participant engagement, to the practices of writing and dissemination. The book aims to provide social science researchers with practical and conceptual heuristics for the 'opening up' of research practice so that it better engages with, but also better provokes, the possibilities that are entailed in the doing of social research.

Inventively and entertainingly, the book draws on many of the author's own empirical examples to illustrate critically the use and value of these heuristics. As a research event in itself, this book is a speculation on prospective methodologies and an invitation to explore the possibilities of social research. This book will appeal to a broad range of social science researchers, from advanced undergraduates to established scholars. It will be a key reading in advanced BA and MA courses on alternative research methodologies, or a supplementary reading on more traditional courses aiming to include emerging methods.

Mike Michael is a sociologist of science and technology, and a professor in the Department of Sociology, Philosophy and Anthropology, University of Exeter. His research interests include everyday life and technoscience; culture and bioscience; and prospective methodologies. He is author of *Actor–Network Theory* (2017).

THE RESEARCH EVENT

Towards Prospective Methodologies in Sociology

Mike Michael

LONDON AND NEW YORK

First published 2022
by Routledge
2 Park Square, Milton Park, Abingdon, Oxon OX14 4RN

and by Routledge
605 Third Avenue, New York, NY 10158

Routledge is an imprint of the Taylor & Francis Group, an informa business

© 2022 Mike Michael

The right of Mike Michael to be identified as author of this work has been asserted by him in accordance with sections 77 and 78 of the Copyright, Designs and Patents Act 1988.

All rights reserved. No part of this book may be reprinted or reproduced or utilised in any form or by any electronic, mechanical, or other means, now known or hereafter invented, including photocopying and recording, or in any information storage or retrieval system, without permission in writing from the publishers.

Trademark notice: Product or corporate names may be trademarks or registered trademarks, and are used only for identification and explanation without intent to infringe.

British Library Cataloguing-in-Publication Data
A catalogue record for this book is available from the British Library

Library of Congress Cataloging-in-Publication Data
Names: Michael, Mike, author.
Title: The research event: towards prospective methodologies in sociology / Mike Michael.
Description: Milton Park, Abingdon, Oxon; New York, NY: Routledge, 2022. | Includes bibliographical references and index.
Identifiers: LCCN 2021033154 (print) | LCCN 2021033155 (ebook) | ISBN 9780815354239 (hardback) | ISBN 9780815354277 (paperback) | ISBN 9781351133555 (ebook)
Subjects: LCSH: Social sciences–Research. | Social sciences–Methodology.
Classification: LCC H62 .M4297 2022 (print) | LCC H62 (ebook) | DDC 300.72–dc23
LC record available at https://lccn.loc.gov/2021033154
LC ebook record available at https://lccn.loc.gov/2021033155

ISBN: 978-0-8153-5423-9 (hbk)
ISBN: 978-0-8153-5427-7 (pbk)
ISBN: 978-1-351-13355-5 (ebk)

DOI: 10.4324/9781351133555

Typeset in Bembo
by Newgen Publishing UK

CONTENTS

1	Introduction: the research event	1
2	Research questions and the sub-topical	18
3	The research event's fit: anecdote, affect and attunement	33
4	Idiot and parasite: on productive disconcertment	57
5	Speculation: fabulating and fabricating the idiot	79
6	Interdisciplinarity and practice: we are all practitioners …	101
7	The event of analysis: patterns, abstraction, expression	123
8	Concluding … but not ending	146

References *150*
Index *164*

1
INTRODUCTION
The research event

In the beginning ... or the middle

As a condition of the funding grant for my PhD studentship in Social Psychology, I was obliged to attend a methods training session organized for all first-year UK Psychology PhD students who were funded in the same way. We were each asked to provide a precis of our research topic and approach. These summaries were pinned to a board so that we (and our instructors) could get a sense of the sorts and range of interests within the cohort. One evening, we were treated to a keynote talk by a well-known senior psychologist. Standing next to an old battered heater, the professor assured us that one day we would be standing where he was. We were the future generation of famous psychologists. He then offered advice on how to gain a PhD in Psychology quickly and efficiently. Find an anomaly in a sequence of experiments in one's chosen field (say, on some aspect of cognitive processing) and then work on that through one's own series of experiments. What one should not do, he said, was ... and then he started reading out my precis.

In retrospect, I am in no doubt that my little summary was pretentious, overambitious, arrogant and not a little devoid of empirical substance. It would have been replete with postmodern bombast and post-structuralist jargon, all of which was alien to Experimental Psychologists. At the time, needless to say, I was outraged by such unfair treatment at the hands of a senior academic.

Why do I begin with this anecdote? Is it because the events described in it had a formative effect on me? No doubt there is some sort of continuing catharsis going on — especially in light of the number of times I've repeated the story (names have been left out to protect the guilty). More relevantly, it is an anecdote that serves the purpose of opening up what might be meant by the 'research event'. Located at a distance 'in' time and place, it nevertheless — I would argue — can still be thought as an element, albeit small and of perhaps dwindling significance, in the emergence

DOI: 10.4324/9781351133555-1

and unfolding of a research event that I'm subsequently involved in. It is indicative of the heterogeneity of elements, more or less proximal 'in' space and time, that feed into what it is we do when we do research, and what is done through (and to and with) us. Moreover, in the retelling of the anecdote, there is a refreshing (and altering) of the affects associated with the original event that is now caught up in a reconfiguration of times and places: and all these too feed into the research event.

This affective dimension of doing research should come as no surprise. After all, the doing of empirical research is one of the most affecting things we can do as social scientists, at whatever stage in a career. These affects are shaped by numerous factors of which a subset might include our personal investment in – or disillusion with – the 'identity of researcher'; the more or less urgent topics we are investigating; our participants (sometimes called co-researchers) and their more or less disadvantaged conditions; our collaborators drawn from different walks of academic life; and our institutions with their chronic rivalries and contested injustices, and their formal and informal requirements for research productivity, global relevance and, increasingly, high-profile 'impact'. Of course, these affects are not so easily separable in the everyday experience of the researcher. Our sense of self as a researcher is influenced by our collaborations, our participants reconfigure our research questions, our institutions have an influence over what is viably researchable as a topic, and our intellectual community affects the framing of our research field (just as the so-called affective turn has affected the foregoing framing in terms of affect). We might say, drawing loosely on actor–network theory, that we are enmeshed in a nexus of networks or assemblages that affects us in a number of ways, even as we are busily trying to put together something like our own research network to affect the world around us. Such a network might minimally include recruiting various constituencies to identify with our research topic, drawing on colleagues' expertise to formulate and refine research questions and associated research design, working with administrators to develop a research proposal that might successfully attract funding, forging research collaborations and finding research participants, doing the actual empirical research in the midst of teaching and administration demands, subjecting the data to analysis and writing up the results and finding the time initially to craft, and then negotiate, the acceptance of a journal paper or a monograph.

One might read these paragraphs above as a type of vignette – a simple storying of the research process. There are number of features to note. First, the storyline is linear – we move straightforwardly in time from topic to question to proposal to participant recruitment to empirical engagement and data collection to data analysis to write up and publication. Except, as hinted, things turn out not to be quite so linear. For example, as many writers on methodology comment, our research participants can influence the research questions, and our collaborators can shape our sense of self as researchers (which might encompass how we think about data or practise analysis). So, there is also something about the research process that is messy – it can take unexpected turns in relation to what and who and how we're researching (with). Further, especially in comparison to many methods textbooks, this vignette addresses parts of the research process that sit outside 'methodology' as it is usually narrated. Institutions can thus lend their support to research projects on the basis of criteria that are not strictly 'intellectual' (for instance, they might rank projects on the basis of which are more likely to yield articles that can be placed in high-ranking journals). The point is that research is shaped by elements that sit at a temporal and spatial 'remove' from the 'actual doing of research' which is what methods textbooks tend to focus on (a noteworthy exception is Tim May's (2011) 4th edition *Social Research: Issues, Methods and Process* where he comments on how, within a context of frenetic, contract-research fund-seeking, spaces for critical reflection had to be consciously built-in, rather than assumed).

If these aspects of the research tend to get neglected in typical accounts, there are also other neglected elements that lie within the timeframe of the 'actual doing of research'. These include, for example, actions of participants that are so far removed from the framing of the research that they are automatically bracketed by the researchers, or even go unnoticed. In other words, research is potentially full of elements that to a lesser or greater degree make no 'sense'. The argument is that such nonsensicality might be an interesting resource for the extended 'actual doing of research' that will be developed over the course of this book.

One can think this expansion of the research both 'in' time (e.g. the institutional pressures on research productivity) and space (e.g. the co-present 'nonsensical' actions of participants) in terms of 'the research event'. This term does a number of things. It highlights the fact: that research is made up of many disparate elements (that are 'extended' temporally and spatially); that there are elements 'pertinent' to the research that remain systemically and systematically unaddressed; that these elements can affect and reshape one another; and that, as a result, this opens up new possibilities, including what ultimately counts as research. The 'research event' thus serves as a particular heuristic for thinking about a subset of events in the world – those that concern social research and how these events might unfold.

The rest of this chapter situates the research event in a number of literatures. At the outset, we can note that the present book *The Research Event* is itself a 'research event'. There is thus an attempt not only to show how research is composed of heterogeneous elements that co-become with one another, thereby potentially transforming the research event, but also to self-exemplify this. As noted later, the usual hierarchical structure that warrants a research design is eschewed: rather ontology, epistemology and method, and experience with data are held mutually to affect one another. Just as the research event can encompass many otherwise marginal and othered aspects of academic life, so too does this book try to evoke ways of enfolding autobiographical anecdotes, institutional settings as well various 'others'. In this respect, as an event, the book ideally (and perhaps delusionally) can contribute to a sort of punctuation in the seemingly unceasing flow of research methods texts. This is partly because, along with a number of other similar-minded writings, very few of the concerns typically addressed by traditional research methods texts are tackled, and where they are discussed this is not in the standard terms. Rather, such notions as 'data analysis' and 'research question' are opened up to creative scrutiny by being embedded within an expanded version of research, that is, by being grasped through the 'research event'.

So what is the 'research event'? In the rest of this introductory chapter, I address this in a number of ways. First, I lightly situate the book in the relation to a loose agglomeration of work that addresses such cognate concepts as assemblage, care, affect, invention, otherness. This will lead on to a discussion of the idea of the 'event' and in particular how it links to a world conceptualized as 'in process' – that is, to a 'world of becoming'. The implications of such a vision of the event for the social research process are then elaborated, and the notion of 'research event' is re-introduced and expanded. The chapter ends with an outline of the chapters.

Situating this book

It has become increasingly apparent through a number of recent debates around the nature of the empirical (e.g. Adkins and Lury, 2009; Ruppert et al., 2013), the 'inventiveness' and 'liveness' of methods (e.g. Lury and Wakeford, 2012; Back and Puwar, 2012) and the involutions of interdisciplinarity (e.g. Barry and Born, 2013a; Lury et al., 2018) that social scientific methodology is at something of a crossroads. In light of the performativity of their methods, the complexity and sociomateriality of their data, and the processuality of their research questions, social scientists are increasingly turning their attention towards new theoretical and practical techniques. Thus, we find growing interest in thinking in terms of, and operationalizing, care and otherness, engagement, participation and experimentation, multiplicity and mutual becoming, to name but a few of the more obvious developments. All of these serve as means for incorporating, on the one hand, a sense of the ways in which social scientists construct their objects of study and constitute others that are more or less neglected, and, on the other hand, a reflection on how researchers themselves, in the process of doing research, are emergent along with their human and nonhuman co-participants.

The volume will draw on several discussions that inhabit this dispersed landscape of emerging social scientific methodology (and associated theory). In particular, it will draw inspiration from recent process-oriented work in the social sciences, comingling several theoretical and methodological issues that have arisen in discussions about how best to engage empirically in a sociomaterial world marked by process and emergence. Central here are such concerns as heterogeneity and otherness (e.g. Law, 2004; Hinchliffe, 2007; Braidotti, 2013), affect and care (e.g. Anderson, 2014; Puig, 2011), multiplicity and co-becoming (Barad, 2007; Mol, 2002), speculation and virtuality (e.g. Wilkie et al., 2017; Ardevol et al., 2016), temporality and futurity (e.g. Adam and Groves, 2007; Coleman and Tutton, 2017), topology, performativity and assemblage (e.g. Lury et al., 2012; Law, 2004), aesthetics and experience (e.g. Highmore, 2002, Massumi, 2011), accountability and interdisciplinarity (e.g. Barry and Born, 2013a; Lury et al., 2018), multi-sensoriality and more-than-representationality (e.g. Pink, 2012; Thrift, 2008). It goes without saying that this is a hugely underpopulated list: many more authors could have been mobilized, and several more concepts and frameworks could have been referenced. But then, that is ever the case.

With this partial backdrop in place, my aim is to provide a, hopefully, distinctive and novel contribution to the methodological elements of this shifting intellectual terrain. In particular, I will introduce and expand on the notion of the 'research event' (along with related concepts and techniques – see next). The 'research event' as deployed here serves several interwoven heuristic functions. For example, it allows us:

- to question what goes into a research event, especially, the heterogeneity of its constitutive elements;
- to consider the performativity entailed in the research event – how does research practice compose the sociomaterial world by engaging with it through the particular research event?
- to address how those elements affect one another, co-becoming in the process, and potentially altering the character and status of the research event;
- to speculate on the emergence of new possibilities through the research event – that is, instead of 'solutions' to a research question, how is the prospect of 'inventive problems' enabled?
- to reflect on the parameters or borders of the research event – how far can it stretch to enfold divergent entities and elements and encompass different times and spaces?
- to explore what it is that is left out of the making of the research event – that is, what are the otherings that take place, and what are the 'qualities' of these otherings?
- to investigate the means by which a research event is judged 'complete' – when do we know that a research event has accomplished a degree of 'cogency' or 'satisfaction'?
- to examine the various impacts of affect in conducting a research event – in what ways is a researcher attuning themselves, and being attuned, to the unfolding of a research event? And conversely, in what ways is affect disconcerted by, and disruptive of, the research event?

As a condensed list of problematics associated with the idea of the research event, the above might give the impression of a series of cleanly demarcated foci. However, these issues intimately interdigitate in a number of ways, so reference to (admixtures of) them will be made throughout the volume. Moreover, the notion of the research event will be attached to a range of other concepts that cut across these issues. For instance, the idea of 'pre-propositions' alerts us to the ways in which the process of research can engender novel relationalities that require new ways of thinking about empirical connections and units of analysis. Here, the composition and performativity of the research event are related to the prospect of inventive research problems and the possible extension of the research event temporally (proposition) and spatially (preposition). Another example: the concept of the anecdote illuminates the practices and affects, and the emergence and transition, of the researcher as they go about enmeshing heterogeneous elements and disparate others in the process of a research event. The simple point is that the research event is meant to sensitize us to a nexus of concerns, to encourage sensibilities that engage with possibilities of research that otherwise might remain opaque or blurred.

One upshot of this focus on the research event is that the present text is not a typical research methods book. While it touches on specific technique – methodological practices that in one way or another yield useful data and facilitate interesting analysis – that is not its primary focus. Rather, the purpose is to suggest some ways of thinking and doing that heuristically enable researchers to explore what it means to conduct research in a world that is conceived as fundamentally in process. Of course, this processuality also applies to the research event itself. So, the book is about becoming practically – 'methodologically', if one insists – sensitized to being entangled in a world characterized by heterogeneity, emergence and possibility. How does one explore, engage and enact this processual world of which 'one' is indissolubly a part?

Now, what is meant by 'sensibility'? For present purposes, I suggest that it embodies a nexus of features. If I were to set these out, included would be aspirations towards openness, incompleteness, partiality, possibility, relationality, attunement, intimacy, curiosity, riskiness, differentiality, reflexivity, response-ability, compromise, care, compassion. These terms are iterative between and within themselves: one can ask what are the partialities entailed in reflexivity, but also how can one be reflexive about partiality? What does it mean to be incomplete about incompleteness (e.g. when does one stop acknowledging the incompleteness of a data set and its analysis in order to write, and what are the incomplete conditions under which one feels obliged to write)? In other words, sensibility is recursive insofar as to be sensible is to be sensible about sensibility: when is it too constrained, too exorbitant? And that includes an engagement with 'self-standing' as it were: how is the self situated as an event – both cogent and emergent, or both subject and, in Whitehead's (1978) terms, superject? I don't even pretend to be able to answer, nor in some cases even address, all these points and problematics; rather, in keeping with the idea of sensibility, I would like to encourage a sensibility that engages these sorts of questionings. Another implication of this sense of sensibility is that it can serve as a 'basis' – or more, realistically, a resource – for the invention of methods. That is to say, the questions, issues, concerns, problems raised through the research event can contribute to the emergence of specific empirical techniques and their contingencies – at least that is the aspiration. In keeping with this, none of the techniques, practices and framings presented in the pages below are assumed to be definitive: they might prove to be useful tools, they might act as helpful illustrations or they might inspire 'methods' more appropriate to the unfolding of other research events.

To reiterate, the present text is itself also part of a research event – after all, it reports on various research events (very often involving the author), and in many cases reworks them so that they yield something approaching insights into the process of doing research. In so doing, the present text, in constituting and composing a particular research event, also reflects on the heuristic functions listed previously. In this respect, this book is engaged in a process of othering while simultaneously attempting to 'recover', or articulate with, some of these others. For instance, past research events are discussed as being affected by otherwise opaque institutional conditions (that is, institutional elements were ingredient to those research events). More specifically, this means that those institutional elements shaped what could count as 'pertinent' behaviour among such participants as members of the lay public, even affecting the status of participants' talk as interpretable data. The book as research event thus attempts to rehabilitate previously 'othered' data not only as a way of exploring the process of othering, but also as a means of reminding oneself of the othering happening even in the moment of rehabilitation. The basic point is that the research event is addressed from within the research event, as it were.

It might be asked, what is the relation of these neglected-now-partially-recovered otherings (the particular institutional conditions, the unanalysed interviews) to broader contexts of gender, class, colonial or linguistic differentiations? As will become apparent, there is not much reference to the impact of such 'large-scale contexts' on, and within, the research event (see Asdal and Moser, 2012). This is because, how such social factors play out in the concrete unfolding of the research event is an empirical matter in its specificity. For the moment, I will simply refer the reader to later discussions of the 'fallacy of misplaced concreteness', and primary and secondary qualities. This means that, in general, the 'others' I do attempt to engage with in this book are of a limited sort – they are the local or proximal, micro-sociomaterial and practical elements that are neglected in, or excised from, the research event. Having said that, in the Conclusion, I will return to the matter of how the research event is related to these macro structures and processes that have rightly been of such central importance to the social sciences.

In its concern with the processuality of research, the volume builds on the work of process philosophers (notably Alfred North Whitehead, Gilles Deleuze, Michel Serres, Isabelle Stengers, William Connolly) and social science scholars (for example, John Law, Bruno Latour, Donna Haraway, Maria Puig de la Bellacasa, Kathleen Stewart). However, this theoretical work is reconfigured in the encounter with a number of original empirical case studies developed – in collaboration with many co-workers – by the author over many years, even as that empirical work has been reconfigured through the encounter with the theory. In what is to follow, I regard the discussion of the event to be deeply affected by my – always already mediated (not least by theory) – experience as an empirical researcher. I don't for a moment imagine that I can fully address the philosophical complexities of the idea of event – there are others much better qualified who have done this (e.g. Fraser, 2006). However, in thinking about the event (and, in particular, the research event) as a specific combination and co-becoming of heterogeneous elements, it seems only appropriate that the understanding of the event itself should emerge out of the concrete specificity of combining, or the 'concrescence' of (see below), 'heterogeneous theoretical and empirical elements. In light of this, I provide a broad outline of what I take the event to be and how it can be deployed for the purposes of doing a particular version social scientific research. Put otherwise, the event is, to borrow a phrase from Claude Levi-Strauss and Donna Haraway 'good to think with', not as a concept that addresses the nature of reality, but as a prompt or lure that might go some way to opening up the doing of empirical social research. That is to say …

On the event …

… I want to draw attention to some aspects of the event as a way of exploring a range of questions that it raises for the doing of social research. Now, the event is often understood as a juncture at which some sort of difference takes place: something changes because of the event (e.g. Deleuze, 1990; Stengers, 2000). For example, a new technology is innovated and precipitates a new way of doing things (the vacuum cleaner makes housecleaning easier; the smartphone transforms how we communicate). And yet, in both these cases, things also stay pretty much the same: women still do the bulk of the household chores; people still gossip energetically about one another. It is hard to imagine the event as a 'singularity' at which change happens. The innovation of these technologies also means regulation and standardization, marketing and publicity, domestication into, and resistance through, existing domestic routines. In a sense, such an event of innovation is a sort of moment of punctuation in a flow of activities (and indeed other events) among humans and nonhumans. If there is change, there is also the reinforcement of what already is: the irony, as we shall see, is that it is not always easy to tell these apart – each can engender their opposite. Perhaps, more importantly, we can understand the event as entailing a more modest version of change. Instead of a juncture wherein a major change takes shape, the event can be grasped as a moment at which possibilities or potentialities emerge. The possibilities might or might not be realized, but something new or different becomes available.

To be sure, the event is conceptually considerably more complex and contested than this empirical example suggests. However, what the illustration does is implicate a number of considerations as to what we would like to address when we think in terms of the research event. Within a limited set of parameters, say housework, then perhaps the invention of a technology does institute something socially and materially novel; it is a punctuation and an emergent possibility in the unfurling of 'normality'. But include, or notice, other factors or elements, and perhaps that 'normality' is reinforced (e.g. Cockburn and Ormerod, 1993; Wajcman, 1995). So, the questions arise: what is included or excluded as parts of the event? And what are the boundaries of the event such that it has cogency, or is somehow discrete?

But, before we unpack this, let us consider what comprise the constituents of an event. Here, I draw especially on Alfred North Whitehead (and, on his various followers, including Deleuze who famously took on Whitehead's schema – Shaviro, 2007; Livesey, 2007). For Whitehead (1978), the world is in-process: things are constantly unfolding, emerging. As Connolly (2011) puts it, we are enmeshed within 'a world of becoming', though as he (p.10) also remarks it not possible to warrant this model of the world 'by the force of argument alone'.

Crucially, this unfolding is also punctuated: thus, while things – people, atoms, galaxies – are in flux (and as Connolly, 2011, says, the unfolding of these entities takes place in relation to different timescales), they nevertheless also attain a certain concreteness or unity. The event serves as a heuristic through which to capture both that process of unfolding (and flow) and those moments of emergence when things 'settle out' in their particularity and specificity. In Whitehead's terminology, the event is framed in terms of an 'actual occasion' and an 'actual entity'. These are interchangeable, not least insofar as an actual occasion is a moment in which actual entities emerge in their specificity, while a specific actual occasion only emerges through the emergence of actual entities.

So, what does actually enter into an event (or an actual occasion or entity)? Anything, according to Whitehead. In innovating the vacuum cleaner, people, atoms, galaxies all contributed, to a lesser or greater degree. For present purposes (and this will be all too recognizable to those familiar with actor–network theory, assemblage theory and related traditions), any seemingly discrete entity is itself a network composed of a multitude of heterogeneous elements, which are themselves composed of a multitude of heterogeneous elements. By heterogeneous, Whitehead means human and nonhuman, conscious and unconscious, material and social, cognitive and affective, macro and micro. Into an event, therefore come – 'ingress' – all manner of elements, or what Whitehead calls 'prehensions' which combine or 'concresce' to produce an actual occasion and actual entities. The moment of 'concrescence' – or the completion of the combination – Whitehead refers to as 'satisfaction': here, the event attains a unity or cogency.

There are number of further points to add to this broad-brush sketch of Whitehead's ontological perspective. First, as noted, the discreteness and cogency of the event has to be situated within the processual flow of the world (both social and otherwise). In this respect, every actual entity or occasion, once it has emerged, then becomes a prehension that feeds (that is, flows) into the becoming – that is, the concrescence – of other actual entities or occasions. There are, to reiterate, both punctualization and process in this approach. One of the implications of this, as shall be discussed at length below, is that the relationship to participants, methodological techniques or social data (as prehensions) is not just one of 'comprehension' wherein one is 'separate' from those participants, methodological techniques, or social data, and one can thus 'grasp' them cognitively. Rather, one is also concresced through the encounter with these elements: as prehensions they can shape how one also emerges as an actual entity and an actual occasion. A parallel here is with the ethnomethodological (Garfinkel, 1967) injunction to recognize that there is 'no time out'. Accordingly, we cannot step outside the flow of social action: every interpretation of social data is itself a social act generative of more social data. We could understand Whitehead's analytic as a heterogeneous version of this injunction: we do not step out of the process of becoming: as participants, technique, data emerge (concresced as actual entities or occasions) in the process of its becoming, so it contributes to our researcherly becoming.

The second point is that the 'moment' of satisfaction wherein the diverse prehensions concresce into a unity, a cogent actual entity or occasion entails a selective process. Not everything 'fits' equally into the process of emergence: concrescence is not completely promiscuous. Some elements are more 'acceptable' than others in that they are better 'suited' to that which is emerging. Whitehead suggests that this selectivity renders the process of concrescence 'teleological': in light of how an actual occasion takes shape, there is a preference for some prehensions over others. Indeed, according to Connolly (2013, p.159), more complex entities are characterized by their ability 'to transfigure more incompatible or antagonistic elements into contrasts that are brought into some kind of harmony in the same entity'.

The mention of harmony implicates the issue of aesthetics as Connolly notes, who regards Whitehead as especially sensitive to the 'human-nonhuman dimensions of aesthetic relations' (p.170). Shaviro (2014) also emphasizes the role of the aesthetic in Whitehead for whom '… aesthetics are universal structures, not specifically human ones' (p.61). Approvingly, he quotes Whitehead's definition of beauty as 'the internal conformation of the various items of experience with each other' (p.78). To unpack, this means that prehensions – which are both the 'objects' and 'subjects' of experience (where 'experience' broadly means 'ways of relating') – accommodate or conform 'harmoniously' to each other within the actual occasion or event. At base, aesthetics inheres in the ontological process of becoming.

However, the final form of this aesthetic accommodation or conformation in the process of concrescence is not predictable. That is to say, how the different elements combine – fit with each other – does not necessarily tell us what will emerge as an actual entity or occasion. This is partly because, as these entities concresce, they also go about changing one another. They co-become. In the process of this co-becoming, what actual occasion or entity emerges, itself becomes open, unfolding towards the not-as-yet. In Whitehead's (1978) terms (see also Latour, 1999), this event is becoming is propositional in the sense that it 'proposes' particular possibilities. In other words, the event as an emergent prehension 'proposes' potential links to – or ingressions into – the concrescence of other 'subsequent' occasions and entities (see also Delanda, 2002). Put simply, events are part of processual flows, but how these unfold is an open matter: as events flow from one another, there is entailed a succession of propositions – or potentialities. One implication of this is that trying to grasp an event (which is an event in its own right) inevitably involves an element of speculation.

Before moving on to discuss the notion of event when it takes the form of a 'research event', I want briefly to expand on how we might usefully engage with an event's unfolding, in particular, with how it becomes a prehension in subsequent events.

Here, I draw on the work of Michel Serres, and especially his call for a philosophy of prepositions (Serres and Latour, 1995). Now Serres' is a very different sort of philosophy to Whitehead and while both have an interest in how heterogeneous elements 'combine', for Serres (1982a, 1982b, 1995b), the overarching motif for such combination is communication broadly understood, whereas for Whitehead it is concrescence. More importantly, they both evoke heterogeneous connectivity and change in which entities of very different kinds (at least in the Western tradition) transfer properties and agglomerate. If events 'proposition' such possible combinations, they open up new relationalities that can be approached through the idea of prepositions. As suggested here, a simultaneous focus on prepositions as well as propositions sensitizes us to the potential array and pattern of new relationalities that emerge with an event's unfolding. More importantly, to think with prepositions ideally alerts us to our own presuppositions: are the relations we initially detect analytically as useful as we presume? Can we develop more inventive and interesting units of analysis (say combinations of the human and nonhuman with their appropriate prepositions) that open up more interesting problems? What heterogeneous relationalities do we neglect in the process of doing research?

In this rendition of the event, to focus on the preposition is to supplement its propositional character. If an event 'proposes', it does so through 'prepositions' that might reflect new relations and combinations – relations and combinations that might be open to exploration. In light of this formulation, the heuristic notion of pre-propositions will play the role of a key lure for thinking the research event in what is to follow.

On the research event

In this section, we draw out some of the general implications of thinking in terms of the 'research event'. Inevitably, these are preliminary and we shall elaborate them in various ways in subsequent chapters.

It goes without saying that the research event is as with all events embedded in a world that is in process, emergent. For John Law (2004), in his germinal work, *After Method*, this world of becoming with all its multiplicity and processuality can be grasped through what he calls a 'method assemblage'. According to Deleuze and Guattari's (e.g. 1988) conception, an assemblage can be minimally understood as composed of heterogeneous elements (e.g. statements and matter or the enunciatory and the machinic, people and objects, bodies and thoughts) and their relations. These can both settle into particular patterns of relations (territorializations) and become unsettled (or deterritorialized) where any element of an assemblage can potentially connect to any other part. According to Deleuze and Guattari, these territorializations and deterritorializations go hand in hand. For Law, a 'method assemblage' entails an array of techniques, practices, skills, assumptions, conceptualizations, theorizations that are a recognizable part of the academic (social scientific) world. Yet, the method assemblage also incorporates elements that derive from other domains too more or less distanciated from academia (e.g. commercial, political, economic). The methodological assemblage is the complex medium by which social scientists engage empirically with 'reality'. However, this reality is itself also a world of becoming, of course; it is an assemblage too. We therefore have an encounter between two worlds of becoming: the method assemblage and reality. It is at this point of encounter that I situate the 'research event'.

As Law argues, this is a complex encounter in which reality comes to be shaped or performed by the method assemblage. The method assemblage is thus performative not least insofar as it involves the 'crafting of a bundle of ramifying relations that generates presence, manifest absence, and Otherness' (Law, 2004, p.45). In other words, the types of methodological techniques that are used, the forms of analysis that are applied, and the conceptual framings that are mobilized, together shape what can be positively apprehended, what is situationally neglected, and what is systemically negated. Stated bluntly, the process of research partially makes its object of study.

The notion of the research event supplements Law's brilliant account in a number of ways. First, as the point of encounter between method assemblage and reality, the research event is an occasion for co-becoming. There can be a 'deterritorialization' of the research event which can even disrupt the very identity of that event – is it research any longer? As such, and this is the second supplement, not only is reality 'performed' or 'enacted', but so too is the method assemblage (including the researchers, the research techniques, and the research questions) through this eventful enmeshment with reality. Put otherwise, reality can not only be performatively 'othered', but it can introduce otherness into the very unfolding of the research event. In a sense, giving some sort of voice to this otherness is the point of this entire book (though as stated previously, this will be of a limited sort).

As we shall see throughout this volume, there are various forms of otherness that can be prehended, pursued or precipitated. However, key to all of them is that they are 'problematic' and 'possibilistic'. By this, I mean that what unfolds from the research event as an occasion in which otherness emerges is not necessarily a 'solution' (a rigorous sampling of the social world; a pattern to research data; an answer to a research question). Rather, as Fraser (2010) notes, this is an event in which (and this is the third supplement) interesting questions might be posed, and inventive problems emerge and be addressed. The fact that in the specificities of a 'research event', there is something 'other' (unforeseen, alien, disruptive, disorienting, aggravating, etc.) that emerges is not an obstacle to be overcome (or sidelined, or silenced) nor a hindrance to the finding of a 'solution' to the research question. Rather, what is opened up is an opportunity to ask new questions about the phenomena in which one is interested, to explore the parameters of an emerging problem, how it might be indicative of unforeseen pre-propositions. The problems that a research event yields are thus, echoing Savransky (2021), not the technocratic commonplaces of blocks to progress, but the possibilities of alighting on new ways – thoughts, practices, relations – for engaging with a world of becoming.

This can also be understood in terms of speculation (the fourth supplement). The otherness at the heart of the research event reflects the openness of that event. Researcher and researched co-become within the research event, the research can even become 'othered' in the process – no longer a process of research *per se*. On this score, it is also unclear what it has become: a number of possibilities become available. The task then is to address these possibilities, to speculate on what these 'research events' might potentially mean and on how they might become sociomaterially reordered: we need an approach that, as Isabelle Stengers (2010, p.57) has put it: 'affirms the possible … actively resists the plausible and the probable targeted by approaches that claim to be neutral'.

The fifth and final supplement to Law's notion of the method assemblage lies in how we go about enacting speculation. Of course, we can certainly attempt to attune ourselves to the emergence of 'others' and the possibilistic within research events that are more or less typical of the social sciences. Interviews, focus groups, ethnographic studies, participatory engagements can be mined for those moments of otherness which throw the research event into doubt, and open up the opportunity for speculating about the possible meanings and orderings of that event. However, we can also seek out examples of such possibilistic happenings more broadly: possibilistic events that do not make much sense to us and require us to craft more interesting questions. Often, these are happenings that generally fall beneath our intellectual radar: they are too trivial, or marginal, or invisible even, to draw or merit our empirical or analytic attention. Here, we might turn our speculative efforts to what might be called sub-topical phenomena where we purposively seek out those elements of the research event that, within the presiding empirical and/or theoretical framework, remain out of reach. By contrast, we can also go about engendering – or at least, inviting – openness around a particular social phenomenon. That is to say, we can draw on more or less experimental techniques that in precipitating forms of uncertainty or openness or playfulness – encourage people to explore, or speculate upon, the possibilities that might be associated with particular issues (for example energy use, or air traffic).

By the end of this book, the (idealized) reader should – ideally – emerge with a sensibility that reorients them to a way of doing research that is directed towards the prospective, the not-as-yet, the emergent. As such, and within my limited capabilities, I propose a number of newly wrought or re-wrought terms (pre-propositions and the research event are the first two) that will hopefully serve as triggers or lures for this sensibility, I suggest some practices that might help in enacting this sensibility, and I provide examples of how such a sensibility plays out at a number of junctures in the research event, from formulating a research question, to 'writing up one's findings'. In all cases, these are heuristics: one cannot be too precious about these suggestions as these too will co-become to the extent that they are ever employed as ingredients in others' research events.

Structure of the book

The book is structured in an ostensibly linear fashion: it begins within an account of how research questions emerge and ends with thoughts about how research is written up. In between, there are discussions about how a researcher engages with the research event in ways through which the prospective is variously, and broadly put, articulated, detected, enabled, engendered, negotiated and enacted. However, throughout, there are reminders that all these moments in the research event can flow into one other, can involute.

If that is the broad arc of the book, there are a number of features that might appear unusual, or even frustrating, within a text ostensibly concerned with social methodology. First, while I more or less explicitly refer to various qualitative research methods – semi- and unstructured interviews, focus groups, participant and non-participant observation, ethnographic and engagement techniques – these are barely differentiated and certainly not discussed in terms of their practical and 'rigorous' implementation. There are plenty of texts (some of which will be cited as the text unfolds) that do a fine job of explicating how one goes about systematically, reflexively and critically applying qualitative research methods. Instead, I range across several of these methods mainly as a way of illustrating how, as means of conducting empirical research, they are embroiled in emerging pre-propositions, in the not-as-yet, whether that is because they are marked by, say, disconcertment, or attunement, or speculative interjection. In other words, the idealized application of these methods is less important than their concrete role in the unfolding of a research event, a role that is by no means straightforward, let alone predictable. Similarly, I do not engage with the usual hierarchies that supposedly structure the research process, for example, from ontology, to epistemology, to theory, to methodology, to method (e.g. Carter and Little, 2007). This should come as little surprise given the previous comments on the impact of empirical experience in affecting the unfolding of the research event. Thus, we might argue that the choice of a given method (that, say, excavates the institutional establishment of philosophical or methodological schools in a particular way) can affect which ontology is privileged – rather than (just) the usual account in which ontology predisposes us to a set of methods. The broader point is that these classes of knowledge and practice need to be grasped within the specificities of the research event. For example, though the disastrous interview discussed in Chapter 4 is not framed in these terms, an epistemology and a method are partly unravelled and opened to transformation by the interventions of a playful cat and a recalcitrant dog.

As mentioned several times already, another key aspect of present book is the emphasis on my own experience as a researcher. This manifests most noticeably in the anecdote that opens each chapter, and especially in the concept of anecdote and the practice of anecdotalization. Given, that experience is understood to be heterogeneous – not just the preserve of living beings (see the references to aesthetics throughout) – and that anecdotalization attempts to grapple with the emergence of the researcher, the aim is distinctly not to prioritize my experience, but to trace it as a product of the sociomateriality of the research event. That is to say, the research self that appears over the course of this book is a composition of, as well as a component in, the research event. In any case, I would be mortified if this book was read as an exercise in self-indulgence (sic).

With those orienting comments in place, we can turn to the structure of the book. Chapter 2, Research questions and the sub-topical, focuses on the emergence of research questions as partly shaped by three broad strands that feed into the research event. These are the institutional opportunities for research funding, the local practical possibilities of research, and the constraints on available conceptual framing of the research questions. These are rather obvious elements of the research process, being as they are a routine part of the everyday narratives that circulate within research communities. However, they feature only rarely, or not frequently enough, in formal accounts of method, and especially with regard to their impact on the emergence of research questions. As such, the main aim of the chapter is to propose a few lures for thinking about how the research question can be opened up differently. Indeed, there is a shift of emphasis from research questions that are in need of solutions to the derivation inventive problems which can incorporate the ways in which these broad strands are to be addressed. Chapter 2 also shifts emphasis from the 'topical' research questions as framed through the broad strands mentioned previously to focus on the sub-topical – those aspects of sociomaterial life that by and large remain invisible but may, with judicious attention and a few practical suggestions, serve in enabling inventive problems.

Chapter 3, The research event's fit: anecdote, affect and attunement, approaches the matter of 'fit' between researcher, research and researched, where 'fit' is indicative of the ways in which the elements of a research event cohere, achieve a certain cogency. This is initially discussed in terms of the anecdote (and anecdotalization) – a topological process in which distance 'in' time and space shifts as different constitutive events are brought into alignment. Second, the affective dimensions of the anecdote are foregrounded, and the borrowed concept of attunement is put into play as way of grasping the role of affect in the unfolding of the research event which accommodates its multi-sensorial and more-than-representational qualities. Finally, the relation of fit and affect is considered through the lens of the 'aesthetic' wherein the 'harmony' or 'consonance' of a research event can entail their seeming opposites.

And it is to dissonance or disharmony that we turn in Chapter 4, Idiot and parasite: on productive disconcertment. Here, there is a shift in tenor from an attuned seeking out of the prospective, to a confrontation with it. In other words, how can we make use of the disconcertment caused by that which is disruptive or makes no sense within a research event. Here, two concepts are a central: Michel Serres' notion of the parasite and especially Isabelle Stengers' figure of the idiot. To start, there is an account of how disconcertment can take different forms within the research event, while 'disruptions' can also be chronically ignored because of the methodological and theoretical framing of the research event. I then examine the parasite as a heuristic that can serve to uncover unforeseen complexity and potentiality in the research event. The idiot is useful less as a revelatory tool, and more as a way of introducing hesitancy into the research event. Whether detected, sought or introduced, the idiot 'obliges' us to question our confidence in the meanings and practices that we presuppose in the research event.

Chapter 5, Speculation: fabulating and fabricating the idiot, picks up on themes introduced in Chapter 4 to chart ways in which the idiotic can be deployed proactively to enable or to encourage the prospective and the pre-propositional within the research event. There is an initial examination of the roles speculative fabulation, essentially understood as a storying and narrativizing, can play within the research event. This is followed by an extended treatment of speculative fabrication in which the idiotic is proactively introduced into the research event. Drawing especially on 'speculative design', I trace how, what Massumi (2011) calls, 'semblance' can operate in the opening of the research event to pre-propositions and inventive problems. However, it is recognized that both fabulation and fabrication are not straightforwardly speculative insofar as they can prompt more 'standard' responses that fail to engage the prospective.

In Chapter 6, Interdisciplinarity and practice: we are all practitioners ..., attention turns to the ways in which interdisciplinarity, broadly conceptualized, features in the research event. In particular, we approach interdisciplinarity through the notions of practice and practitioner, arguing that the participants with whom we engage can be understood as practitioners too. The research event can thus be re-framed in terms of what Stengers has variously called cosmopolitics, or the ecology of practices. This is further explored through the concepts of composition, comprehension, compromise, compassion and composting, which are offered as lures for thinking anew about common concerns such as ethics and collaboration.

Chapter 7, The event of analysis: patterns, abstraction, expression, tackles the issue of 'analysis' of qualitative empirical materials. The 'bringing to light' of patterns in the data set is contrasted to, for example, abductive or idiosyncratically scholarly heuristics which engage with the potentialities of data. Once again, aesthetics is discussed this time as a feature of the analytic process, not least in relation to the fit between empirical materials and other elements that have entered into the research event. There will also be a reflection on practices of generalizing analytic claims, that is, on the abstraction from one case to another. I also touch on the ways in which writing, and the prospect and process of dissemination and circulation, impact analysis. The chapter ends with some thoughts on how we value, as oppose to validate, analysis in relation to a research event oriented towards the prospective. Finally, Chapter 8 concludes with a review of some of the many shortcomings of the book, not least in order to imagine how they might be fruitfully developed. In keeping with the pervasive sensibility of openness, I 'end' with a few 'idiotic slogans'.

Acknowledgements

The Research Event has drawn on many studies that I've been involved with over many years. While I draw on parts of prior publications, all have been rewritten for the purposes of this book. I would like to thank all the many co-practitioners – whether academics or not – who were central to those studies.

Without the support of many friends, family, collaborators, colleagues and students this book could not have been written. There will be several names missing from the list below. My apologies will have to supplement my thanks.

Gratitude is deserved, though perhaps not desired, by James Auger, Thomas Binder, Lynda Birke, Andy Boucher, Caragh Brosnan, Nik Brown, Simon Carter, Rebecca Coleman, Tridibesh Dey, Carl DiSalvo, Miquel Domenech, Pelle Ehn, Catriona Elder, Ignacio Farías, Uli Felt, Mariam Fraser, Masato Fukushima, Jennifer Gabrys, Bill Gaver, Priska Gisler, Michael Guggenheim, Mick Halewood, Gay Hawkins, Steve Hinchliffe, Maja Horst, Michael Humphrey, Alan Irwin, Tobie Kerridge, Joanna Latimer, Jimmy Loizeau, Daniel López, Deborah Lupton, Celia Lury, Noortje Marres, Rosemary McKechnie, Annemarie Mol, Maggie Mort, Tahani Nadim, Liliana Ovalle, Sarah Pink, Kane Race, Israel Rodríguez-Giralt, Marsha Rosengarten, Martin Savransky, Michael Schillmeier, Vicky Singleton, Kath Smart, Paul Stronge, Manuel Tironi, Robert van Krieken, Steve Wainwright, Alex Wilkie, Claire Williams and Brian Wynne. Tor Brandon, Susan Condor, Grahame Jenkins, Gavin and Trish Kendall, Marios Michael and family, Bethan Rees, the Russells and Chris Todd have proved themselves masterly distractions over the years.

This book is dedicated to Nye and Yanna Rees who have remained resolutely indifferent, but in an eventful way.

2
RESEARCH QUESTIONS AND THE SUB-TOPICAL

Introduction

Nowadays, one might call it a postdoc: the job that follows more or less immediately after the award of a PhD. This post was less immediately after my PhD than I would have liked. In the constrained circumstances of the mid-1980s United Kingdom, there were not so many research posts available, and my first year of being a 'Dr' was financed by a mixture of unemployment benefit and casual teaching. Then I got a job researching into the Public Understanding of Science. Specifically, we were concerned with the sorts of 'mental models' – cognitive structures – that shaped lay people's understandings of ionizing radiation. I was not party to the crafting of the research proposal, so I can't speak authoritatively about how the project took shape. However, I can, with all due circumspection, retrospectively concoct a narrative which traces the experience of putting together a research project outline. This is simply a device to explore, in a preliminary way, what elements enter into the formulation of a project, the questions it asks and the problems it addresses.

In relation to this project, particularly important was the interest in the field of 'public understanding of science'. This was partly prompted by the Royal Society's (1985) then-recent report on the public understanding of science, and the subsequent research programme (1986–1992) funded by the UK's Economic and Social Research Council (ESRC). As I later came to learn, research not uncommonly follows the money. Second, there was the choice of ionizing radiation as the 'object' of understanding. In fact, there were several options that were discussed, including the rise of information and communications technologies or ICTs (how did people understand these – at the time – novel technologies?). After several visits to a number of sites into which ICTs were being introduced, we settled on ionizing radiation for a number of reasons, not least of which was that we were living and working in an area (Lancaster) with a number of nuclear installations

DOI: 10.4324/9781351133555-2

close by (Heysham nuclear power station, the Sellafield nuclear reprocessing plant and Barrow's nuclear submarine facility). In addition to this, nearby countryside in Cumbria had been seriously affected by the radiation fallout from the Chernobyl nuclear power station accident. So, in some ways, for all its controversiality, ionizing radiation was a convenient topic. Third, there was the choice of 'mental models' as the theoretical framework. To be sure, this was allied to Sociology of Scientific Knowledge, then fast establishing itself as a major force in the social sciences. The overarching idea was how to explore mental models of ionizing radiation (which are socially and experientially derived) in the structuring of lay people's relations to scientific institutions, and vice versa. That is to say, how does trust in scientific institutions affect lay people's understanding of ionizing radiation. This combination reflected the intellectual interests of the principals in the project. As it turned out, people didn't possess mental models of ionizing radiation.

What this short account points to is an assemblage – a nexus of mutually shaping elements – minimally comprised of three strands: the institutional opportunities of research funding, the local practical possibilities of research and the available conceptual framing of the research questions. These are part of what Law (2004) calls the method assemblage's 'hinterland' – those elements that underpin the production of knowledge (or in the present case, a research question). For Law, these include various devices and routines that resource the way that particular realities are manifested.

Having made these observations, we need to be wary of portraying the emerging research question as too simple or singular. These three elements are also entangled with others, not least disciplinary, which will shape how the question is grasped, both conceptually and practically. I recall the fiery discussions with my co-researcher over a whole range of issues, including the purpose of the research. As we shall note in Chapter 6, there is a multiplicity of ways of enacting reality that reflects differences in practical and conceptual embeddedness (see Mol, 2002). But for present purposes, I just want to reiterate that any version of reality is actualized through a panoply – an assemblage – of texts, devices, routines, architectures, etc. All I have drawn out here is that this hinterland also applies to rendering a version of reality that is not yet well-enough known. That is to say, the crafting of a research question – 'what are people's mental models of ionizing radiation?' – itself rests on version of reality, and is 'askable' only by virtue of that reality. Underpinned by a hinterland composed nominally of institutional opportunity, local practicalities and intellectual framing, it is assumed that there are such things as mental models (as opposed to cognitive constructs of relatively limited generalizability), and there is such a phenomenon as ionizing radiation (as opposed to a highly politicized range of sociomaterial risks).

However, as has been pointed out numerous times (e.g. Phillips, 2006), and as Law himself is only too aware, the English translation of the French term 'agencement' as 'assemblage' belies the dynamic qualities of assemblages: they unfold in various ways that are more or less predictable, more or less open. So, how our three strands shape the research question is not settled. The research question – as it is 'operationalized' or implemented as a series of activities (developing questionnaires, arranging meetings, reading literature, talking with colleagues) – can itself be reconfigured such that 'its' relation to those strands shifts. Moreover, it goes without saying that these three strands do not do justice to the complex of elements that constitute them. So, for example, if we dig down into the strand of intellectual framing, all sorts of elements can be said to be present, ranging from theoretical fashion in the social science (with all the subtleties of identification and differentiation that entails) through to the affective proclivities and craft skills (both methodological and social) that partially and fluidly characterize particular scholars.

In relation to our central notion of the research event, what the foregoing discussion highlights are some of those constituents (or prehensions) that affect the eventuation of the research question. Further, the discussion also raises the issue of the temporal and spatial parameters of the research event. In the present case, the research event has been spatially extended to encompass the Royal Society's report, but this could be further expanded to draw in, for example, accounts of the crisis of scientific expertise in the 1980s, captured in Lyotard's (1984) narrative of the end of grand narratives, including that of science, or indexed in Holton's (1992) claim that contemporary society is marred by the rise of anti-science. In the main, however, the idea of the research event alerts us to the ways in which the research question and the realities it presupposes and enacts are emergent.

In what follows, these three strands – limited though they are – are revisited and expanded upon. Here, the main aim is to provide a series of lures for thinking about how the research question can be opened up. Indeed, in keeping with previous discussion, there is a shift from thinking in terms of questions (for which solutions must be found) and deriving inventive problems (with which renewed explorations can be launched).

Following the money (… and not)

In my home sub-discipline (or multidiscipline), Science and Technology Studies, and my sub-sub-discipline of the Sociology of Science and Technology, there has long been an interest in the ways in which research priorities emerge, and how these reflect a range of interconnected conditions, including philanthropic organizational preference through national university career structures to individual academic risk-taking (e.g. Whitley, 2000). Obviously enough, certain research priorities will routinely be set by governments. For example, Gordon Brown – the then UK's Chancellor of the Exchequer – ring-fenced funds for translational research, that is, the movement of laboratory-based science into the clinic in which laboratory-based findings were translated into clinically viable interventions such as drugs or medical technologies (Watts, 2008). Relatedly, this involved not only the funding of the translation of particular experimental findings (say, from stem cell or neurological research into specific therapies), but also the social scientific study of the translation process (see, for example, the UK's ESRC's Stem Cell Initiative[1]). The imprimatur of important politicians can be less overtly instrumental but no less influential.

Witness Margaret Thatcher's late 1980s speeches to the Royal Society and United Nations General Assembly where she stated that anthropogenic changes to the environment were leading to hitherto unknown negative impacts on the planet. In such a context, it becomes possible for the ESRC to fund its long-running (some ten years) Global Environmental Research programme (1991–2000). Subsequently, funds were directed towards the social scientific study of genetics and genomics in the form of the ESRC Genomics network which was composed of four major centres (2002–2013). At the time of writing, the overarching government body responsible for research funding (under which sit nine specialist councils), the UK Research Innovation (UKRI) has instituted rapid-response funding initiative for COVID-19-related research. This includes an invitation to 'Switch existing funding to a COVID-related priority area'.[2]

I cannot say I haven't benefited from these research programmes, whether directly (by being part of research groups funded through such programmes) or indirectly, by virtue of being among colleagues who were working in these fields (who influenced my thinking on various topics, such as the supposed genetic determination of animals resulting in a dilution of their symbolic potency, or the historical specificity of nature being mediated by mundane technology such as walking boots – Michael, 2000a, 2001). Put otherwise, there is nothing *necessarily* problematic about such programmes, initiatives and agendas. In any case, these research agendas, programmes, etc. were not uninfluenced by the research 'community': researchers themselves have an input into their development and final content, after all. Having noted that, it is also worth bearing in mind that inputs from certain disciplines, institutions and individuals carry more weight than those from others. As ever, the devil is in the detail – each programme needs to be assessed in its specificity, as should its influence on researchers' questions.

Now, I do not want to give too deterministic an impression of how research follows funding streams that are allocated according to apparent 'relevance' or importance. After all research councils still have a 'responsive mode' through which other sorts of research can be pursued. In addition, there are opportunities within academic assemblages to find a space where it is possible to pose 'sub-topical' questions – questions that do not map in any easy way onto 'matters of concern' (in both the colloquial and Latourian sense – see below). Nevertheless, these large-scale research initiatives (along with such factors as emancipatory traditions within disciplines and particular high-profile sociomaterial phenomena) can enable an 'affective atmosphere' (Anderson, 2014) which can influence what might be counted as 'seeming' research questions.

But even within the apparent constraints of an agenda-led research funding process, there is room for emergence – even research funding operates within a world of becoming. On this score, research funding committees like all decision-making bodies are potentially open affairs – they (within certain legal and economic bounds) occasionally become something other. I have sat on a variety of such committees, and, not untypically, I have been frustrated by the way in which particular traditions predominate, even when the aim is to support high risk or blue skies research. Yet, I am also every so often delighted by the shift in the tenor of the committee which might suddenly decide to support something rather 'outré' – that given the composition of the panel, or the parameters of the research programme, should have no chance of funding.

This is what seems to have happened when colleagues and I were funded by RCUK (Research Councils UK) for our sociology/design project 'Sustainability Invention and Energy-Demand Reduction: Co-designing Communities and Practice' in 2011.[3] We were all rather dumfounded at the award, for while the project addressed the main rationale of the programme,[4] I at least was painfully conscious of the fact that we had pulled together and composed the proposal in a mad rush of breathless exchanges. More importantly, or so it seemed to me, we were promising to design a methodology (for which we had set the vaguest of parameters), to engage ethnographically and through design processes with communities (for which we had as yet no contacts), in order to generate materials and 'data' (whose form remained opaque at the very best). But perhaps this is what the committee found exciting – a group doing something radically different from the more usual social scientific research. This was certainly high risk, but it might nonetheless yield high gains …

The point of this short and very partial anecdote is that it not only points to the expandable borders of the research event, but also to how openness and potentiality can arise at different moments in its unfolding. As a cosmopolitical event entailing an ecology of practices (Stengers, 2005a, 2005b), research funding committees can be open to unforeseen decisions – where a proposal that is untypically novel or unfamiliar prompts not a rejection but triggers an interest, invites intrigue in its pre-propositions. If a positive decision follows, then this can resource the openness of the research event subsequently. We shall return to the notions of cosmopolitical event and ecology of practices when we discuss interdisciplinarity in Chapter 6.

Thus far I have focused mainly on government-sourced research funding. Of course, funds also come from charities (e.g. the Wellcome Trust). Now, as Callon and his colleagues (2001) have traced, some types of research priorities are shaped in part by lay actors who have key positions within charities. These are people who are not experts in the usual credentialized sense, but who have been sufficiently central to the raising of research funds that they can have a say in how those funds are disbursed. As Callon et al. document, this process is not straightforward, and there are complex and delicate negotiations among experts and laypeople to navigate. The point is that the setting of priorities in these 'hybrid forums' is not always shaped by experts or politicians, but also by laypeople. Once again, there is openness at play: as Callon et al. put it: the 'identity of the groups making up the collective (of the hybrid forum) and the very composition of the collective are left open for debate' (Callon et al., 2001, p.128). In other words, as hinted previously, the identities of participants may alter, new connections among participants might be made, different sorts of groupings might emerge, and the research focus or agenda might change.

Needless to say, there are other sources of funding that are tied to much tighter agendas, where particular bodies – governmental or commercial – require a sort of 'service', or quasi-consultative, research to illuminate this or that pre-specified social, medical or environmental problem or issue. I will not be addressing these types of research, nor will I address the in-house social research that happens within such organizations. However, we can address the role local institutional forms of funding or support play in directing research. It would seem that with the increasing competition for research council funds, universities have taken a much more proactive role in directing researchers' attention to this or that source of funding. Administrators are tasked with surveying the research funding landscape for announcements of new programmes, schemes, initiatives and so on and so forth, and disseminating news of these to more or less targeted academic groups. While this can be understood as a service – one that is on occasion backed up with seed corn funding, it is also a form of pressure. Allied to various types of audit (ranging from the institutional research assessment, through to unit and individual performance evaluation, to research grant capture assessment for the purposes of promotion or probation completion), the regular flow of information about research opportunities serve as an ongoing reminder that one should be applying for funds, or developing a project for funding, or thinking about developing a project for funding. These more or less subtle signifiers and accompanying practices contribute to an affective backdrop or atmosphere, partially configuring the sort of emotional orientation towards what can be seen as a 'feasible' or 'valued' research question. And by emotional orientation, I mean not simply the content of the research question, but also the 'effort' one puts into delineating it – an effort that can vary from frantic (desperate attempts to render one's research relevant to funding bodies), to tactical (putting in research bids that simply tick off a probationary requirement for an early career researcher). Having painted this rather depressing picture, there are nevertheless occasions when the constraints imposed by someone else's research agenda, advice or 'service' can possibly be generatively creative in the sense of opening up interesting research problems. As designers and artists have long known, adding constraints and removing possibilities is a means of enabling openness or creativity (see, for example, Lars von Trier's film, *The Five Obstructions*; also see Lange, 2012, on the use of such constraints in creativity training).

In summary, research questions are shaped by a range complex and diverse institutional elements that can influence the unfolding research event by opening up and closing down possibilities in the articulation and elaboration of a research question or problem. As an aside, I should be clear that I am using the terms 'opening up' and 'closing down' in an ontological sense – it is in the concrescence of the research event that potentiality is made apparent, or not. This stands in contrast to the more limited sense of these terms as applied to the politics of engagement in Science and Technology Studies (see Stirling, 2008).

It should be noted again that I have only touched on a very limited – and no doubt sorely obvious – array of such institutional elements (others include ethical and informational practices, under-resourcing of research and finance administrative support, and the demands of workload allocation). In the next sections, there is a shift of focus, from research questions fashioned through the exigent prehensions of institutions, to those that emerge in the process of doing research. That is to say, we consider how particular forms of engagement with(in) the sociomaterialities of a research event or opportunity can unexpectedly open up and invite new research problems.

Sensibility, sub-topicality and everyday life

Now, even when a research question has been formally or effectively settled for the purposes of a project outline, a research application, or even a research interest, as one ventures into the field, it is not uncommon for the question to begin shift and change. Confronted with various impracticalities or barriers, or presented with pressing prospects (the emergence of an unforeseen controversy or phenomenon), or exposed to empirical observations that are peculiarly resonant or novel, research can take on different trajectories. In the process, a research event can evolve different themes, precipitate the identification of replacement field sites or incite the adoption of alternative methods. This is all part and parcel of doing research: there is a reflexive recalibration to the constraints and opportunities made apparent through the research process.

Put in a different way, the research event is 'unsatisfactory' in some way – it doesn't fit together but is indeed rather inchoate. We shall return to the matter of satisfaction and its relation to aesthetics in a later chapter. For now, the focus is on how we can become responsive to this 'unsatisfactoriness' of the research event, its lack of cogency. We might begin with the idea that perhaps this should not be surprising, after all the world is one of becoming, we are surrounded by moments of emergence. These can encompass both the grandly theoretical and the local empirical.

With regard to the former, in certain corners of the social sciences (and arts and humanities), new conceptual frameworks arise with some regularity. Claims to another intellectual turn (linguistic, material, affective, speculative to name but a few) render analyses ripe for revisitation as research events become 'unsatisfactory'. In my own case, working on publics' relation to scientific institutions, I drew on the then emerging work on consumption, and especially the relation of the consumer to the citizen (Featherstone, 1991; Keat et al.,1994; Lury, 1996), to argue for the need to expand the notion of the layperson (in public understanding of science) from one situated within the confines of a local community, to one that is subject to global flows of information and goods (Michael, 1998). A few years later, now influenced by the increasing centrality of arguments on hybridity (Haraway, 1991; Latour, 1999), I argued that the public should be understood not in terms of its comprehension of scientific knowledge, or its apprehension of scientific institutions, but its prehension of all manner of relations, knowledges, affects, technologies, etc. that served in the constitution of that specific public (Michael, 2002).

Here, a new research question took shape in part out of theory-in-vogue. But this is also a reflection of a sensibility within the everyday life of being in academia (or at least certain sections of it). To draw on a particular turn as a means of critiquing or expanding an existing field of empirical research in order to pose new questions is to be, at the very least, alert to the 'dizziness of turns' (Michael, 2016a) that characterizes one's academic field. This alertness can apply no less to other everyday aspects of academic life – emerging methodologies, emerging research topics and emerging sociomaterial phenomena. This alertness however can also be a reflection of the nature of academia as a terrain of (reputational) competition (Michael, 2018a, 2018c): the questions that arise can end up being more 'business-as-usual' rather than inventive problems with their prospective pre-propositions.

This is not to dismiss such alertness (after all the present volume is an example of it). However, perhaps, we can try to think of an alternative way of – or at least, a metaphor for – doing academic everyday life that is attuned to less self-evident forms of becoming. William Connolly (2011), in addressing how the researcher might attune themselves – become exquisitely sensitive – to a world of becoming, draws on the figure of the Nutty Professor. This Jerry Lewis character suffered from constant distraction – a chronic physical reaction realized in a corporeal jerkiness – as he was assailed by the changing, shifting mundane world about him. The purpose is to marshal this sensibility in order to become attuned to those shifts and changes in the world that do not necessarily rise to prominence whether popularly, or in an academia with its more or less explicit or implicit research priorities or agendas. Here, the aim is to find sociomaterial phenomena that are sub-topical, so to speak: that loiter below the academic radar, as it were.

In the last section, there was a discussion, albeit limited, of the institutional shaping of research. To a greater or lesser extent, we witnessed examples of how the Exchequer, governmental policy makers, or (quasi-)expert constituencies exercised influence within the research event, pre-designated what could count as an important topic – what deserves to be addressed by virtue of its signal relevance to society. The topicality of any research framing, and the research questions that can nest within it, need to be treated with appropriate circumspection and criticism. This is not to say that such framings and questions are not in urgent need of research attention – the present discussion is not meant to detract from them. Rather, the aim is to suggest that in engaging with the processuality or eventfulness of the world, one can also turn to the sub-topicality of everyday life (including that of academia). The upshot of this is that it opens up the possibility for new inventive research questions and problems to emerge, along with new pre-propositions. As a corollary, there might also arise a potential for the productive rethinking of the topical.

So how does one go about doing sub-topical research? The first thing to note is that the everyday should not be seen as a static counterpoint to the dynamism of the workplace, or politics, or the battlefield (e.g. Featherstone, 1992; Felski, 1999–2000). For a start, each of these arenas are part of someone's everyday life. Crucially, everyday life has something ineffable about it: it is both a domain that is exceedingly familiar yet hard to grasp. It is what we are immersed in, and as researchers include both empirical field sites and our academic setting (that is the elements we import from our institutions into fieldwork, and vice versa). It is also a world of becoming – full of little and not so little shifts and changes. For many scholars, to study it requires not only empirical observation, but the mobilization of a panoply of resources beyond social scientific method and theory to include literature and art (Highmore, 2002; also see Michael, 2016b).

For present purposes, I will suggest a number of empirical and affective tactics which, though by no means mutually exclusive, serve as heuristics through to engage with and articulate the sub-topical.

Noticing and asking

In pursuit of the sub-topical, we might exercise what we might call, for want of a better phrase, 'noticing and asking'. The present version of 'noticing' inflects with that of others (e.g. Gan et al., 2017; Tsing, 2015 on the 'art of noticing') but instead of an emphasis on becoming sensitive to the ghosts of human and nonhuman actors whose prior activities leave traces across a particular more or less damaged landscape, noticing here means that we remain alert to what is seemingly trivial and unworthy of attention in our everyday lives. Sometimes, this alertness is incidental in the sense that the world knocks at our affective door.

For example, while idly following threads on YouTube, I encountered a video of someone destroying an iPhone. The very notion of someone purposely destroying an iPhone was intriguing enough, but what really took hold of me was the elaborate manner in which this was accomplished (as I recall now, this entailed throwing the iPhone out of a helicopter). What further intrigued me was this video had views numbering in the low millions. I began to follow this up, snowballing through a range of such videos in which iPhones were subject to forms of destruction that included the application of force (shotgun, a grinder, or a hydraulic press), heat (home-made flame thrower, molten gold or a platform of a 10,000 matches) or chemical assault (Gallium, Bromine or Fluoroantimonic acid). At first, this was just driven by an unreflexive curiosity but I soon began to ask questions: why were these versions of iPhone destruction posed as quasi-scientific experiments, even if they lacked all manner of the usual paraphernalia and practices that are associated with science? What might this genre of YouTube videos tell us about our presuppositions about science, especially as enacted by non-specialists, or what are sometimes called 'citizen scientists'. Is this an example of citizen science or something else (for instance, a form of fandom for a 'closed technology' as opposed to an 'open text')? In any case, from a genre largely invisible to social scientists, a series of interesting problems began to emerge that could be addressed to such fields as the Public Understanding of Science and Technology, Citizen Science and Science Communication (see Michael, 2017a).

I should add two notes to this short account. First, this genre can be treated as 'idiotic' in a technical sense that will be addressed in Chapter 4: its otherness can serve to prompt a slowing down of our usual ways of thinking. Second, as mentioned, everyday life is not a distinct domain, it is something we all inhabit whatever the 'role' or position we are currently ostensibly occupying. Thus, in the everyday life of a social science researcher – in an interview or focus group study, for example – unexpected happenings occur all the time, though usually they are, or are rendered, sub-topical.

A second brief example. I was at a workshop on academic administration which was held deep in rural Kent. During a break in the proceedings, I took a walk along a country lane only to encounter a dead badger lying by the side of the road. I had seen plenty of roadkill over the years, not least when out cycling. Usually, this roadkill comprised birds, or small mammals (mainly rabbits). This was my first view of a dead badger and it struck me very forcefully. Indeed, it made me wonder about the ways in which roadkill was socially enacted, and beyond that, what roadkill might teach us about the patterns and processes whereby animal and human paths crossed. More specifically, it set me to thinking about how roadkill 'speaks' to the then emerging mobilities literature. Could there be interesting questions to pose about the relation between 'automobilities', that is, the movements of various types of vehicle and their sociomaterial 'shaping' of the social, and the movements of animals, or what might be called 'animobilities' that might likewise affect naturecultures? (see Michael, 2004a).

Both of these examples could have been dismissed as 'mere trivialities' – they might have sparked off an affect, but this affect might have been individualized in the sense of being confined to oneself, or one's non-academic self. Nothing of 'import' is signalled in these responses of, respectively, intrigue and upset – the phenomena remain sub-topical. Yet, both ended up raising questions for particular more or less prominent topics: what is presupposed by the literatures on Citizen Science and Public Understanding of Science and Technology? What is missing in the mobilities literature's treatment of the relation between cars and animals?

Remembering and reflecting

The second heuristic I propose is 'remembering and reflecting'. Here, the 'interesting problem' emerges through a reflection on occurrences that, while 'dormant', have been brought to one's attention. This is another inchoate process and many elements can contribute to the recovery of a memory of an event that might potentially be social scientifically interesting. Reading theory, something on TV, a developing interest in a new empirical field, even a colleague's throwaway comment or request – all of these can become trigger to an event in the past that can be rethought in ways that, potentially at least, point towards the rearticulation of a problem. Below, I present two examples.

The first example of memory coming to mind concerns a trip to Samaria Gorge in Crete. I had been thinking about writing something on the heterogeneous construction of nature and the memory of this particular event stood out, not least because I was still suffering its aftermath – a replacement nail growing on the big toe of my left foot. On a previous visit to Crete, because of adverse weather conditions, I had been unable to walk the length of the gorge. As reputedly one of the 'natural wonders' of Europe, I was deeply disappointed. In a subsequent trip,

I was at last able to go. The now fervid expectation was that I would be utterly enthralled by the majesty of the gorge. As I later realized, I was aligning myself with a well-established account of aesthetic experience – namely that relating to the notion of the sublime. However, despite having – or so I thought – broken in a pair of walking boots, the trip to the gorge turned out to be an agonizing disaster. Descending the steep xiloskalon that led from the Omalos Plain to the gorge floor, I quickly realized that the boots were simply too tight, my big toes pressing painfully against the toe cap with each downward step. This only intensified the further I walked. It became apparent that that day I would not be experiencing the sublime of the Samaria Gorge. It also led me, in retrospect, to recognize that the sublime is not simply about an abstracted experience of nature, but that it required a whole panoply of sociomaterial relations to be in place in order for that experience to be even feasible. Over and above comfortable boots (and other garments), this panoply included such widely separate elements as transport systems (that ensured one could get to the gorge in the first place) and relations of identification and differentiation with locals (and their seemingly unserious use of street shoes in such an aesthetically serious place). The research question that arose in the face of this memory of pain and theory was: how does mundane technology – as a sociomaterial arrangement – play a role in mediating more or less skilful corporeal and social relations to the environment (see Michael, 2000a)?

The second example relates to a different sort of memorial trigger: a colleague's request. I was asked if I might be interested in contributing a chapter to a proposed volume, what would eventually be published as: *Walking through Social Research* (Bates and Rhys-Taylor, 2017). I was a little stumped about what I could contribute at first – apart from the above-mentioned work on walking boots, I hadn't really addressed walking (except perhaps observations about people walking with dogs and dog leads, Michael, 2000b). So, I started thinking about examples of walking, and something that came to mind was a walk in Cader Idris, a mountain in mid-Wales, where on a slight decline I had fallen and hurt my hand. This triggered another thought, namely that walking was occasionally punctuated by falling. So, I started to think about the ways in which falling might also be used as a means of discussing sociomaterial practices. To that end, I remembered two additional examples of falling (down the stairs while moving assorted bits of packaging; and 'out-of-nowhere' – where standing on the pavement with my son I slipped and fell, but had no recollection why it happened, or even where, though the affect resounded both for my son and me). The upshot of all this was a consideration of the way that falling played out in relation to different and extended eventuations: the event of falling down the stairs was part of a broader event of a family visit – it mattered in relation to a projected sequence of family happenings; falling on a mountain side, could be situated in relation to the enactment of a particular sort of masculinity and its challenges and subversions; slipping on a pavement highlighted the role of non-representational affect, or at least meagrely represented affect, in shaping the subsequent unfolding of intergenerational relations (the shock of paternal vulnerability).

In these examples of falling, in response to a particular analytic task (to think walking as method), I felt 'obliged' to dredge up memories long since dormant. One of those memories wasn't even specifically about a fall, but about the affect associated with the discussion of a fall. However, what each memory did was trigger unexpected associations. In the process, the research question can be said to have shifted from how 'does the fall serve to illuminate particular (walking) events?', to 'how does the memory of a fall render sub-topical relations to manifest, and thus allows them to re-configure the event of which the fall is a part?'. Along the way, a different sort of research problem comes into view.

These two illustrations are meant simply to hint at the ways that memories might be brought forth in a number of ways: collegial suggestion, developing intellectual interests, even exposure to popular culture (my desire to experience the wonders of the Samaria Gorge owed not a little to the photographs I had seen in holiday brochures). However, there is a proviso to add here. I do not want to suggest that the drawing on memory as an empirical resource is unproblematic. Such memories are always already mediated – they are narratives shaped by subsequent experience, even while the event entailed in the memory impacted on that subsequent experience. This is, in other words, a memorial eventuation in which there is mutual becoming between the memorial event and its subsequent mobilization as a memory. This is discussed in much greater detail in Chapter 3, in terms of the concepts of anecdote and anecdotalization.

Posing and querying

The third heuristic is 'posing and querying'. Here, one presses oneself to think up something that one has simply not seen treated academically – or at least not addressed within one's own sub-discipline – before. As such, the aim is to find an empirical (sub-)topic that has remained invisible, all the while hiding in plain sight. By beginning to explore such a sub-topic, one potentially begins to pose interesting questions to, for example, the family of topics to which a sub-topic belongs. However, I also want to draw on the more corporeal connotations of the term 'pose': one that nurtures something like an unfamiliar posture that might pick up on what is usually overlooked and under-recognized. Again, I discuss two examples.

A while ago, I was invited to write a paper on standardization. This is a classic topic in Science and Technology Studies which focuses on the process by which standards are derived across scientific groups, disciplines or domains (each of which might have divergent ideas and practices in relation to what counts as evidence or causality), and the rhetorical role such standards might play within scientific controversies or contested science policy development (e.g. Bowker and Star, 1999; O'Connell, 1993). My first thought was to find a case study through which standards were contested (for example, how regulatory standards concerning the safety or efficacy of xenotransplantation are articulated in the context of uneven biomedical globalization processes – see Cook et al., 2011). However, I also began asking myself what is the 'stupidest' example of standardization I could study. By 'stupid' I didn't mean foolish, or even idiotic (whether in the technical sense or not – see Chapter 4). Rather, I was trying to identify an empirical example that was trivial in the sense of being so common a part of the backdrop to everyday life that it didn't invite attention, let alone analysis. So, I did some thinking and cycled through a number of examples: I recall chewing gum was one possible case study, but I wasn't sure how well it lent itself to a discussion of standardization. In the end, I settled on sticking plasters (or band-aids). I did actually manage to find some academic writing on these – focused on the standardization of white-skin colour for the plasters, and the innovation of different shades of black-skin colours. My interest, however, focused on why the packets of plasters have standardized distributions of shapes and sizes (Michael, 2010). What were the assumptions that went into this or that number of small, medium and large plasters? What did these – and the various shapes of round or square or rectangular plasters – connote about the typical distribution of cuts, punctures and grazes? In light of this, one could begin to derive what are hopefully more inventive problems insofar as they are suggestive of novel connections and possibilities (pre-propositions). For example, one might pose such questions as: how do these shapes, sizes and distributions serve in the mundane practical procedures whereby wounds are classified as 'domestic', as opposed to medical or criminal, or private rather than public? In other words, does the standardization of plasters and their size and shape combinations serve in the enactment of various sociomaterial and naturecultural boundaries?

The second example of the 'unobvious obvious' arose out of another invitation, this time to give a talk at a department of geography. The invitation came about because of a shared interest in the role of everyday technology in the mediation of the 'natural environment' (see the discussion of walking boots above). Again, I set about trying to think about a 'stupid' object. What triggered my choice of object was the not infrequent teasing that my then partner directed at me. Whenever we went on holiday or the odd weekend away, I would always pack a more or less – usually more – complicated Swiss army knife. On seeing this, my ex-partner would, almost unfailingly, comment 'you're going on a different holiday'. That is to say, while she and the rest of family were going to enjoy the comforts of wherever we were going (definitively not camping), I seemed to be imagining some sort of adventure into some sort of wilderness. This got me thinking about the knife as my object of study. So, I began researching the Swiss army knife, but also began comparing it to other sorts of knife – specifically, the hunting knife and the mushroom knife. On this basis, I went about examining the online materials through which these various knives were represented, discussed and marketed. As it turned out, perhaps not unexpectedly, each of these three types of knife seemed to be associated with the enactment of a different version of nature, each with its respective spatio-temporality. In summary, these can be set out as follows: for the Swiss army knife, with its many separate functions, nature was portrayed in terms of an instrumental environment structured as a multiplicity of discrete tasks serially identified by the manufacturer and presented to the user; the mushroom knife involved the mediation of a timeless, romantic nature of leisurely foraging and increasing knowledgeability; and the hunting knife entailed the performance of a natural environment of personal challenge and pliable adaptability through which self-identity could be developed and expressed. As it turned out, the paper was never delivered as most of the geographers who would have made up the audience were stuck, post-conference, in the United States because of flight disruptions in the face of volcanic activity at Eyjafjallajökull in Iceland. In sum, this example points towards how a particular trivial, or mundane, object – suggested through the intersection of academic and domestic moments – allowed for a particular exploration of different versions of the natural environment. However, it also invites us to think about designing a knife through which to explore more 'marginal' natural environments such as Tsing's (2014, 2015) blasted landscapes, or to craft speculative fabulations of future naturecultures such as Haraway's (2015, 2016) Chthulucene. Here, what are more or less well-known thematizations of the (not so) 'natural environment' are 'sub-topicalized' by being approached through a mundane artefact: what unexpected pre-propositions might thinking these through a knife afford?

Concluding remarks

This chapter has attempted to address how research questions take shape in the midst of a panoply of elements that were, for the sake of convenience, condensed into three strands: the institutional opportunities of research funding, the local practical possibilities of research and the available conceptual framing of the research questions. While these were seen to exert a certain pressure on the emergence of research questions, it was also suggested that there might be more openness at play than might initially appear to be the case. Needless to say, these were only a selection of the constituents that enter the research event through which a research question takes shape. Not dealt with were those 'Other' elements (with a capital 'O' to echo Law, 2004) such as those imaginaries of economic benefit and growth that underpin research policies at funding body and university levels (with all their attendant postcolonial implications). In a small way, then, by listing a few of the ingredients that enter into and make themselves felt within the research event, the chapter was also an attempt to chart some ways of altering research questions that are so formed and formulated that they constrain the possibility of detecting the emergent, the not-as-yet and the potential.

In this regard, the chapter also pointed towards an engagement with the 'sub-topical' – those areas and objects of research that remain under the empirical radar, so to speak. Here, the figure of the Nutty Professor served as an initial medium through which to think how to access the sub-topical. However, this figure tends towards the inchoate, the distracted, and indeed the destructive. The main part of the chapter was therefore taken up with sketching and illustrating a tentative selection of sensibilities that might help access the sub-topical and related research questions. Through 'noticing and asking', 'remembering and reflecting' and 'posing and querying', the hope (there are no guarantees, of course) is that we engage with the sub-topical and thereby enhance the possibility of shaping research questions for the detection of the emergent, the not-as-yet and the potential.

However, a note of caution needs to be sounded here. The account in this chapter is rather too linear. As many texts on developing a research proposal indicate, the process of deriving a research question is an iterative process, a to-ing and fro-ing between, say, literature review, findings and questions (e.g. Agee, 2009; Bailey, 2017). As such the research question does not always prompt or structure the research, but can emerge at some point over the extended course of research. As we shall see, we might think we are engaged in a particular research event when, somewhere over its course, it dawns on us that we are doing something very different (see Chapter 4). Even within a highly structured research question embedded within an established problematique, we might well find that we have been asking something of our research participants about which we are barely aware (see Despret, 2016, for just this point beautifully elaborated in relation to research into animal behaviour). Indeed, initially unbeknownst to us, we might be asking a totally different research question, or 'not a research question at all'.

Notes

1 See www.york.ac.uk/res/sci/introduction.htm.
2 See www.ukri.org/apply-for-funding/coronavirus-funding/switch-existing-funding-to-a-covid-related-priority-area/.
3 'Sustainability Invention and Energy-Demand Reduction: Co-designing Communities and Practice' funded by RCUK and led by the Engineering and Physical Sciences Research Council (EPSRC) (project code ES/1007318/1).
4 This was the 'Energy Programme' initiative, overseen by the RCUK, and led by the ESRC and the EPSRC. The central aim was to investigate the role of community in environmental action funded and especially energy-demand.

3
THE RESEARCH EVENT'S FIT
Anecdote, affect and attunement

Introduction

In the course of our research into the public understanding of science, specifically ionizing radiation, my colleague, Rosemary McKechnie, and I made a visit (around 1988) to the Sellafield nuclear reprocessing plant's visitor centre. This included a coach trip around the Sellafield site, during which we noted the disjunction between, on the one hand, the clean and orderly internal working environment as portrayed on the TV monitors inside the coach and, on the other, the seemingly dirty and disordered external world of plastic debris and unkempt building materials witnessed on the site tour. As we exited the coach to re-enter the main exhibition area we were approached by the retired scientist who had provided the tour commentary. I recall how, without much preamble, he directly asked us if we agreed with the then-current Greenpeace campaign against nuclear energy. We began to mumble something indistinct (perhaps boldly trying to remain neutral for the sake of not sullying our fieldwork, perhaps timidly trying to avoid a confrontation) but before we could even formulate a politic response let alone finish, he had launched into a scathing attack on Greenpeace. I can recall quite vividly the image of this elderly man becoming more and more agitated, working up a temper, giving vent to his outrage. I remember especially the spittle shooting out of his mouth. And all this emotion was expressed to condemn the over-emotionality of Greenpeace's campaigns.

This anecdote recounts a formative event that, arguably and circuitously, came to shape my interest in the role of affect in how both participants and researchers engaged with the each other, as well as the issue at stake. Or at least, that is how I've come to understand this episode. Though it might also be the case, that the significance that has attached to this episode has been affected by the ways in which affect came to be a privileged site of investigation in subsequent years – the

DOI: 10.4324/9781351133555-3

famous affective turn (and modulations thereof). Though, in turn, my interest and involvement in the affective turn might be affected by that early affective encounter with affect. I can also say something similar with regard to aesthetics: the disjunction between the video presentation of the interior of Sellafield, and the 'direct observations' of its exterior were a memorable aesthetic juxtaposition. This sort of unintended aesthetic juxtaposition was redoubled in the exhibition space in which mock boron rods dropped terrifyingly above one's head as a means of reassuring the visitor that a reactor emergency could readily be controlled. Again, this retrospective aesthetic view of the visit to Sellafield might be at once a reflection of an emerging interest in aesthetics in Science and Technology Studies (STS), and the social sciences more broadly, and a partial result of my attraction to this aesthetic turn very partially born of the aesthetic juxtapositions of that visit.

In these accounts, there is a to-ing and fro-ing between past and present, as each constitutes the other through the initial anecdote and subsequent narratives, including iterations of that anecdote. While the anecdote above is one based on an incident nominally situated in the relatively distant past, anecdotes are part and parcel of the ongoing process of doing research, not least because they are instrumental in shaping, and being shaped by, affect, both in relation to specific research interests, but also in relation to the mediation of wider institutional relations. That is to say, they are a part of the research event that relays its shifting, constitutive and heterogeneous relationalities. As mentioned in the Introduction, each chapter begins with an anecdote: this serves critically and creatively as a reminder that the subsequent discussions are processual – grounded in, and constitutive of, prior events, while at the same time (sic) oriented toward pre-propositions of the research event.

Now, what anecdotes also hint at is that their enactment serves in affording research events a certain (albeit contingent) 'coherence'. The disparate – and disparately situated – elements that compose the research event come together and concresce in a 'satisfactory' way that affords the research event a certain completion and cogency (with which that research event can enter into subsequent events). Here these elements 'fit' together whether positively (by ingression) or negatively (by exclusion). Key in all this is the way that we as researchers also 'fit' into the research event, and the research event 'fits' us as researchers. The underpinning point is that there is an aesthetic, as well as a more broadly affective, dimension to the unfolding of the research event; the chapter aims to explore this through a number of lenses.

In what follows, this sense of the 'fit' among researcher, research and researched is approached initially through the motif of the anecdote (and its recursive enactment or anecdotalization). As we shall see, this is a deeply topological process in which distance 'in' time (and space) shifts as different constitutive events are brought into alignment. Second, the anecdote is expanded into more affective territory. Here the notion of attunement is discussed, not least in terms of how it might be exercised multisensorially or more-than-representationally. Finally, we take a closer look at the aesthetics of the research event in order to examine several of the forms the aesthetic might take. As we shall note, the 'fittingness' or 'satisfactoriness' of a research event can entail their seeming opposites.

Telling stories in/about the organization

Let us propose that the research event is situated within and partly constituted by the circulation of stories. After all, researchers are constantly telling about their research – in formal venues, in informal settings, in elaborated narratives and passing comments. At the same time, the research event is a source of such stories as they are both circulated through various institutions, and partly constitute those institutions. From universities and research institutes, through to scholarly societies and publishing outlets, such stories are part and parcel of their constitutive associations.

As organizational theorist Barbara Czarniawska (2004, 2008), Pippan and Czarniawska (2010), Czarniawska and Hernes (2005) has shown through her 'action nets' variant of actor–network theory (Michael, 2017a), actors actively engage in constructing their organizations. Indeed, institutions emerge out of the actors' ongoing perceptions, interpretations and practices not least in relation to other actors' – colleagues' – ongoing perceptions, interpretations and practices. Given the variety of actors within an organization, such ongoing perceptions, interpretations and practices will vary such that there will be multiple and disparate constructions of the organization (or as Mol, 2002, would put it, multiple ontologies). As might be expected, some interpretations have more resonance than others: the anecdote coming from a CEO is likely to carry more weight and reach further than a complaint from a cleaner. In this respect, stories are also central to the doing of hierarchies of various sorts.

The social science researcher will likewise be constructing a version of an organization they are studying. This is because, like those actors – or practitioners – 'within' the organization, a researcher has access only to fragments of the organization and is party only to a selection of the stories that are composed and circulated within the organization. The 'within' the organization is set within scare quotes for two reasons. First, the researcher is of course 'within' the organization and might even have greater access than some practitioners (though may also not – see Law, 1994). Further, in their own partial circulation within an organization, the researcher may become an element in practitioners' storying of that organization. Practitioners' relations to researchers can take on numerous guises that might include enacting the researcher as, for example, confidante (who listens empathetically to their experiences), intermediary (who hopefully serves as a conduit to actors in the upper reaches of the institutional hierarchy) or managerial stooge (acting as another medium of surveillance). Second, practitioners themselves are also partially outside the organization. As Czarniawska demonstrates, organizations are necessarily highly porous, and the different 'departments' or 'professions' of an organization connect with their counterparts in other organizations. In following the associations of different sorts of actors, links can be drawn, for instance, across organizations' various specialized practitioners – management conferences, accountants' professional associations, marketing training, manual workers' unions, etc. However, there are also other sorts of relationalities that also compose the organization: some of these are formalized (e.g. contracts), some are broadly financial (e.g. relations of economic dependency), some cultural (e.g. gender- or ethnicity-based forms of discrimination) and some are personal (e.g. friendship).

In sum, Czarniawska provides a picture of organizations that are ongoingly and disparately constituted through various practices (I have focused mainly on narratives here, though, as Czarniawska insists, various nonhumans are also central to organizational functioning). This approach does not deny that organizations can be stable but sees them as a more or less temporary accomplishment: organizations are 'temporary reifications, because organizing never ceases' (Czarniawska, 2004, p.780).

Now this foray into a particular perspective within Organizational Studies is simply a way of introducing the role of narratives, stories, tales, etc. that are key to the process of doing research within an organizational setting. As researchers we ply our own stories about our own institutions, our own colleagues, our own relations, as well as our own (and others') research: this is all part of the research event as articulated in this book. In the United Kingdom, we might complain about the overweening managerialism of our universities and the sector in general, we might sometimes sing the praises of young researchers in our fields of interest, we might gossip about recalcitrant colleagues who don't pull their weight in our departments. And of course, we tell stories about our own research activities – how this research engagement went well or badly, how those data made no sense or fell so easily into an elegant interpretive pattern, or how this conference audience provided such fabulously useful feedback, or how that journal's referees provided such wildly contradictory assessments.

These tellings of experience clearly mediate affect (see below) – as a matter of course, we enact particular affects about forms of surveillance, moments of accomplishment or hints of communitas. In what follows, I initially focus, on the one hand, on a variant of these forms of tellings, namely anecdotes, and, on the other, on a subset of these affects, namely those born of doing empirical research. As we shall see, anecdotes can be rethought to sensitize us to the recursive affective processes whereby research, researcher and researched can reconfigure one another, and ongoingly unfold. Subsequently, I broaden this picture to take in other elements that might contribute to this recursivity. In particular, I focus on the processes of attunement in the doing of research: how it is that we align with other elements (the discourses and practices of others) in the composition of a research event. This is subsequently discussed through the notion of aesthetics. On the one hand, this relates to a subset of affects that is concerned with form – with the way in which participants and researchers attune themselves to one another. On the other, aesthetics sensitizes us to how a sense of 'fit', or 'satisfaction' (or 'conformation') of a research event is derived. That is to say, we ask, how is it that a research event comes to attain a wholeness, or a 'completeness', or a sort of unity?

Anecdote/anecdotalization

I take the anecdote to entail a short story about this or that event that is of interest and has some sort of point – say, a moral, an insight into the workings of the world, a performance of a version of self. Not untypically, the anecdote is humourous. Insofar as anecdotes comprise narratives about this or that individual or happening, they might be considered another component within the methodological toolkit of qualitative social science.

However, the anecdote can also be said to have other properties that extend methodology into epistemology and ontology. It can be conceptually re-crafted to address the ways in which particular knowledge is performed and valued, and how that particular performance and valuation emerges.

The following observations about the anecdote can be listed:

- The anecdote is both a literary fabrication (it is a story that has been constructed) and a mode or reportage (it is constitutively an account of something that is assumed to have actually happened). As such, it is necessarily ambiguous in form in that it encompasses what is real and what is constructed (see Fineman, 1989; Boettger, 1998). In this respect, the anecdote shares characteristics with Latour's (2010a) notion of a factish, an entity that is at once regarded as objectively representing something real and as sociomaterially constructed that serves in the mediation of heterogeneous associations. As Meghan Morris (2006) has suggested, anecdotes while functional, need not be true.
- The anecdote is a component part of the historical record insofar as it is documented and circulated within 'history', as it were. Because of this, and the specific interpretation of an incident that it enacts, it can have a performative impact on historical events as they unfold. If an anecdote tells what did happen, it also intimates what could happen. For Morris (2006), this impact is likely to be small-scale – an introduction of a minor opening that barely specifies what is to follow.
- The anecdote also enacts similarities and differences. To the extent that an anecdote distils a happening that is worth distilling, it is drawing connections to other like happenings, while differentiating that happening from others that are in one way or another different. In these ways, it performs both the-out-of-the-ordinary and the taken-for-granted.
- The anecdote can facilitate the process of abstraction in which lessons are drawn and links made from the singular event to a class of events. As such, a specific singular event can come to be a marker for a broader phenomenon, or a deeper lesson that illuminates wider sets of relations.
- The anecdote is not unusually concerned with identifiable individuals, not least the anecdote's author. It relays an incident in which the enunciator of the anecdote has become embroiled. But the anecdote can also relay the changes undergone by the individual because of that embroilment. However, the process of narrating the anecdote entails, as we have noted earlier, a partial

fabrication. The telling of the anecdote – or 'anecdotalization' – thus takes the form of a recursion in which past events shape the speaker even as the speaker 'makes' those past events using representational resources partially made available through those events (e.g. narrative analytic techniques or discourse analytic tools that enable a rethinking of the event that the anecdote relays).

- The 'telling' will itself be adapted and modified in future tellings as the anecdote develops and the event is enacted in different ways, that is to say, takes on different ontologies. This is because, the anecdote gathers together new or alternative, or more or fewer, relationalities that recompose the event.
- The means by which past events impact on their anecdotalization is not always – indeed, is rarely – explicit: events can operate corporeally or affectively, shaping the sensibilities of their teller. The teller's retelling can recursively modulate this impact, sometimes reinforcing it, sometimes diffusing or modifying as different ways of telling are performed (and different relationalities mobilized).
- In relation to the research event, the anecdote might seem to 'sit within' it, in the sense of telling a particular more or less expansive incident (from a 'disastrous' interview to the wrong-headed-ness of a research design) that is a component of the research event. But it might also seem to 'sit outside' the research event, capturing and conveying a narrative about the research event 'as a whole'. But this is not quite right. Anecdotalization is, rather, processual: it performs a sort of distillation of the research event, it enacts a moment of completion or 'satisfaction' as Whitehead would put it. As noted, this can be characterized as 'aesthetic' in that a certain form is given to the event. Yet, that aesthetic form can also be 'dissatisfying' by virtue of making available new potentialities or possibilities. In Massumi's (2011) terms, there is a 'semblance' – a semblance that applies to the eventualizations of anecdotalization. This reflects the dual aspect of Whitehead's metaphysical schema which is at once processual and atomistic or punctuated (see Chapter 1).

This is no doubt a highly condensed and inexhaustive rendering of the anecdote and anecdotalization (cf. Adams and Thompson, 2016), and much of the rest of this chapter will be devoted to clarifying, elaborating and illustrating the points listed in the foregoing. We begin with some thoughts on the role of affect within the research event and 'its' anecdotalization.

However, before that, we need to distinguish anecdotalization from perhaps its ostensibly closest methodological relative, auto-ethnography. No doubt some readers are understandably wondering what the difference is between anecdotalization and auto-ethnography: is not the former simply an over-theorized way of engaging empirically with the researcher and their experiences, interpreting both in terms of broader social and cultural processes, and social scientific categories? According to Chang (2008), auto-ethnography involves the interpretation of the self in which the self is subject to a consideration in terms of its similarity, difference or opposition to an array of others (categorized in terms of, say, classes, ethnicities and sexualities). For Ellis et al. (2011), the form of an auto-ethnography reflects the extent to which there is focus on the researcher self, on relations of power, on the how others are brought into the analysis. Ellis et al., in describing auto-ethnography as entailing aspects of both ethnography and autobiography, draw attention to the role of epiphanies – key moments in a biography that take on a disjunctive status because they index a major change in a culture or cultural identity. Such epiphanies can serve to structure auto-ethnographies not least because they can be subjected to close scrutiny and analysis.

Auto-ethnography has been criticized on a number of grounds, notably by Delamont (2007). In her six objections, Delamont is critical of the insights auto-ethnography is able to yield because it does not gather new data, is too experiential and is ethically suspect (in that it draws non-consenting others into its narratives). Most scathingly, she insists that researchers are simply not interesting enough – we are the privileged and the powerful. In contrast, Ellis et al. argue that auto-ethnography can indeed involve the collection of novel data, is analytic as well experiential and entails a relational ethics in which potential impacts on implicated others are discussed and negotiated with them. On top of this, there is a consideration of the validity of analysis which is seen less in terms of verisimilitude, and more in terms of performativity (how does an auto-ethnography empower, facilitate social connectivity, afford a better world?). One might also counter Delamont's point about the privilege of the auto-ethnographer. Certainly, the unitariness assigned to this figure belies the possibility that auto-ethnographers have complex – intersectional – backgrounds that are not simply 'privileged'.

However, both criticisms and rejoinders seem to share a number of positions. First, there is a commitment to pre-existing social scientific categories (e.g. class, gender and ethnicity) which can capture the situatedness of the auto-ethnographer. By comparison, anecdotalization eschews the analytic use of such more or less standardized categories, except insofar as they are a part of the anecdote (that is how they feature in exchanges relayed through the anecdote). On this score, anecdotalization follows the analytic ethos of such perspectives as (post)actor–network theory that regard such categories as something to be explained rather than as serving as explanations of the events portrayed in the anecdote (see Michael, 2017c, for a summary). That is to say, there is a sort of reversal in which counter to auto-ethnography's tendency towards the use of existing categories to grasp and theorize the self's experience, anecdotalization looks at the ways in which the self at once performs those categories (if it does so at all), and emerges out of and through specific events which might incorporate these categories. As a corollary of this, and this is a second difference, the self is not presupposed as a pre-existing site of experience, rather, in the process of anecdotalization the self emerges both as the 'thing' being told through the anecdote, and the subject doing the telling.

So, instead of the stable subject that is assumed to run from the content of the auto-ethnographic account through to its author, anecdotalization takes it that there is a mutual constitution of the subject of the anecdote and the teller of the anecdote through which a version of the subject emerges (what Whitehead would call a 'superject'). In this regard, the telling of the anecdote is shaped by the events – including persons – that affect the experiences of the teller, who tells the events of the anecdotes which affect their own telling through their impact on the teller. Put otherwise, and this is a third difference, there is a topological – Moebius strip – quality to anecdotalization where an anecdote is tellable by virtue of subsequent experience, but subsequent experience is shaped by the content of the anecdote, which partly becomes tellable by virtue of subsequent experience which … and so on. Anecdotalization is simultaneously 'in' and 'of' the research event. More concretely, if we return to the story of Samaria Gorge and the badly fitting walking boots, this becomes 'anecdotalizable' in a particular way because it had affected me in ways which, in one way or another, fed my interests in actor–network theory; the ongoing sense of the pain and the other experiences in the gorge made Actor-Network Theory (ANT) more 'feelable' or useable; and in so doing, the anecdote could take on a particular ANT-tinged narrative and analytic form. Of course, the present telling is itself an anecdotalization – which in turn reinforces the anecdote's topological character.

Central to the above account is the role of affect. The painful experience of ill-fitting walking boots affected what subsequently made theoretical 'sense' while that theoretical sense made that pain graspable, even as that graspability came to shape subsequent tellings (including the present framing in terms of anecdotalization). It is to the complex role of affect that the next section turns.

Anecdote and affect

As mentioned earlier, anecdotes are part and parcel of doing organizations, including research organizations such as universities. A regular element of such anecdotes is the narrativization of affects and emotions: how this manager upset me, how that colleague made me angry, how this administrator's kindness brought about a feeling of humility. This list is near-endless. When we wish to study such performances of emotion or affect (I conflate these for the moment, but see below), we might ask participants to give specific examples, to tell us anecdotes. Thus, when a scientific practitioner displays concern and care with regard to the experimental use of animals, we might ask for, or seek out an, an anecdote (e.g. the keeping of a menagerie at home – Michael and Birke, 1994a). And when a stem cell scientist enacts embarrassment at the rise of a particularly problematic experimental protocol or system, we might ask for a specific incident that precipitated this feeling (e.g. a close colleague who hitched themselves to a failed experimental bandwagon; see below). The point is that anecdotes might serve partly to situate such performances of emotion in relation to specific moments. But they also serve as a way of tracing how such anecdotalization partly constructs those moments (or events).

However, it is clear that these emotions as described are more or less identifiable. In one account, this is what differentiates emotions from affect. Where the latter entails the material impact upon bodies that set up corporeal intensities, the former is a sort of domestication or socialization of affect whereby it is translated into conventional emotion categories (Massumi, 2002). One problem is that it is not clear how, or indeed whether, we can access this version of affect, nor trace how affect manifests as emotion as there seems to be an abyssal difference between them – one is mechanical, the other enunciatory, to draw on terminology of Deleuze and Guattari (1988). As various scholars have noted, this dramatic differentiation between emotion and affect might not do justice to their actual entanglement. For Wetherell (2012), the emphasis should be on the conventionality of emotion as the filter through which affect can have effect: affect necessarily passes through the embodied discursivity of emotion categories. By contrast, Anderson (2014) provides a more heterogeneous and relational perspective on affect. Accordingly affect is circulatory in the sense that it impacts and enables (or hinders) bodies, which in turn are themselves affective in particular ways, more or less able to affect heterogeneous others. Affects are mediated by complexes or assemblages of entities composed of humans and nonhumans: these assemblages vary in their structure (though they are not mutually exclusive), from the highly directed and discrete (e.g. governmental apparatuses) to the rather diffuse and dispersed (e.g. crowd feelings or atmospheres).

Within this formulation of affect (and there are several formulations within the extended affective turn – e.g. Harre, 1986; Clough and Halley, 2007; Gregg and Seigworth, 2010; Blackman and Venn, 2010), the anecdote can serve as a means of tracing the circulation of affect, and its various transformations as people at once mediate, reflect on and enact affect. We can initially examine this through a particular example, the Lumelsky protocol event. By way of preview, we can note that scientists' account of a particular experimental protocol, which, after being lauded and adopted, was found to be fundamentally flawed and was abandoned. But further, as we shall see subsequently, in addressing the Lumelsky protocol event in terms of affect, we as researchers also reconfigure what that event is (or has become). Yet, in keeping with our framing of anecdotalization, we do not see this as some sort of arbitrary or self-interested re-articulation of the Lumelsky protocol event. Rather, that event could be understood as itself an affective resource that perhaps, albeit circuitously, contributed to, or reinforced, our own analytic turn toward the affective. That is to say, the affects displayed by the scientists affect us as researchers in not always transparent ways. Here, affect is a topic and resource, the importance (or value) of which was reinforced by virtue of our being touched by the scientists' affective struggles as they tried to equilibrate the scientific community's momentary overabundance of hope and underappreciation of hype, and to bring a balanced view to colleagues' actions that straddled a disparagement of gullibility and an acceptance of overenthusiasm.

More specifically, Michael et al. (2007) consider the ways in which stem cell scientists discussed their own and their peers' responses to the emergence of a promising technique for differentiating embryonic stem cells into pancreatic beta cells that produce insulin. The relevance of this technique was that, if successfully developed, it might have furnished the basis for curing type I diabetes. Importantly for present purposes, these participants' responses are anecdotal insofar as they are narrations of the reactions and emotions that arose over the course of the rise and fall of this technique, that is, what came to be known as the Lumelsky protocol.

I will not dwell on the technical details (see Michael et al., 2007), suffice it to say that in the early 2000s, experimental findings seemed to show that under the appropriate biochemical environmental conditions, mouse embryonic stem cells seemed to differentiate into pancreatic cells. The subsequent report published in Science was initially widely lauded and the techniques laid out there were adopted by many scientists working in what was a highly interdisciplinary field. Subsequently, it was noted that the insulin that seemed to be being produced by the newly differentiated cells had already been present in the culture medium in which the cells were supposedly differentiating, and it looked as if all that had happened was that insulin had been absorbed then secreted by the cells (the secretion being an indication of differentiation). One irony was that this could have been deduced from the original paper. In the retrospections of the participant scientists, several observations were made about those who had jumped onto the 'Lumelsky bandwagon'. First, the problems were understandable given how hard the science was; but further, many of those scientists who were involved were not 'experts' according to Michael et al.'s participants. The latter meant that these scientists did not always interpret results as cautiously as they should, or had become too invested in the new technique.

In terms of affect, Michael et al.'s participants' anecdotes pointed to the ways in which others had been overly enthusiastic about the Lumelsky findings and the promise of the new method. However, some also reflected that in the past they too might have been more positive about the protocol – willing it to succeed as it were. In part this meant that they were hesitant to denounce those scientists that did commit to the Lumelsky protocol (this was in contrast to previous social scientific – specifically, STS – treatments that might have placed emphasis on derogation as a means of claiming more credibility for the participant scientist – e.g. Collins, 1985). Indeed, scientists were able partially to identify with those scientists who had jumped onto the Lumelsky bandwagon – a few years ago they themselves might have done so too. Michael et al. discuss this in terms of the 'but for the grace of god' presumption. Indeed, as these authors also comment, it might be the case that the participant scientists were at the time of the interviews clinging on to a different bandwagon, they were just not aware of it yet – though they were no doubt aware of this possibility (that is, they were aware of a future awareness). While Michael et al. focus on the different sorts of more or less agonistic relations within the scientific community, here I have partially reinterpreted that material through the lens of affect and anecdotalization. Arguably, the scientists were themselves telling tales about enthusiasm and bandwagoning which were misplaced but which nevertheless might have been indicative of their own past situation and might be symptomatic of their own then-current circumstances. More broadly, this could be read as a tacit account of being affected by competitive atmospheres and governance mechanisms that shaped the affects of scientists to succeed, to publish, to keep their institutions and funders happy. Most scientists, not least those further down the pecking order, are subject to cultures and regimes which demand sacrifices, and, potentially at least, increasingly place pressure on practitioners for breakthroughs and discoveries.

The irony of this will not have escaped the reader's attention. The present affect-laden reinterpretation can itself be read as a parallel reflection of the same affective atmospheres and governmentalities this time as instanced in the social sciences. One has to wonder, therefore, whether we are affectively attached to an affective bandwagon even if that bandwagon is perhaps (momentarily) best approached through an affective analytic. So, even if the interview data take on different meanings by being placed in relation to the affective turn, we should nevertheless entertain the idea that the data themselves played an affective part in this particular turn to the affective turn.

Here, then, we need to rethink data in their sociomateriality, in the sense that the process of gathering them leaves particular affective traces in the researcher – after all, one has entered into several sociomaterial relations in order to generate those data (not least with the participants, but also with funding agencies and a host of local institutional actors). Similarly, the analytic engagement with the data is a sociomaterial process (for further, see Chapter 7) in which the processes of arranging, patterning, connecting, differentiating and abstracting in relation to the transcriptions, photographs, recordings and so on and so forth are affectively charged. In all this, the data themselves can relay the affects of the participants, and, on this score, the data are particularly likely to ask of us – indeed to demand of us – a response equal to their qualities as Souriau might say (we elaborate on this point below). That is to say, we are engaged by the data affectively to do them some sort of analytic justice (though this will always be contingent). In any case, we need to treat data (in this sense of evoking relationalities into which we are tied) respectfully, that is, 'carefully' as they can 'construct' (us) as well as be 'constructed' (by us) through the analytic process.

In the preceding example, we have seen hints of how affect and anecdotalization serve in the process of enactment of disparate relations and their links (between cells, methods, scientists, institutions, and social science as well). What anecdotalization offers is one means of opening up this process to inspection that resources the asking of more interesting questions about how, for instance, affect circulates across acts of theorization, data collection, analysis and so on. Moreover, it alerts us to the performance of temporality in research, in which pasts, presents and futures and their respective conditionalities interweave (I could have been on a bandwagon, I might be on a bandwagon, I hope to succeed by not being on a bandwagon).

I now want to expand on this use of anecdotalization to explore these extended and involuted temporal relations with another example: in this case where the affect is present but fails in its connection to a specific episode – that is to say, the affect remains, but the incident can longer be recovered or remembered.

As discussed in Chapter 2, I wrote a piece on the memory of falling as a means of reflecting on how a mundane mishap (that is, a misstep and fall) could act as a lens through which to explore a range of relationalities that affectively entailed family, gender and intergenerational elements. At the same time, the aim was to explore how these incidents of falling were partly composed through these elements. That is to say, the purpose of the analysis was to complexify these incidents, to see them as markers of a nexus of heterogeneous processes – a nexus which served as a cautionary tale against too simple or singular an account of the incident. One particular incident was especially resonant, not least because while the affect was potent, the memory of the incident to which it was initially attached had long since faded.

So, here is the anecdote. I can't recall how I fell to the ground but I think I slipped, or somehow lost my balance, on a pavement, in an urban setting. I'm still not sure if I was standing or walking. I think there was something slimy – leaf litter? – underfoot (but on further reflection, perhaps this is an attempt to explain away the fall). I ended up on my bottom before I had a chance to extend my hands out and break my fall. Witness to all this was my son. This is particularly significant because after all the repair work and joking as I got to my feet, he subsequently told my then-partner (who then told me) that he had had a big shock seeing me fall. It was the first concrete indication of my ageing, and my growing vulnerability, of my impermanence. In writing the chapter in which this episode featured, I asked my son whether he remembered it: he said he remembered the fall but could recover very few details about either the place or the time.

Now, a straightforward social scientific perspective might treat the fall as an object of study *per se* – an incident independent of its telling that could be subjected to a variety of analyses. For example, it could be understood in terms of: Elias' (1994/1939) notion civilization as a moment of lack of control that in the 'civilized' present period deserved explanation; the dramaturgical model developed by Goffman (1959) in which a fall is a sudden exposure of the 'back' of a performance of fatherhood; Bourdieusian practice theory (e.g. Bourdieu, 1977, 1984), in which falling down and getting up was an expression of a specific habitus and its links to particular class positioning; a Foucauldian failure of discipline along with an enactment of responsibilization (e.g. Foucault, 1979; Dean, 1999: cf. Woolgar and Neyland, 2013). As we can see, this anecdote can become entangled in a series of conceptual frameworks that each brings with it particular relationalities and in the process enacts the anecdote in a more or less divergent way.

However, as mentioned, what is of particular interest in the present context is the contrast between the vagueness of the detail and the strength of the affect that attach to the 'incident' (partially and inchoately narrated as it is). To clarify, my son's affectedness had a huge affect on me: not only because it put up a mirror to my own growing infirmity, but also because it echoed my relation to my own father. The specific parallel incident took place when on an extended family trip, a cousin motioned toward my father (then in his mid-sixties) who was struggling to walk and mentioned nonchalantly that he had become an old man. This really shocked me, partly because I could, for the first time, see all too clearly his all too rapid ageing. Here, what is important about the anecdote is the affects it set in train, how it begins to shift the nature of the research question and the research event (rather than be entangled within pre-existing frameworks). Instead, we can sketch a circulation of affect (my son's shock at my vulnerability, my then-partner's need to tell about this, my own recognition of my growing infirmity, my sadness at my father's growing infirmity, my upset at my cousin's seeming indifference) that reflects and performs spatio-temporal relationalities across people (cousin, father, son, then-partner, self) and moments (present pasts, past futures, present, present futures, future pasts). Here, there is a connectivity between these space-times that is topological insofar as it is emergent and involuted: 'prior' affects are re-called and connected, and, in being, so affect the affects that enabled that recall in the first place. Here, it becomes difficult to discern and stabilize external, linear spatial and temporal indices through which this anecdotalization of affect can be mapped (e.g. Mol and Law, 1994; Lash and Lury, 2007; Lury et al., 2012).

Another way of thinking about this is in terms of prepositions and propositions (and their combination as pre-propositions). As we saw in our discussion of Michel Serres (see Chapter 1), he is interested in the relations between entities, whether human or nonhuman, and he has considered how such relations may be established (through various figures such as Hermes and angels) or disrupted and complexified (through the operations of the parasite – see Chapter 4). In elaborating on how to understand these relationalities more broadly, Serres' call for a 'philosophy of prepositions' can be regarded as an appeal for an expansion of terms which can be used to describe the relations between entities, beyond physical relations to incorporate social and communicative relations. In brief, he is asking that we imagine that such a 'philosophy' formulates a range of heterogeneous prepositions that straddle the multiplicity of entities and their relations. We return to this matter when we discuss the role hybrid categories in the doing of data analysis.

A parallel question is: how might we address such connectivity temporally, where entities are entangled with heterogeneous pasts, presents and futures? In this specific case, anecdotalization encompasses how a specific affective past (my falling) evoked a distinctive remembered past (my father's ailing body and my cousin's commentary) through my son's past anxiety about my own ailing body, and together my son's and my own concern for our respective fathers, might well proposition a prospective future in which my son remembers a past where these parallels became narrated. Here different 'points' in time enfold one another: anecdotalization thus serves as a lure for thinking about how the events we narrate are enmeshed within temporalities that are complex, involuted. Serres formulates this version of temporality in the following way:

> (Time is) is not laminar (flowing smoothly). The usual theory supposes time to be always and everywhere laminar. With geometrically rigid and measurable distances – at least constant … No, time flows in a turbulent and chaotic manner; it percolates … this time can be schematized by a kind of crumpling, a multiple, foldable diversity.
>
> *Serres and Latour, 1995, p.59*

The event's temporality as a 'multiple, foldable diversity' – as topological – is what anecdotalization, hopefully, sensitizes us to.

In summary, the 'falling down' anecdote, properly anecdotalized, has made apparent unexpected new entanglements out of which involuted temporalities (incidents) and spaces (people) emerge. We will encounter anecdotalizations throughout the rest of the book, and while we will use them to shed light on other aspects of the research event (as, say, an occasion of collaboration, or disconcertment), we will be alert to the 'multiple foldable diversities' they import. However, in the context of the current discussion, there is another point to pursue. We have already mentioned that aesthetics can be understood as a subset of affect. In what follows, I aim to explore how aesthetics might fit into this Whiteheadian view of the research event, and what it might afford.

Attunement and affect

In this section, I will address the notion of attunement, especially those elements of the research event that are not openly, or noticeably, influential but rather operate at an 'infra-sensible' level. Here, I draw on the notion of the 'infra-sensible' as indicative of those affects that, as Hawkins (2011, p.542) neatly summarizes, 'operate below the culturally organized logics of conscious thinking, feeling and judgement'. And by affects, I mean, following Ben Anderson (2014), the heterogeneous material-semiotic impacts upon the body that set up resonances and reactions and, potentially at least, open up possibilities for subsequent responses. As such, affect can also be regarded as relational insofar as it is emergent within patterns of relationships with the human and nonhuman, discursive and material, arrays that can, as mentioned earlier, range from the distinctly discrete (e.g. disciplinary apparatuses) through to the dissipated and diffuse (e.g. more or less localizable atmospheres). Further, affect should be understood as processual and specific: it is dynamic in that being affected is linked to being able to affect, and such dynamics are specific to the particular patterns of relations which affect and are affected.

As noted in Chapter 1, for the research event, composed as it is of heterogeneous elements, affect is central. And yet, of course, it routinely operates at an infrasensible level – it impacts us corporeally and cognitively in ways that are not always readily available to consciousness or to overt articulation. The general question taken up in this section is how do we as researchers become sensible to such affects as they circulate through, by and as us?

Now, there are several aspects to this question that need to be unpacked. The first concerns the ways in which we might attune ourselves to such affects as they manifest in the research events into which we enter and out of which we emerge. As we shall see, there are various techniques that have been suggested. Crucially, and this is the second aspect, this requires an expansion of the sensorium as usually enacted in social scientific events. In other words, we try to encompass more than the typically visual and verbal – to do research in a 'more' multisensorial or multimodal way. In addition to touching upon some of the innovations in multisensory methods, I will provide my own suggestions – one linguistically oriented, the other more corporeal – which aim to afford an attunement to, and a sense of, the infrasensible (and its multiplicity). Third, such attunement is concerned with potentiality: the relationality and circulation of affect not only reflect sequences of prior events (sometimes these are combined and condensed as 'late capitalism' or neoliberalism, for example) and the closing down of possibilities, but they can also open up potentialities, and prospective avenues of affect (and being able to affect). Fourth, in academic work, the usual expectation is that these affective possibilities which are at once infrasensible and multisensory are 'conveyed' – enacted and put into circulation so that various constituencies can access them. The task of such enactment is routinely linked to non- or more-than-representational techniques and there have been numerous innovations in 'doing' the non- or more-than-representational through different sorts of performances (e.g. Thrift, 2008; Lorimer, 2005; Vannini, 2015). Here, however, we will focus on particular forms of fabulation – our telling of academic fables – in order to explore more-than-representational in the textual: where writing is fabulation, it can serve as a conduit and mediator of affect, one that points to possibilistic futures (this will be taken up again in Chapter 5). Fifth, and finally, we reflect on the 'broader relationalities' entailed in this attunement to affect: we are ourselves enmeshed within disciplinary apparatuses (e.g. the institutional requirements to 'produce' or be 'productive' in specifiable ways), heterogeneous atmospheres (e.g. reputational circuits) and admixtures of these (e.g. commonly available metrics such as the H-index). That is to say, our attunements to affect are themselves affected by the attunements of others – we too are entangled in the circulations of affect even as we at once identify, mediate and resist such circulations.

For Kathleen Stewart (2007), what she calls ordinary affects 'are public feelings that begin and end in the broad circulation, but they're also the stuff that seemingly intimate lives are made of' (p.2). In other words, these affects circulate across expanses of relations (e.g. the shared sense of precarity) but also eventuate in the specificity of particular relations. In the process, these 'wider forces' have both an overbearing influence but also an immanence in which 'things are ... both hardwired and flighty, shifty and unsteady' (p.3). There are then, intrinsic possibilities attached to such affective circulations, possibilities that might be promising and threatening, or simply 'dissipate, leaving you standing' (p.13). As Stewart (2011) subsequently notes, accessing these ordinary affects requires a certain attunement, not least to the inchoate circulations in which they are caught up – she calls these 'atmospheres'. Thus 'atmospheric attunements are ... an intimate, compositional process of dwelling in spaces that bears, gestures, gestates, worlds. Here, things matter not because of how they are represented but because they have qualities, rhythms, forces, relations and movements' (p.445). The proactive or performative elements of atmospheric attunements, and their prospective openness to the not-as-yet, are underscored when Stewart goes on to write:

> An atmosphere is not an inert context but a force field in which people find themselves. It is not an effect of other forces but a lived effect – a capacity to affect and be affected that pushes a present into a composition, an expressivity, the sense of potentiality and event.
>
> *p.452*

For Stewart, this process of atmospheric attunement in everyday lives, with its multiple, variable responses, is also what characterises the researcher. They too must attune themselves to the ordinary attunements and affects of others – exercising a kind of attention that is 'immersed in forms of the ordinary but noticing things too' (2007, p.27). This is a 'hypervigilance' (which, it has been critically argued, seems to be employed less in ordinary settings than in hyper-paranoid milieus, Barmwell, 2016).

For Stewart objects are central to atmospheres. Jane Bennett (2010) similarly focuses on the role of objects in such affective circulations, where objects are regarded as 'things' which have a certain 'vitality' or openness. This means that objects escape ready correlation with particular impacts or affects that they might precipitate. They are 'vivid entities not entirely reducible to the contexts in which (human) subjects set them, never entirely exhausted by their semiotics' (Bennett, 2010, p.5). In other words, objects too are possessed of potentiality and, as such, they evade easy empirical or analytic capture. Engaging with these objects is thus simultaneously a recognition of their excess, their intractability in terms of their affectivity, but also in terms of their representability. That is to say, while they do stuff, what 'it' is they are doing is never discrete but always complex and unfolding, and accounting for this 'it' is always at best an estimation that necessarily fails to hit its mark. Bennett, drawing on the negative dialectics of Adorno, says that 'we knowers are haunted ... by a painful, nagging feeling that something's being forgotten or left out. This discomforting sense of inadequacy of representation remains no matter how refined or analytically precise one's concepts become' (p.14). In summary, there is a nonidentity between the object and the concept. In this situation, we need 'The self-criticism of conceptualization, a sensory attentiveness to the qualitative singularities of the object, the exercise of an unrealistic imagination, and the courage of a clown' (p.15) in order to afford nonidentity the respect that it is due.

In both the cases of Bennett and Stewart, the issue of how we assimilate, represent or convey 'analytically' these affective circulations in their specific eventuations is a matter of focused concern. For present purposes, I will concentrate on some means to attunement, hypervigilance or attentiveness to the qualitative singularities of the object.

Now, we might frame the issues addressed by Stewart and Bennett as a question of attuning ourselves to others' (both human and nonhuman) attunements, of being affected by (and affecting) the ways others are affected and affect – or placing ourselves in relation to the circulations of affects in which others are caught. As noted previously, affects operate in many disparate and heterogeneous ways – they impact bodies in their multiplicity, cutting across senses. This clearly evokes the need for some sort of a multisensorial engagement. If we are to register even an albeit contingent and incomplete sense of the affects that circulate in a given field of study, we will need to deploy more than the usual modalities (visual and aural, in the main). Fortunately, the social sciences have begun in recent years to develop ways of doing research which incorporates other senses. Below we recount some of these approaches, while also pressing them with regard to what comprises the senses within the unfolding of research events (shifting sensorium, emerging situated senses, attuning to attunement). So, to become attuned to the infrasensible entails, at least partly, a reconfiguring of the senses. This might mean raising the sensitivity of those senses that are usually attended to, or attending to senses that are routinely neglected, or, changing the inter-relations of the senses so that unexpected categories of affect might emerge.

So, for example, we can become better attuned to those aspects of the visual and aural that we would typically neglect: this might involve nurturing a capacity for being disconcerted (see below), or at least curious about what seems to be obvious. For example, we might learn how to alter our usual modes of attention: in looking at a scene, we can practise resting our view on the utterly mundane – a stain on a bus seat, the grass between paving stones, the lone drawing pin on a message board. As Lefebvre (1947) insisted – these little events and objects can be pursued analytically to unravel the broader historical process of which they are a part (for Lefebvre, the object was a bag of sugar and the process was Capitalism). But carefully looking at, or listening to, such miniscule eventuations can be unpacked through a simple procedure of asking such questions as: 'why is this X so mundane or how has it become so?' and 'Whose problem might this be or become?' But we might also explore the conditions of this perception (or lack of it): 'Why have I not noticed this before?' In all these cases, the aim is to foreground what is perceptually backgrounded and make it 'data-able' in that it can become an object or event of inquiry that might tell us something about the sociomaterial assemblages in which the object or event is imbricated.

Let us take an everyday example: we notice – tune in to – chewing gum ground-in as a stain on the carpet-like cover of a bus seat. From this visual cue, we can open up a more multisensory perspective on a series of possible questions. What happens when we imagine an encounter with a freshly discarded piece of chewing gum – the way it sticks to clothing, the work and technique necessary to remove it, the standards of overt stainlessness that we are willing to tolerate when the chewing gum stain fails to be completely removed. Then we can ask how this particular chewing gum stain got to be on this particular bus seat: the feelings the gum-chewer experienced through their gum-chewing and in the action of discarding the gum in particular way. Here we can begin to ask questions about contemporary chewing gum consumption and disposal habits and the tradition of chewing gum in the West, especially as a mode of enacting difference and identity (Redclift, 2004). But we can also open questions about why we had to put effort into the process of noticing. What does this tell us about our own expectations around the micropolitics of public stains, about the standards entailed in bus-cleaning regimes and in seat-cover design? Beyond this, can we query the position of chewing gum as a Western sociomaterial commonplace and its relation to a history of international expropriation (Redclift, 2004)? Perhaps this suggests that the effort entailed in attunement is indicative of how we as researchers are thoroughly interwoven into the assemblages of chewing gum: here the infrasensible relates not only to the everyday practices of chewing gum, but also its complex histories (also see Tsing's 'art of noticing' – mentioned in Chapter 2). In any case, we have used the visual modality to engage with several others, including touch (e.g. the tackiness of chewing gum), proprioception, flavour and taste (e.g. the chewing of gum) and even the sense of being observed (e.g. the act of secretly depositing the gum). But further this process of noticing, of attuning, and expanding the researcher sensorium, pre-propositionally prompts a different set of questions: are there other critical-creative ways of using spent chewing gum in everyday life that propose and proliferate new relationalities?

We can also delve a little deeper into how the senses are themselves shaped. Shove (2002) has argued that our corporeal assumptions about what is comfortably viewable (e.g. levels of lighting) are historically and geographically contingent. The same applies to levels of warmth, or more general senses of cleanliness (including touch and smell). In certain settings, such as office buildings, these have been standardized according to model human bodies. Shove's key observation is that these standards shape our senses so that what becomes comfortably or uncomfortably sensible affects what can be perceived. For Shove, one upshot is that consumption operates at particular environmentally wasteful levels as people aspire to accomplish their habitual levels of visibility, or warmth, or cleanliness. For present purposes, and keeping with the chewing gum example, seat fabric design is broadly standardized in such ways that stains are better disguised and thus less visible than had that fabric had a different design.[1] Here, then, assumptions about the 'normal' human visual system serve in backgrounding visibilities that might potentially lead to interesting questions. This example is a reminder of a key Whiteheadian tenet: while the processes of noticing and attuning are embroiled in wider histories (of, in this case, chewing gum), these histories are manifested as local concrete elements within the research event.

If we have so far focused on enhancing and supplementing predominant senses, these are predominant because others are marginalized. Or to put it another way, we inevitably engage multisensorially with the world, it's just that we don't always access and recount that engagement with reference to those senses – these are muted in our accounts, as it were. The sense of smell, touch, taste, proprioception, heat, etc. all serve in how we perceive. In Gibson's (1966) terms, we perceive as a system that encompasses all senses. Again, returning to the example of the chewing gum stain, our visual sense of this might well be shaped by how other senses are impacted. If the feel of the seat fabric is 'clean', if the smell of the bus is 'fresh', if the sun is gently warming through the bus windows – how does this 'ambient' sensing affect our ability to visually attune the stain in a particular way?

Further, once one has attuned to a particular object or event one can pose another question to oneself: in attempting to reprioritize subordinated senses – and thus to open up the empirical and analytic horizons of the object or event – one can systematically ask: 'what in addition to "seeing" am I perceiving across other senses and how might this affect the ways I am seeing?'. For example, Gallagher and Prior (2017) have addressed the technique of 'Listening Walks' as a method of researching into place. Here, participants walk in single file (say, around

Edinburgh), don't speak, stop at certain points and listen. In the process, they also engage other senses – smell and hearing (particular areas have smells attached to them which can also be related to the noise one hears e.g. traffic, fume smells), and these combine with other sensations such as vibrations, feel underfoot, rhythms and speeds of walking. In this way, the sense of place becomes far more deeply textured and the sorts of questions that arise become, potentially, more interestingly pre-propositional.

However, in pursuing this multisensoriality, it behoves us to exercise a little circumspection. Indeed, perhaps we also need to ask the question 'what precisely do we means by "senses"?'. That is to say, we need to address the composition of the sensorium. The five senses of the Western tradition are simply one version of the sensorium, and following a scholar such as Pink (2012, 2015) we can be highly critical about what counts as part of the sensorium and thus what can contribute to a sensory methodology. Other cultures have different sensoriums which might include kinaesthesia, balance, sensitivity to spirits and so on and so forth. Further, people can mix up in odd ways the five Western senses – in the case of synaesthesia numbers, letters or words are grasped as inherently coloured; and, more mildly, as we have suggested, the sight of a stain is suggestive of other sensory perceptions – textures, smells, feel. For Mason and Davies (2009), there is even the possibility where senses that detect 'what is there' are enmeshed with intangible sensoriality where people detect (or project) 'what is not there'. There are echoes here of such social psychological findings as the impact of majority or minority influence on the individual perception (say of comparative length). Bracketing the question of the 'reality' of 'what is or is not there', Mason and Davies' observation indicate how sociomaterial conditions such as the pressures exerted by certain social expectations (as well the ambient sensoriality discussed previously) shape the process of perceiving. The broader issue here is that the senses (or the researcher as well as the participant) are not fixed but emergent in the process of the research event (also see, Mann et al., 2011).

We can also begin to explore this in relation to language. Pink (2012) has documented the sensorial complexity of terms such as 'freshness' in the context of everyday domestic cleaning. 'Freshness' cuts across the senses – it suggests a particular clean smoothness, the sound of squeakiness, the smell of pine or lemon, as well as the visual cues of stainlessness and dustlessness, tidiness and reflectiveness. This suggests another method for a multisensory engagement, one mediated by language. It would seem that there are linguistic terms that evoke a particular configuration of multisensory engagements. Succulent, autumnal, medicinal – all these traverse, differentiate and connect the senses in particular ways. How might we use – or invent – such terms as a means of sensitizing ourselves to, and exploring, the complexity of both the infrasensible and the senses?

Now, what the preceding discussion has been attempting is a gradual shift from thinking in terms of 'attunement to the affects entailed in an event', toward thinking about 'the way the elements entailed in a research event affect the faculties of attunement, the senses'. In other words, how are our senses emergent within the specificities of the research event? And what are the sorts of inventive problems that arise in the process?

If we accept that the senses can be 'attuned' within the research event, then given its heterogeneity, we would expect such attunement to be variegated: as we have seen, it is mediated by ambient conditions, social expectations, and particular linguistic terms. But technologies can also play their part in the process of attunement. Let us return to the example of becoming attuned to a chewing gum stain. The seat one is sitting on affords a position and posture from which to attune to the gum. If it is comfortable, it facilitates the easy engagement with the chewing gum. If it is not comfortable or not comfortable enough, we can become distracted, our attention tends to be pulled elsewhere (corporeally). In other words, we attune through a nexus of senses that are more or less sensible (Michael, 2000a). One obvious question to pose here is: how do such backgrounded technologies shape attunement to the infrasensible? In some ways, this is a parallel question to that addressed by Law (2011) in his discussion of collateral realities – those taken-for-granted realities that allow for the ready enactment of particular social situations. Echoing Law, we ask what presuppositional corporeal backdrop affects how particular affects affect? Importantly, the technologies that set these backdrops are not those that that serve as sensory extensions, in the way that digital video camera or sound recorder might do (they allow for changing temporalities, zooming and focusing in the ways that are 'beyond' usual human sensorial capacities), but rather those technologies that are co-constitutive of existing sensibilities. They are the mundane technologies that contribute to what we might call an affective landscape – or ecology of affects – in which the affective specificities of the research event play out. One implication is that in engaging in the research event, we might consider ways of altering the sensorial backdrop (for example, implementing technologies that engender small discomforts or pleasures), as a way of opening up new possibilities for engaging with the infrasensible, for attunement.

This last proposal reflects a broader issue. While we could be adjusting the affective landscape technologically, we also need to take into account that we are constantly adjusting to our sociomaterial environment anyway. As Gibson (1979) noted long ago, perception is not passive, it is part of a process of engaging with, and moving through the world – of being affective, not least on oneself as one constantly alters the bodily circumstance of engagement as one moves through the world. This is partly shaped by the plans that we are 'executing' and 'adapting' to the sociomaterial conditions that confront us. The implication is that we are attuning our process of attunement, affecting our capacity to be affected. We are, in other words, constantly opening up new ways of engaging with the infrasensible – expanding pre-propositional horizons – even if these are in a minor register, or certainly not as dramatic as the technological interventions suggested earlier.

Together, the foregoing discussions crystallize the observation that the process of attuning to the affects of a research event is complex, fluid and variegated. Moreover, it implicates a process of attuning to attunement in which the researcher engages with how their own senses and sensibilities emerge out of the research event iteratively with the affects to which they attune, which are themselves affected by the process of attunement. This suggests a sort of infrasensible fitting – an affective calibration and reverberation across researcher and researched – in a word, an aesthetics of the research event. In the next section, we unpack a little further what is meant by just this phrase: 'an aesthetics of the research event'.

Attuning to aesthetics

If aesthetics is an underappreciated element in our understanding and practice of the research process, it is central to the idea of the research event. How things fit together to produce (or fail to produce) a form that somehow is 'pleasing' or yields a certain satisfaction is a key element in how we assess the 'success' and indeed the value of a research event. This operates in several ways across the unfolding of the research event – from the 'elegance' of a research proposal, through the experience of the research engagement (and the sometime 'euphoria' of a good empirical session), to the 'beauty' of data analysis and the 'satisfaction' of the pattern thus derived, aesthetics, in this run-of-the-mill sense, plays its part in how we 'appreciate' a research event. Such aesthetic feelings seem to be a part of all research practice (including in the natural or physical sciences). Now, insofar as 'aesthetics' captures part of the mutual 'fit' of the elements that comprise any research event, it can be differentiated from the plethora of art-based methods that have become part of the social sciences methodological repertoire (see, for example, Coleman, 2020; Jungnickel and Hjorth, 2014; Woodward, 2020). In Chapter 5, we will consider in more detail some ways in which the aesthetics of empirical engagement can serve in the opening up or closing down of participants' responses. In particular, we will discuss how particular arts-related methods of engagement (or what can be called 'proactive idiocy') can enable more speculative responses. There, we deploy a more 'troubling' version of aesthetics, namely the idea of semblance (Massumi, 2011).

However, for present purposes, we want to look at aesthetics as an ontological category. By this, I mean that any event attains a certain singularity, or integrity, satisfaction, or conformation – a unity that identifies it as bounded. To recapitulate comments in Chapter 1, the Whiteheadian view of the event entails the coming together of a multitude of heterogeneous components which Whitehead (1978) calls 'prehensions'. These 'prehensions' can encompass different scales and statuses and can therefore include both the human and nonhuman, the cognitive and the affective, the conscious and the unconscious, the micro and the macro, the social and the natural. In coming together they combine or in Whitehead's terminology, 'concresce'. How precisely this concrescence takes place is what comprises the actual occasion or actual entity that emerges – that is to say, it constitutes an event. There are a number of things to take note of here.

First, the prehensions that flow into this concrescent event were themselves once concresced, and that which is concresced as an actual entity say, will in due course become the prehension of another actual entity. Thus, we see a flow – or becoming – of prehensions and concrescences that is also, as Whitehead notes, 'atomistic'. There is a clear echo here of Dewey's (1934) account of experience as both flow and distinctive part. The key difference is that Whitehead has generalized experience to the world at large. For him, everything 'experiences' where experience is a primitive or basic form by which entities 'feel' other entities.

The second point is that this concrescent process is not indiscriminate: some prehensions go better together than other prehensions. There is thus a degree of situated teleology at play within (this part of) Whitehead's schema, in that some prehensions are accommodated within an event, while others are not.

Having remarked on this process of harmonization, and this is the third point, there is nothing deterministic or inevitable about it. The elements that come together can, as Fraser (2010) has noted, affect one another, co-become in ways that are not necessarily predictable (not least when they derive from different 'force fields' that include the human estate, and all manner of physical and biological arenas – see Connolly, 2013). There is, in other words, an intractable degree of 'creativity' in the process of concrescence which means that we can never grasp it fully. This is simply redoubled when the process of grasping entails various social scientific methodological procedures: these comprise another prehension (Michael, 2012a) that is 'experienced' and 'experiences' in ways that are not always readily accessible (also see Law, 2004). What this implies is that we would do best to regard our own situatedness within research events as, to reiterate, entailing moments of speculation in which one, to quote Stengers again (2010, p.57) 'affirms the possible … actively resists the plausible and the probable targeted by approaches that claim to be neutral'. In other words, we ourselves are caught up in an event which we 'bring into some kind of harmony' but in which we ourselves are also subject to harmonization: the various inclusions and exclusions, concrescences and contrasts that make up our research event are not necessarily predictable, especially as 'we' ourselves might be 'being brought into some kind of harmony'.

In summary, a research event aesthetically coheres as a unity, a satisfaction in Whitehead's terms. But also, that moment of satisfaction is fleeting, as that event becomes a component – a prehension – in another's concrescence, satisfaction. But, further, satisfaction need not imply a static unified form – it can be open, becoming, uncertain (more on this in Chapter 4). At base, the research event can be both dissatisfied with satisfaction (as a cogent singularity) and satisfied with dissatisfaction (as an unresolved event still in process).

This is something, I suggest, researchers routinely 'experience' in the expanded sense used here. We can elaborate on this through a rather different perspective. In their introduction to Souriau's *Different Modes of Existence*, Stengers and Latour (2015) point out that for an object of art that is in the process of being crafted (indeed, for anything – including a research artefact – that is made by a person), a demand is placed upon the maker. They are required to 'work it out', that is, to realize that object in its fullness, to 'care' for it appropriately. Unsurprisingly, this process is not seamless: things go wrong as well as right. This 'demand' can be understood as the event's momentum toward satisfaction, and the inclusion or exclusion of elements that add to, or detract from, that 'satisfaction'. Further, in the 'making' of the research event, the researcher is 'party' to this satisfaction, in the emergence of both the 'artwork' – the study – *and* themselves. In other words, the research artefacts that emerge out of the research event (papers, presentations, engagements, etc.), and the technique that goes into designing a project, gathering the data, analysing the material, drafting the paper – all these also yield the researcher as they engage with the minutiae of the sociomaterial 'stuff' with which they work. Like the artist, the researcher responds to the exigencies of the 'sociomaterials' with which they work which also includes the persons with whom they engage, as well as the research peers with whom they collaborate. 'Working it out', attaining 'satisfaction' – these are thus terms that lure reflection on what ingredients of the research event prompt the sense of completion in the emerging researcher.

It is worth re-emphasizing that the finished work (the satisfied event) is never finished. As it enters into subsequent events, what it 'is' shifts in much the same way that a work of art is serially reappraised as it becomes entangled in different patterns of heterogeneous relationalities, in changing fashions and mores. It becomes other in its encounters with others. Of course, that other might be the 'originating' researcher that some way down the line has themselves become other, that themselves re-engage their 'own' work in a more or less dramatically different way. Both work and author are pre-propositionally 'in progress'.

What does this detour through an ontological version aesthetics afford? At minimum, it orients us toward the ways in which affects – that circulate as part of the research event – form patterns that are aesthetically 'satisfactory' (possibly in multiple ways). We are not necessarily aware of these, being caught up as we are in the process of such satisfaction. However, we can be possessed of an 'aesthetic' sense that a 'satisfaction' is indeed emerging and, as such, we can be circumspect about it. In other words, this is another framing of how we might become attuned to the process of attunement.

Concluding remark

In this chapter, I have tried to think through a number of ways in which the process of doing research entails forms of attunement. The anecdote and anecdotalization, affect, the senses, and the infrasensible, and aesthetics were presented as concepts through which to think and do attunement, while also recognizing that the 'fit' with and within the empirical is complex, iterative, heterogeneous, topological, extended and pre-propositionally uncertain. It goes without saying, the themes taken up here are partial – I do not claim that they are anything other than particular heuristics among a range of others (e.g. formulations of intimacy; see Latimer and López Gómez, 2019). Throughout this chapter, I have attempted to be careful about attunement, to recognize how it can fail (for another example, see Brown et al., 2019) but also to hint at how attunement can also be intimately tied to disruption, to breakdown, to interference. This is taken up more fully in the next chapter in which I discuss 'disconcertment' (not least as mediated by such figures as the parasite and the idiot) as a chronic dimension of the research event.

Note

1 www.bbc.com/autos/story/20160804-why-are-trains-seats-so-hideous.

4
IDIOT AND PARASITE
On productive disconcertment

Introduction

While engaged in fieldwork into the public understanding of ionizing radiation, I conducted numerous interviews with lay people in and around the city of Lancaster in the United Kingdom. In some cases there were follow-up interviews, to see if people's views on ionizing radiation had changed since the initial interview some six months previously. In this specific interview, I was interviewing a woman in her late 20s in her home for the second time. The participant had told me she had been a drug user, but had, after an extended period of time during which she was unemployed, stopped using and got a job at the local Burger King. I settled onto the sofa, while the participant sat on the armchair to my right. I placed the tape recorder on the floor, attempting to ensure that it picked up both our voices. As we chatted, prior to the interview proper, her dog – a pit bull terrier – trotted in and turning herself around, sat on my feet. The participant reassured me that the dog did this because 'she liked to know where people are'. As I tried to direct discussion towards the issue of ionizing radiation (and the risks she might or might not associate with it, and the relations of trust that she might or might not have with the relevant scientific institutions), it was quickly apparent that this topic was not uppermost in her mind. In fact, she was far keener to talk about her new job at Burger King and described at length her prospects for promotion. In the meantime, her cat entered the room, and immediately made for the tape recorder. After pawing at the tape recorder strap for a little while, it caught hold of it with its claws and proceeded to pull the recorder towards the other side of the room. As we humans dropped out of recording range, it became clear that the participant had no intention of addressing herself to ionizing radiation. With the pit bull terrier (at the time the breed had been dubbed 'devil dog' by the UK press) on my feet, I could find neither the will nor the courage to spend too much effort on turning the interview

DOI: 10.4324/9781351133555-4

around. The participant received £5, and I put the whole disastrous episode down to a mixture of inexperience and ineptitude (see Michael, 2004b, for more sorry detail).

Within this story lie clues to the ways in which we routinely exclude or neglect elements that are core parts of the research event, both by virtue of their inclusion and, especially, their exclusion. That is to say, chronic to the research event are a range of 'misbehaviours', 'in-actions', 'anti-activities' or 'contra-practices' that do not fall within the parameters of the research question at stake. These can be at once noticed and not-noticed, have the impact of having to be rendered non-impactful, or are treated as an inconvenience to be managed in a way that re-establishes the convenience of the research event. The very process of 'gathering' data is thus based on a complex act of exclusion, or othering, of indeed a sort of wilful ignorance.

However, by more explicitly attending to this exclusion, othering or ignoring – that is by putting potential disruptions to work – it might become possible to enrich the data one gathers, complexify the research question and open up the pre-propositionality of the research event, and move more towards an inventive problem-making. Here, the figures of the parasite and idiot will be central to our discussions of how we might speculatively engage with these others.

Having identified these figures as key, it should be noted that there are numerous others that could have been deployed, notably the trickster and the coyote (e.g. Haraway, 1992). As such, care needs to be exercised: the concepts of parasite and idiot are, as ever heuristic, and one need not be too precious about their status or utility.

Now, before explicating and illustrating these, we should note some of their differences. The parasite tends to apply as a figure that disrupts pre-existing sociomaterial associations. It intervenes in heterogeneous ways that undermine the usual arrangements among protagonists (whether human or nonhuman). In the process, there is opened up a possibility for new, more complex arrangements and associations to emerge. By comparison, the idiot works in a different way: it makes no sense to us within our prevailing understandings of the situation. By paying it due attention, we can begin to question those understandings. That is, by seeing its nonsensicalness as a challenge to our presuppositions, we can begin to open up alternative possible meanings for that situation. Whereas the parasite in a sense tends to force itself upon us, the idiot needs to be embraced (rather than ignored). However, this is a matter of degree – parasites can be ignored or explained away too, and idiots (perhaps those that are least 'embraceable') can be forceful interlopers as well.

In any case, in what follows, I will examine the parasite and the idiot in some detail, instantiating each with a number of cases, while also considering some of these figures' limitations. In light of the key functions of the idiot or parasite – namely to disconcert the researcher as well as 'disorient' the research event – I begin with a consideration of disconcertment. I then develop an account of the concept of the parasite as proposed by Michel Serres, then illustrate it with examples in order to derive a series of methodological tactics whereby it can be put to use. This is followed, in similar fashion, with an explication of the idiot, especially as advocated by Isabelle Stengers, and again I provide exemplifications of its deployment, and suggestions as to its broader methodological application (as encountered, sought and proactively introduced). The chapter ends by reflecting on the ways in which attunement and disconcertment can topologically enfold one another in practice.

Doing disconcertment

In a research interview with a high-ranking government scientist, I found myself (as a still relatively inexperienced researcher) scrambling to ask my questions. I had my list of questions on my lap, yet when it came to it, I was struggling to ask, in a prompt and timely manner, the next question. It was about a quarter of the way into the interview that I realized that the participant was giving none of those cues (so elegantly studied by conversation analysts, see Heritage, 1984) that signalled the end of his answer, and, in this case, invited my next question. This meant that I was not able to judge when to start turning my attention towards the next question. I became embarrassed as this had the effect of making me appear unprepared, even more amateurish than I was. Now, I certainly felt this as a loss of professional face, so responded by paying little attention to his response (it was being recorded after all), and focusing on the next question so that as soon as his response stopped abruptly, I could immediately (and hopefully seamlessly) ask the next question. I can't say whether this lack of cues was a quirk, indicative of a condition, or a deliberate attempt to disconcert me. For a long time, I thought it was the last of these, especially in light of what appeared to be major tensions within the institution, and the senior scientist's own later resistance to the research we were conducting (which his institution was partly funding). In this respect, I was taking a critical analytic perspective on the form of this exchange.

There are a number of features to this instance of disconcertment that are worth taking time over. The first is that it was, in part, a reflection of a difference in status. This was, after all, an interview with an elite participant who responded to my questions with a standard institutional narrative – that the research undertaken by his institution bore the usual hallmarks of rational, objective science. In this respect, the interview evidences some of the problems typically identified with interviews with elites (e.g. Stephens, 2007; Delaney, 2007).

However, and this is the second point, paralleling Jerak-Zuiderent's (2015) analysis of the 'fleeting subtleties' (p.904) of interruptions that take place in interviews (laughter as tacit expressions of fear, in her examples), the abrupt cessation of talk on the part of the scientist could be read as something more than a way of simply curtailing (or, perhaps, derailing) further follow-up questions. Instead of such moments of disconcertment being regarded as a marker of misdirection and a pointer to 'something being hidden', they can be treated with due care (Puig de la Bellacasa, 2011, see Chapter 6) in the sense that we try to take into account the practices and sociomaterialities that are their conditions of emergence. In other words, we do not focus on status differentials or relations of power or the righteousness of our epistemological conventions. So, as Jerak-Zuiderent argues, rather than draw on such moments of disconcertment as a basis for launching critique (or launching a defence of our good name), we might use this as an opportunity to explore the potential of the matters at stake. For Jerak-Zuiderent, in her case study, this means seeking in the laughter of her respondents the sense of disconcertment through which she can open up what is potential or prospective within the area of 'Dutch healthcare indicator implementation'. In the process, there is the possibility of asking how things might be done otherwise, how the problems that can be posed are more inventive. In the instance of my own interview with the senior scientist, his conversational style could be understood as a way of asserting the normative view of science as a means of defending his institution against the close government scrutiny and the threat of restructuring to which it was at the time being subjected. This points to the constraints under which he was operating and hints at potential other versions of science that could be entertained within his institution under different circumstances (in fact, alternative versions of science were indeed in evidence among other members of the institution who were enacting a range of roles). At the very least, there arises a way of engaging with the interview and the material it produced that is more inventive, and that, to paraphrase Puig de la Bellacasa (2011, p.100), remakes our relationships with our 'objects of study', that is, opens us up to participants as prospective cosmopolitical partners – co-practitioners – with whom we can negotiate our mutual and disparate concerns (see Chapter 6).

A third point further addresses the nature of what disconcertment might allow. Jerak-Zuiderent wants to practice a 'generative critique' which, drawing on Helen Verran (2001, p.20), entails 'the possibility of innovation, a way that things might be done differently to affect futures different from pasts'. However, we should elaborate here on what is meant by this. As Latour (2004b) famously argued in his 'critique of critique', our aim should not be to unpick – to revel in – the determinants of another's practices (which are known to the analyst if not the practitioner) – after all, one's own critical account can be subject to a parallel critique. Rather, one needs to engage with the ways in which a plethora of heterogeneous elements are assembled – composed – to render any reality (Latour, 2010b), while acknowledging that the process of engagement is likewise composed. For Latour,

> The critic is not the one who debunks, but the one who assembles. The critic is not the one who lifts the rugs from under the feet of the naïve believers, but the one who offers the participants arenas in which to gather. The critic is … the one for whom, if something is constructed, then it means it is fragile and thus in great need of care and caution.
>
> *2004b, p.246; also see Chapter 6*

Arguably, the senior scientist's truncated turn-taking could be read as a tacit critique of my own political naivete and youthful overenthusiasm. In light of Latour's re-casting of critique, we might ask in this specific case how might we have practically sidestepped a position where the scientist's tacit accusatory critique was met with immediate 'avoidance', or subsequent retaliatory critique? How might this research event be turned towards a process of composition in which there was an opening up of the exchange, a possibility of different relationalities emerging.

Let me tentatively and circumspectly propose the heuristic motif of 'teasing'. Teasing is here understood as a form of more or less gentle critique, in that to tease someone or something is to propose aspects of them of which they are not aware, or not aware enough. This taps into another connotation of teasing – to tease apart: to reveal the more or less hidden components that comprise someone or something. But, teasing also entails an invitation to be teased: as a gently humorous mode of interaction, it promotes an atmosphere of common affects, it ideally enables sociability. It is not simply about revealing and exchanging information but is also concerned with the relationalities and mutualities that can be forged. In this sense, teasing is compositional – it serves to set up a relation in which mutuality is possible. As such teasing also entails an openness to being teased: to being attuned to the invitation to compose a mutuality of teasing from others.

Such willingness to be teased might mean being sensitive to what one might consider trivial, or marginal, or unworthy. It maps onto Jerak-Zuiderent's call for a 'generative critique' which can also be understood as a form of mutual revelation that facilitates emergent mutualities (as well as the possibility of generating alternative prospects). Inevitably, there are dangers in store. Teasing, where it lacks mutuality, can slide into bullying, or where there is an excess of mutuality it can slide into a form of collective self-congratulation. Still, this should not stop us from being teased by teasing, and teasing apart some of the ways in which teasing itself operates to enable mutualities – and new relations to be forged, and with that more inventive questions.

Having offered this suggestion, albeit with some considerable hesitation, we can point to another feature of disconcertment – specifically, how it comes to be triggered or invited. In comparison to my spontaneous disconcerted reactions to the abrupt cessation of a conversational turn, Jerak-Zuiderent seems to have had to work hard to nurture her sense of disconcertment, to become alert to, on the one hand, laughter as a punctuation of otherwise fluent narratives, and, on the other, to its potential implications. This suggests that what precipitates (or attracts) disconcertment can vary somewhat. We address this further below and in Chapter 5.

For Law and Lin (2010), disconcertment also came comparatively easily – in particular Law found himself disconcerted by the surprising counterarguments made by members of his seminar audience (as indeed were members of that seminar audience). For Law and Lin (2010), Law's advocacy of noncoherence (e.g. Law, 2011) and the reaction against this reflected metaphysical differences in Western and Taiwanese thought (broadly and contingently understood). Following Verran (1999), they say that 'bodily disconcertment may be understood as an expression of metaphysical disjuncture' (Law and Lin, 2010, p.137).

In light of this relatively 'high-level' metaphysical disconcertment, as against my 'low-level' conversational disconcertment, one can imagine these triggers to disconcertment as arrayed on a spectrum moving, say, from the micro-social to the metaphysical, or ranged in terms of perceptibility (easy-spontaneous to difficult-onerous). I suspect that this framing won't be of much use – after all, as hinted at previously, an abruptly ended conversational turn might signal epistemological difference. In any case, we can perhaps proliferate what it is that might disconcert us, not least because this opens up more ways of inventively engaging with, and enacting, our participants (as co-practitioners – see below).

This suggests that it is useful to enable ways of becoming disconcerted about what is absent (in the sense of tacit or assumed). So, for example, if on this account disconcertment is a means of accessing and creatively enacting difference (from the 'micro-social' to the 'metaphysical'), the fact that disconcertment is oriented to a particular difference suggests that other differences are being ignored, or simply presupposed. Law's (2011) concept of 'collateral realities' is useful here. So, while difference disconcerts, this is situated within a set of implicit practices – collateral realities – that enable social, or, better, sociomaterial, interaction between participants. These collateral realities – for instance, shared conventions about politeness – affect the form disconcertment takes and contribute to an unwillingness or incapacity to articulate disconcertment (in my case, at least, to express my discomfort during the interview with the senior scientist, for example). In other words, we might also be disconcerted by the resilience of various conventions that disable the expression of discomfort. The broader point is that we perhaps need to nurture disconcertment about disconcertment too – what shaped the initial form of disconcertment, and how does that subsequently affect what can be done with disconcertment?

Law and Lin (2010) make a point of noting the corporeality of disconcertment. Given the discussion in the previous chapter, this should not be wholly surprising. In the next section, this is taken up by exploring the figure of the parasite as a disrupting intervention that disconcerts in multiple ways, corporeal and semiotic.

The parasite

As has been illustrated a number of times, things do not always go smoothly within a research event. 'Things' can interrupt and disrupt the even flow of interaction that make an episode of empirical investigation appear to be an utter, dispiriting failure, as in the case of the disastrous interview described in the 'Introduction' section to this chapter. However, let us step back from this despairing picture. The research event will be affected by the researcher's expectations embodied in the research design, in the interview protocols, in a broader sense of the proper conduct of engagement and interaction, for instance. At base, it is assumed that some sort of meaningful exchange will be accomplished, in the dual sense that meanings are exchanged and the exchange has meaning. Of course, this exchange is not simply semiotic or hermeneutic, materials are also exchanged or circulated: an ethics form, a cup of tea, money or a voucher for the participant, possibly stimulus materials, a participant's photographs. These and many other material-semiotic elements are more or less in evidence in such research encounters.

However, just as there are elements, the presence of which together comprise a research encounter, so the research encounter is, as noted earlier, shaped by the absence of certain elements. In Whitehead's account of the actual occasion, what this is (and can become) is affected not only by the actual constituent prehensions, but also by those that are denied entrée, that do not fit into the occasion as it coheres or becomes cogent (as we have seen this can be discussed in terms of satisfaction or harmony or conformation – see Chapter 3). However, in the concrete unfolding of a research event, sometimes these absented elements can invite themselves back in and begin to exercise an impact. Indeed, they can not only disrupt the event, but also serve to both reveal and add to its complexity.

It is at this point we can turn to the work of Michel Serres. As an inspiration in the early emergence of actor–network theory (see Michael, 2000b, 2017b), he provided key insights into the interactions of the material and the cultural, the human and nonhuman. This, according to Serres, could be grasped through such a figure as that of Hermes, the not so reliable messenger of the Greek gods, who delivered 'messages' across humans and nonhumans, binding them in new ways. Such messages can take many forms: ideas, objects (both natural and cultural), energies, thoughts, matters. Moreover, they could change in form – ideas become objects become energies. Crucially, an object passing among and between people could shape their social relations just as it is itself shaped by those social relations (Serres uses the example of the ball and its movements in a football match as shaping the relation of the players as they all orient towards it). Quasi-objects, as Serres calls them, at once produce and are produced by social relations. As such:

> Our relationships, social bonds, would be airy as clouds were there only contracts between subjects. In fact, the object, specific to the Hominidae, stabilises our relationships, it slows down the time of our revolutions. For the unstable bands of baboons, social changes are flaring up every minute … The object, for us, makes our history slow.
>
> *Serres, 1995a, p.87*

So, objects play a crucial role in the realization and stabilization of heterogeneous ordering. Further, over time, this role is progressively socially specified so that objects' contribution tends towards the standardized. If objects and subjects have this mutually constitutive relation that is increasingly entwined, this does not mean, however, that within any particular event, disruption cannot arise. Indeed, For Serres, 'disruption' is a chronic part of the world, and much effort goes into keeping such disruption at arm's length. On this score, Serres (1982a) refers to this as the 'excluded third' which is always on the verge of entering into any ordered relation or communication, in the process bringing with it forms of disordering. Sometimes, this excluded third might emphasize the material (for example, the biting cold disrupting a conversation, kept out with clothes and heating technology), sometimes the social (for example, the exploitation of forests leading to soil erosion, mitigated by crowd-funded reforestation).

When the excluded third, does enter a communication and interrupts it, it is a parasite in the technical sense of something that disrupts the movement of a signal from sender to receiver. In his book, *The Parasite*, Serres (1982a) begins with a series of variations on La Fontaine's parable of city and country rats 'at table'. Thus, the country mouse knocks at the door of the city mouse and disrupts their dinner. In the end, the city mouse invites the country mouse to eat at their dinner table, even when the other has nothing material to exchange. However, what the country mouse can provide is stories – thus there is an exchange of the material and the semiotic. In the process, a more complex arrangement emerges where the disordering of the relation between city mouse and their dinner is replaced by a novel reordering between two strangers.

Revealing complexity

Let us return to the disastrous interview. Any ordering that takes place in a research event necessarily entails dealing with the excluded third. In the case of the research interview, TV sets have to be switched off or muted, the kitchen door needs to be shut in order to dull the noise of the washing machine on its spin cycle, the children and the spouse must be asked to stay out of the living room, and, nowadays, mobile phones must, of course (sic), be switched off. Put otherwise, to conduct an interview or a focus group or some other technique of empirical engagement entails the disciplining of potential parasites, the exclusion of unruly thirds. Needless to say, much of this is automatic insofar as it is structured by the conventions that are constitutive of such research events, and the events on which they draw, such as mundane conversations. Also needless to say, this is contingent in that some cultures are happy to include what, from the perspective of others, might appear unwelcome social intrusions (such as the noisy presence of children).

Now, in certain cases, excluded thirds enter into a research event and comprehensively undermine it. The assumed ordering disintegrates when the companion animals entered parasitically into the interview described at the head of this chapter. And yet, we can look again at this and ask whether these parasites actually served to generate and reflect a more complex heterogeneous ordering.

On reflection, I (see Michael, 2004b) think there were several complexes of ordering being enacted in this seemingly simple research event in which no data was gathered (recall the tape machine dragged out of earshot, the apparent indifference of the participant to the research topic). First, we can note that the entry of the cat and the dog reveals the work that discipline does in the making of any research event. Second, we might ask what enabled the cat and pit bull to behave in the way that they did. In part, it was arguably the co-presence of their human; conversely, it can be suggested that their presence facilitated her 'resistance' to the interview. What this suggests is a more complex ordering in which this is no longer a typical relationship between 'interviewer' and 'interviewee' (to draw on the then-current terminology) but a relationship between two complexes (or hybrids) of humans and nonhumans: participant, cat, dog 'versus' researcher, tape recorder. What this suggests is that the 'gathering' of social data is a deeply heterogeneous affair: it rests not only on the relationships between humans, but also on how these relations inflect with and are partially mediated by nonhumans. This also adds another layer of analytic complexity: rather than see this episode as involving the struggles and alignments of humans and nonhumans, we might wish to switch our units of analysis to focus on the interplay of different hybrids composed of mixtures of the human and non-human (see Chapter 7 for an extended discussion of hybridity).

There is another complexification to this interview episode. Recall, the participant's reluctance to engage with the 'matter in hand' (as determined by the researcher, and agreed with the participant). The preferred topic of conversation was her new job at, and prospects with, Burger King. Here, we can propose that another form of differentiation was being enacted, this time between rather more expansive hybrids. Against the hybrid of the University (and perhaps higher education in general) was being counterposed a hybrid of Burger King (and perhaps the commercial sector in general). What was arguably being performed was the autonomy of the participant (now entangled with Burger King) from the University, its payment, and its representative (the researcher). Notice that central to this is the co-presence of the animals that facilitate the participant's 'obstructiveness'. Put otherwise, the animals are an element in the local enactment of meso-structures (as some might call them), that is, organizations. Once more, we detect another layer of the complexity in which heterogeneous orderings between human and nonhuman animals, technologies and organizations are played out. We shall return to elaborate on how the 'naming' of these hybrids might usefully inform analysis (Chapter 7).

It goes without saying that this analysis is contingent. It focuses on the nonhuman (animal) and the material as an underappreciated dimension in the generation of ostensibly 'social' data. Other researchers might have focused on other differences, even while retaining the emphasis on the nonhuman and material. For instance, there were obvious gender and class differences that might have affected the interaction. However, in keeping with the general Whiteheadian approach adopted here, I would not want to attribute to these a sort of determinative impact (that would be indulging in Whitehead's fallacy of misplaced concreteness). Rather, I would want to look at the ways gender and class were done in this specific context. So, while disparate class and gender (and many other) dispositions (one might even say habitus) might have been brought into the research event, how they were manifested in their specificity might have varied. For example, the role of the animals implicates specific enactments of class, ethnicity and gender: notably, my reluctance to do anything about the pit bull sitting on my feet suggests a further peeling back of further orderings, at the most visceral level, of the contemporary role of media's virulent representation of pit bulls as violent and uncontrollable, and the alignment of this with particular versions of gender, race and class.

The point is that these parasitical disruptions do not necessarily denote failure. They are an opportunity to unravel further the complexities that might emerge from that disruption and to reformulate the research event as an inventive problem: what are the exclusionary sociomaterial means by which research is rendered 'social'? What are the complexities and hybridities that can usefully be said to comprise the research event? What are the novel 'units of analysis' that might illuminate the research event?

Seeking complexity

In the preceding section, we considered the ways in which parasites imposed themselves upon a research event. Even so, it took time to imagine the actions of the various actors in the interview as disruptive: as noted, this was because the predisposition – or, better, the sociocultural norm – is to blame oneself as a more or less incompetent researcher. At other times, parasites are considerably less obvious, and we need to be a little more open to their affects and to the additional layers of complexity they introduce. In part, this is because we have become inured to these tacit or 'interstitial' parasites that operate within the fabric of mundane sociomateriality, disrupting it at an affective or corporeal level, but also complexifying the situation by precipitating minute affective or corporeal modulations. In what follows, two examples are presented.

Velcro is an everyday technology that is, by and large, understood to operate seamlessly (see Michael, 2006). It is even held up as iconic of unproblematic connection, both positively (it allows for ready connection irrespective of alignment) and negatively (Velcro straps enable too easy a connection on children's shoes, thereby denying them the opportunity to learn how to deal with problems in general). Of course, it turns out there are all sorts of problems that are associated with Velcro. Perhaps most obviously, it loses its stickiness with time and the collection of fluff or mud (although there are also many examples of its inappropriate use). However, for present purposes, I want to focus on a much less 'obvious' problem – less obvious because it was solved without explicit reference or reflection.

When my daughter was around the age of two, her very fine hair would get caught in the Velcro that attached the inside padding to the frame of her cycle helmet. This caused her obvious discomfort and initially we had to do a little work disentangling her hair. But this quickly changed into a set of automatic procedures in which she and I would coordinate our movements in such a way that her helmet was put on and secured without fuss.

Here, Velcro acted as a parasite that intervened in the event of the putting on of a helmet, yet it also contributed to an enriching of the parent–child relationship by virtue of requiring a sort of a micro-mutual choreography. Put crudely, a material intervention underpinned the unfolding of a more complex social relationality (Michael, 2006) between father and daughter. However, notice that the technology is central to this – there was an emergence of a new technosociality. The point is that in tracing these 'interstitial' parasites, we get a glimpse of more complex ways of thinking about relationalities, ways which gesture towards the emergence of pre-propositions.

This general perspective on the research event can take on an even more speculative tenor. Let us take the example of rolling luggage. Once again this has been promoted as a seamless technology – one that works unproblematically (Michael, 2011, 2016b). And yet, within the busy transport systems and hubs that travellers must negotiate, rolling luggage can be said to comprise another interstitial parasite. As one moves through these crowds of travellers, one is at once aware both of the problems one is generating with the rolling luggage as it trails behind one (it is potentially blocking or tripping others), and of the problems presented by those others (whose rolling luggage is potentially blocking or tripping one). In order to deal with this, there has arguably been a reconfiguration of body techniques (Mauss, 1973/1935): a redistribution of perception that attends at once to what is behind and what is in front, to dangers posed and faced. Here, the event of travelling has been socially complexified insofar as, where traditional held luggage did not require these sorts of sensorial sensitivity, rolling luggage necessitates a more acute awareness of the sociomaterialities around one.

Of course, this is a highly simplified rendition of the event of travelling with rolling luggage. For instance, rolling luggage itself has not stood still. Innovations such as spinner luggage with its articulated four wheels mean that, as with the older hand-held luggage, luggage can be retained by one's side, therefore not generating the sorts of problems just noted (though other problems arise – spinner luggage has a tendency to roll away when on a slope or on accelerating or decelerating transport, requiring new corporeal techniques). Moreover, there are cultural differences: the care taken in not blocking or tripping others implies a level of a particular sort of 'politeness' that not all cultures share. Finally, we might also mention the rise of such rolling luggage in the relation to 'infrastructural' changes, such as the reduction in the numbers of porters at transport hubs, or the extraordinary rise in tourism, rendering transport hubs so overpopulated, that they can function only by virtue of these minute corporeal repairs – micro-mutual choreography – that facilitate (relative) ease of movement.

This sort of empirical and analytical sensibility to the interstitial parasitism of such technologies can lead in a number of directions. At the level of critical governmentality (e.g. Dean, 1999), we might use the observations above as a way of considering how, as a feature of neoliberal societies, responsibility is re-assigned to citizens, consumers, users, etc. The crowding of transport systems and hubs will not be dealt with by governments or organizations, but by people, 'responsibilized' to negotiate these settings through all sorts of techniques – from the direction lines painted on the floors, through the constant intercom reminders to stay with one's luggage, to the presence of various guards and police. In the process, affects (which here means bodies and sensoriums) are affected either through direct disciplinary instructions or diffuse atmospheres (see, Anderson, 2014). Here, the complexification of relationalities that arises among travellers is a sort of compensatory collective responsibilization that makes transport manageable without raising mildly anti-capitalist questions about the need for investment in infrastructure, or, more radically, about the very need for travel.

Of course, this responsibilization is not as straightforward as implied in the foregoing. As Woolgar and Neyland (2013) have pointed out and beautifully illustrated, such governmental relations do not always unfold smoothly. Instructions whether highly explicit or rather diffuse are not always easy to follow, and people regularly find ways, whether by design or by accident, of sidestepping or mangling them. Yet, people might also find ways of creatively usurping these governed relations. The social relations among travellers as mediated by rolling luggage might indeed involve redistributed attention and reconfigured practices, and might further generate frustration and upset, when the micro-mutual choreographies of negotiating transport hubs goes awry. But there are also other potentialities in play. Travellers might well moan, and grimace, and get angry in the process of such collective negotiation, but they might also mutually recognize these affects in each other, might see the commonality of their lot. One might even posit that there is an emergent technosociality here that pre-propositionally opens up to different sorts of complexified relations – less agonistic and more communitarian, less fraught and more sociable.

Perhaps this last pre-propositional picture is but a dim possibility. After all, while Stengers (2010) insists, we might want to resist the probable and the plausible, and promote the possible, to definitively demarcate the possible might render it too plausible. We thus need to proceed cautiously. In this respect, what the interstitial parasite does, at least in principle, is provide a tool for charting how new more complex orderings – pre-propositions – might emerge through forms of disruption (not forgetting that those forms of disruption apply as much to the researcher as the researched). In this light, the research itself takes on a different tenor, and the question it is addressing can become transformed so that inventive problems come into view.

In the next section, we shift emphasis to a cousin of the parasite, namely the idiot. If their intellectual roots are different, they nevertheless share a disruptive quality. If the parasite disrupts and in so doing reveals or produces more complex orderings, the idiot's nonsensicalness gives us pause ... to question what it is we think we are doing as researchers.

The idiot

The idiot comes in a number of guises not all of which are useful for present purposes. Originally, for the ancient Greeks, the idiot was an individual concerned only with their own private affairs at the expense of their civic duty to get involved in matters of state. Lezaun and Soneryd (2007) summarize this idiot thus: 'by minding exclusively his (sic) own affairs, (the idiot) became useless to the polis' (p.295). This is paralleled in Deleuze's (2004) earlier version of the idiot who Beckman (2009) casts as a 'private thinker', conceptualized as a figure that

> takes the universal capacity to think for granted and ... fails to recognise that his (sic) self-reflection is based on a very strong presupposition regarding his own natural capacity for thought. The idiot, in fact, naturalises these presuppositions of the Image of thought and conceals them as a pure element of common sense.
>
> Beckman, 2009, p.55

However, subsequently, in Deleuze and Guattari's 'What is Philosophy' (1994), the idiot has been transformed into conceptual persona marked by absurdity and its creative potential. As such,

> The old idiot wanted, by himself, to account for what was or was not comprehensible, what was or was not rational, what was lost or saved; but the new idiot wants the lost, the incomprehensible, and the absurd to be restored to him.
>
> p.63

This absurdity opens up potentiality even if it is sometimes disorienting and painful because it makes so little sense. As Mills Todd (2004) writes, in his Introduction to Dostoyevsky's *The Idiot*, Prince Myshkin, 'stands out because he eludes the understanding of the (other characters)' (p.xxvi) and because they cannot 'fit him into their own patterns of distrust, self-hatred, lying and fraud' (p.xxvii). For Isabelle Stengers (2005a), the idiot similarly 'resists the consensual way in which the situation is presented and in which emergencies mobilize thought or action' (p.994). Stengers sees the 'presentation of the situation' as part of 'cosmopolitical' events – political events in which are involved both human and nonhuman participants. The idiot does not 'enter' such events, rather it remains outwith them because what the idiot says and does in relation to the shared understanding of the event is nonsensical. We shall have reason to discuss cosmopolitical events – or the ecology of practice – in more detail in Chapter 6. For present purposes, I will focus on the ways in which this version of the idiot can have impact upon the research event.

Stengers (2005a) suggests that 'the idiot can neither reply nor discuss the issue ... ' (the idiot) does not know ... the idiot demands that we slow down, that we don't consider ourselves authorized to believe we possess the meaning of what we know' (p.995). Accordingly, the inhabitants of the cosmopolitical event are obliged to 'bestow efficacy upon the murmurings of the idiot, the "there is something more important" that is so easy to forget because it "cannot be taken into account", because the idiot neither objects nor proposes anything that "counts"' (p.1001). By addressing seriously the idiot's nonsensical murmurings, the 'standard' or consensual meaning of the event is thrown open.

Before we proceed to discuss how to elaborate and 'operationalize' the figure of the idiot, there are a number of issues to bear in mind. The first is that the idiots we have addressed are modelled as people whose actions remain in one way or another unfathomable. We might ask whether this figure should be reserved for people – can other sorts of entities be 'idiotic'. For instance, can an animal that does something that is unexpected and difficult to interpret within the frame of a behavioural experiment be considered idiotic. Vincianne Despret (2016) certainly suggests that we might want to reconsider the particular experimental framing, to reformulate the question that is being asked of the animal, to rethink the paradigm in which that experiment sits. The point is that we might need to think carefully about who – or what – can take up the role of 'idiot'.

The second point is that the absurdist idiot we are dealing with is comparatively civil or polite. It is not difficult to imagine idiots whose behaviour is so outlandish, or indeed uncontrolled, that the non-sense-making that they engender leads to fear or flight, and perhaps an outright avoidance. Even 'milder' idiots can be distressingly abstruse so that they inspire a profound perplexity, and prompt a panoply of emotional reactions, including frustration, mockery, irritation, anger and rejection. Thus another famous idiot, Melville's Bartleby – whose idiocy manifests in the monotonic response to every request, 'I would prefer not to' – triggers, for instance, aggression, pity, disparagement. Taking these together, we also need to be circumspect about the assumptions we make about the figure of the idiot – not only should we reflect on the presuppositions exposed by attending to the idiot, but also on the presuppositions that allow for such attendance (see Chapter 5).

So, with these circumspections in mind, we can turn to 'operationalizing' the idiot (again this is more as a sensibility than a technique or a tool). Given that the idiot undercuts – prompts a re-visioning of – the meaning of the event, perhaps we need to begin by treating the research event as a site of 'consensus'. Within an interview, or group engagement, or participant observation, there is a routinely deep-seated sense that the participants – researchers and researched – have a shared understanding of the meaning of the event. The collective purpose is to contribute to a process of gathering some sort of social data often for the putative bettering of society. Of course, this can be challenged in various ways – lay people might see the questions as patronizing, or uninformed, or missing the real point – examples of this have been presented previously. In such cases, there nevertheless remains a common sense of what the event is about, even if it is challenged, undermined or usurped by the actions of the participants. By comparison, the idiotic participant acts in ways which do not make any (even oppositional) sense within the parameters of the research event. If those acts are 'endowed with efficacy', they yield a substantively different understanding of the research event – even to the point when it is no longer a *research* event.

At the most basic level, before we can proceed with an 'idiotic approach' we first need to 'bestow efficacy' upon the idiot. This is not as simple as it sounds. This is because as researchers, we are embroiled in the research event. As such, we have designed our research engagements with the aid of a panoply of assumptions about institutional parameters, the appropriate research question, the conceptual framework, the empirical field, the nature of our participants/practitioners, the utility of our chosen methods, the forms of analysis. We are intellectually and institutionally predisposed to a particular reading of research engagement as research engagement. The upshot is that we are not always sensitive to the more or less minor idiocies that inhabit such research engagements – we fail to bestow efficacy upon them.

For example, Michael and Carter (2001), in researching school students' understanding and utilization of educational materials focused on genetic science, ran a number of focus groups with the students. They noticed that in the focus groups, the students reflected on the value of information on genetics in complex ways. In particular, the students assessed the sources of genetic knowledge through a range of criteria, including scientific, pedagogic, affective, biographical, aesthetic and ethical. In trying to come to terms with this variety, we suggested that this might reflect a collective process of serially addressing the value and status of genetic information and its sources. At the time, this made a novel contribution to the literature (specifically in the field of Public Understanding of Science – PUS) by highlighting the hitherto unexpected fluidity of the identities of lay participants (the students). The students seem to display a far more variegated relationship to science than the literature of the time implied. However, reflecting back on this engagement after about a decade, and at some remove from those heady days of PUS, a different meaning to this research event suggests itself. Perhaps the students were behaving idiotically. What we assumed was a straightforward production of data – the students provided their accounts, inspired by one another – was possibly something rather different. In particular, the focus groups might have been a collective enactment of existing competitive group dynamics. The students were not acting as 'respondents' but as 'players' in a competitive game of trying to outdo one another in their responses to us. While we interpreted the focus group as a research engagement, the students ironically enacted it as a game in which they playfully competed to produce more and more ways of addressing the value and status of genetic information. The point is that within our research engagement, participants do 'idiotic' things to which we as researchers find it difficult to be sensitive, burdened as we are by our researcherly presuppositions and enthusiasms.

Michael (2012a) has called these untoward actions of research participants – albeit with a heavy dose of irony – 'misbehaviours'. They inhabit our research engagements in many different forms that, by and large, we ignore, or to which we remain oblivious. Opening ourselves up to these 'misbehaviours' can be regarded as a matter of care (see Chapter 6): an iterative ethical and political sensitivity to the assumptions that have been brought to bear through the research event. This is no easy matter as it also entails a potential re-demarcation of the meaning of the research event and, with that, a revision of the 'researcher'. In other words, research, researcher and researched can co-emerge redefined from such an exercise in idiotic sensibility.

In what follows, I discuss two ways in which we might 'operationalize' the idiot, and point to a third. In the first case, we consider examples of how we might encounter idiots in the process of enacting our research events, and how attending carefully to such idiocy might resource a rethinking of the research event, not least as it is manifested in the engagement with participants. In the second case, we seek out instances of what look like, or might be treated as, idiotic. Here, there is a deliberate reading of a particular social phenomenon as idiotic – as making no sense in relation to a particular academic framework. Out of this might emerge a reinvigorated questioning of that framework and a reorientation towards the research event's pre-propositions. Finally, there is the case of self-consciously enacted idiocy-producing events or artefacts that are designed to be idiotic to those who, respectively, participate in, or use them. The aim here is to open up speculatively possible avenues of thought and action for participants through the concoction of an idiotic research event.

Encountering the idiot

Let me begin with an initial and informal survey of idiots. This is collected from colleagues who have long been involved in engagement or participant research. This is research in which, for instance, members of the public sign up to participate in discussions with scientists and experts around a particular controversial scientific development or technological innovation whose potentially worrying implications are yet to be fully articulated. Colleagues noted that participants don't always display the sort of behaviour that is conventionally expected in such research events: they sometimes turn up drunk, or refuse to contribute, or simply fall asleep. Such 'misbehaviours' might be put down to the rich variety that makes up society, or to the inexperience of researchers, or to the recalcitrance of some members of the public. And yet, we might also stop and bestow a modicum of efficacy on such misbehaviour. Perhaps research engagement is nothing of the sort: it may be a warm place where people can hang out for a while. Such events are part of, or fit into, a 'society' or a 'routine' that can differ between participants and researchers. A focus group is contrastingly a way of countering loneliness, and a medium for producing data; a public engagement event is an opportunity to be entertained by people getting aggravated with one another, and a means of charting a form of politics in action. Indeed, taken together, perhaps these misbehaviours point us towards a taking stock of the stock we place in controversial scientific developments or technological innovations and the debates these engender. The very focus on controversiality might be of less interest to members of the public, than researchers, or might take on a different sense (be concerned with spectacle rather than policy, for example). In any case, such little idiocies or misbehaviours should alert us to the contingency of our very framing of a research event.

A second example is more involved in that not only is more detail provided, but it shows how such misbehaviour might enable a rethinking of the conceptualization of a research field. But further, it elaborates on how researcher and research might enter into and agitate the routines of potential participants, and as such be idiotic in their own right.

Horst and Michael (2011), in reflecting on the science communication installation Landscape of Expectations, which had been assembled in a shopping mall just outside Copenhagen, came to regard some of the actions of visitors as idiotic.

The installation comprised an invitation to participants to engage not only with the political and ethical issues surrounding stem cell research, but also with the political means by which such issues might be debated (not least, the role that laypeople might play in such debates). As such the installation was both a means of conveying technical knowledge and political controversy, but also collecting data from participants about their reaction to that knowledge and controversy, and how these might be politically managed. While many visitors were happy to read the various information panels and engage in the various tasks and exercises presented within the installation, others were less willing to follow the instructions. One particular group of teenage schoolgirls responded in ways that from the perspective of science communication did not make much sense. Thus, in that part of the installation where there was a TV connected to a camera, the girls enacted X-Factor performances to one another, and in response to the posted query: 'what are you most worried about?', one schoolgirl commented: 'my biggest fear is that all shopping centres in the world close'. So here were responses that didn't seem to engage with the installation in any serious way. Rather, the girls appeared to be operating along rather different parameters of relevance.

Now, the girls' responses could be treated in terms of their 'idiocy'. To elaborate idiocy is here understood in 'relational', terms: within the setting of the science communication installation, the 'sense-lessness' or 'non-sense-making' of the girls' actions emerges in relation to a specific 'sense-making' embodied in the installation. And yet, it is perhaps unsurprising that this was the reaction among a group of teenagers presumably out on a shopping trip. Rather, their non-sense-making is very likely to constitute a very serious sense-making within the dynamics of a group of teenagers. To have engaged seriously with the Landscape of Expectations would have been tantamount to challenging those dynamics, and the ongoing, collective enactment of the group's identity.

By treating the non-sense-making seriously, we can begin to interrogate our own assumptions about the research event as mediated by the Landscape of Expectations. As Horst and Michael went on to elaborate, perhaps we need to step back from existing presuppositions about the installation as a means of science communication. On this score, we might say that the Landscape of Expectations drew on the two predominant conceptualizations of science communication (Horst, 2008): the diffusion model (in which knowledge was diffused from experts to lay publics), and the critical model (in which dialogue and participation took place between experts and lay publics). However, what the reaction of the girls (and others did) was point to a third model – one of emergence in which the identities of expert and lay were de-reified, as it were. Who might count as a scientific expert or a member of the lay public depended on how the science communication 'research' event unfolded. At the same time, the event might not turn out to be one of 'research': it might emerge as an event of mutual entertainment and group bonding (as might be posited for the schoolgirls).

Crucially, we might also imagine that from the perspective of the teenage girls, the installation was itself idiotic. After all, here was a strange (for them), uninvited (by them), artefact taking up space in their domain. It was, in relation to their collective sense-making, non-sense-making. On this score, as researchers, perhaps we need to acknowledge that sometimes, the events we organize and the artefacts we craft seem idiotic to others – not least those others with whom we would like to engage. Additionally, even if we treat the idiotic actions of others with care, we cannot necessarily expect that care to be reciprocated. We cannot presume that the idiocy of our research is bestowed efficacy.

This last point again cautions against too ready a use of the idiot. We need to acknowledge a certain 'perspectivism' when mobilizing the figure of the idiot – not least insofar as the idiotic might be precipitated by the idiocy of the research event. This 'reverberative' quality of the idiot is something we will touch upon again when we consider, in Chapter 6, collaboration (whether amongst practitioners from other academic disciplines, or with practitioners from other walks of life) as a cosmopolitical and careful process.

Seeking out the idiot

In the preceding discussion, we have accidentally encountered idiots who, with proper care and attention, have enabled us to slow down our thinking and reflect on our intellectual presuppositions, and thereby entertain new pre-propositions about the research event. By contrast, the present section suggests a tactic of deliberately seeking out the idiotic. Of course, this is fraught with problems. After all, to seek out an idiot, is in some ways to know, or at least have an inkling of, what is worth problematizing within one's existing framework. In other words, there is a danger of domesticating the idiot so that it simply underpins a sort of self-serving or self-fulfilling analysis. Having noted this, it is possible to seek out events or groups whose behaviour makes no immediate sense.

I return to a previous example. In Chapter 2, there was a discussion about how we engage with – notice *and ask about* – the sub-topical. There, I pointed to an encounter with YouTube clips in which iPhones were destroyed in one more or less exotic way or another (for instance, to recapitulate: by being dropped from a selection of heights onto a selection of surfaces; cut, crushed or pierced with technologies ranging across trains, guns, blenders and hydraulic presses; and burnt thermally or chemically with home-made flame throwers, molten gold or aluminium, a bed of 10,000 matches or Fluoroantimonic acid). Entertaining and distracting as all this was, I couldn't help but think that this ostensible genre of YouTube films of iPhone destruction had something idiotic about it that perhaps opened up our typical ways of thinking of the relation of scientific expertise to lay publics. Here was a genre that in several ways enacted the various signifiers of scientific experimentation: there were claims about testing the limits of the iPhone, there were quasi-experimental protocols in place, and there was some degree of measuring and commenting on the results of the experiments (of destruction). But all these were contorted as it were. They deviated substantially from the conventional modes of scientific practice. For instance, the process and setting of the experimentation, as well as forms of address to the audience, were marked by extreme informality; the reasoning behind the experiment was vaguely framed at best (often couched in terms of 'let's see what happens when …'.); there was a lack of precision in the way the experiment is conducted (rough estimates of quantities, routine accidents); the reports to camera were usually exclamatory and often frenzied.

To reiterate, it seemed to me that here was an opportunity to treat this genre as if it were idiotic, in the sense of being afforded an efficacy that slowed some typical ways of thinking about the relation of scientific expertise to lay publics. For example, in the field of 'Citizen Science', the primary concerns are the distribution of scientific knowledge and occasionally scientific skills (along with enthusing citizens about science), but also the recruitment of members of the public who are asked to collect scientific data (very often about wildlife and environmental conditions – see, for example, Cooper et al., 2007; Dickinson et al., 2010; Crain et al., 2014). Understandably, a central issue is the capacity and skills of citizens as 'quasi-scientists' able to produce useable data. Additionally, some of citizen science projects are more collaborative and can involve citizens having a hand in shaping the research question itself (e.g. Woolley et al., 2016; Prainsack, 2014).

Yet in the case of the 'Destroying iPhones' genre, there are several things missing: the lack of a 'serious' research question, the neglect of methodological rigour, the absence of accredited or institutionalized scientific actors. In some ways, as Michael (2017a) proposes, this genre might be thought in terms of a 'feral science' – resistant to domestication by scientific institutions (unlike, say 'science in the wild', which might escape the laboratory but which is nevertheless associated with the projects tied to scientific institutions – see Callon et al., 2001). On this score, there is perhaps also an indifference to being citizenly – what does destroying an iPhone contribute to the polity? Moreover, the genre reflects a sort of surfeit: of enthusiasm (for the iPhone – despite the wanton destruction, there is evidently much affection for this technology); of ostentatious affect in the conduct of the destruction; of knowledge even (in the sense of do we 'really' need to know how an iPhone stands up to a home-made flamethrower, etc.?).

A number of questions suggest themselves that trouble the usual thinking within the field of citizen science (and beyond that, the fields of public engagement with science and technology, and science communication). Perhaps in the Destroying iPhones' genre, we are witness to a sort of 'epistemic excess' which we can counterpose to 'the serious production of serious knowledge'? Or we can contrast the genre's feral science with more domesticated and institutionalized forms of deriving knowledge. Or we might treat the practitioners and audiences of iPhone destruction as a sort of mediated fan community that questions anew the idea of citizen science and indeed figure the scientific citizen (e.g. Irwin, 1995). In all these cases, by carefully paying attention to the idiotic doings that comprise what I've called the 'Destroying iPhones' genre, we can interrogate and potentially rethink the usual categories that apply to the relations between science and publics. There is even a possibility that we might expand our repertoire of categories and open new fruitful ways of doing citizenship in relation to scientific expertise (and vice versa).

Minimally, it would be useful if this seeking out of, and engagement with, the idiocy of the 'Destroying iPhones' genre at least gave us pause – allowed us to scrutinize our usual ways of thinking about the relations between science, communication and publics, and perhaps to imagine new ones. Needless to say, there is no guarantee of such fruitfulness. Nevertheless, in the idiocy of this genre, we can detect pre-propositions that suggest new possibilities and relations. Such a process of speculation implicates a third 'operationalization' of the idiot – the deliberate (as opposed to accidental as was arguably the case for the Landscape of Expectations installation) rendering of idiocy. In this case, it is the researcher who, as a mode of research, generates what might be called, the proactive idiot – the idiot is deliberately introduced into the research event.

The proactive idiot

In the preceding sections, to encounter the idiot is to stumble upon it accidentally, and to seek out the idiot is to deliberately reimagine an event or phenomenon as if it made no sense (by situating it within a familiar sense-making framework such as science communication). In this final section, we briefly point to a third tactic – that of purposefully fabricating or fabulating the idiotic. Here, there is a concerted effort to 'design' an idiotic object or interaction, or to craft an idiotic account, that can act as a sort of provocation that opens up possibilities for those who engage with the object or account or situation, including the researchers. The research event itself becomes knowingly idiotic – brought into its concrescence is a concrete element of the nonsensical that ensures a sort of 'dissatisfaction', or speaking aesthetically, a 'semblance' (Massumi, 2011). We leave detailed discussion and illustration of the proactive idiot to the next chapter not least because there is considerable conceptual ground-clearing needed. Suffice it to say for the moment that there are many ways in which the proactive idiot can be deployed, and that often this will require venturing onto interdisciplinary terrain.

Concluding remarks

In the last chapter, the focus was on various (limited) forms of attunement and the way in which attunement could be understood affectively and aesthetically. This chapter, in contrast, has focused on a different dimension of the speculative, the process of disconcertment variously conceptualized through such figures as the parasite and the idiot. The impression might be that attunement and disconcertment stand in contrast, even in opposition, to one another. If attunement connotes a sort of harmonization, a patterning of relations, and disconcertment implies their dissolution or disruption, it might well seem as if these are contraries.

However, this is not an altogether persuasive dichotomy, especially when we consider that we might well need to attune ourselves to that which disconcerts and be disconcerted by our attunements. Thus, if the idiot is disruptive or gives us pause, it is because we have in one way or another attuned to it, despite the predisposition to neglect it by virtue of our framing of the research event. And if we have attuned to a particular event or figure, it is because we have excised – excluded – some element that might have idiotically disrupted proceedings. In terms of the research event more broadly, it perhaps benefits us to rethink the interweaving of attunement and disconcertment (or non-attunement and concertment) and better to trace the elements that concresce to attain, at once, a 'satisfaction' (or harmony) and a 'dissatisfaction' (or disharmony). In what follows, by way of illustration of this topological relation between attunement and disconcertment, we draw on an example of some – what can be called – 'problematic problems' of everyday life.

Research events such as interviews or focus groups or engagement events entail patterns of attunements and disconcertments. As hinted in this chapter and the last, participants and researchers partly attune to, and are disconcerted by, one another. But such patterns of attunement and disconcertment also apply to the settings of research – the furniture, the buildings, the pictures on the walls, the smells and sounds that are all part of research event. As with everyday life, these sociomaterial arrangements comprise affordances, but they also can constitute 'little problems' – problems which participants attune to, ignore, and are disconcerted by.

The matter of 'little problems' is taken up ironically in Douglas Adams and John Lloyd's book, *The Meaning of Liff* (1983), they write that they are interested in the 'hundreds of common experiences, feelings, situations and even objects which we all know and recognize' but which thus far have had no name attached to them (p.5). In going about addressing these supposedly terrible situations, etc., they exploit the reservoir of place names 'which spend their time doing nothing but loafing about on signposts pointing at places' (p.5). So for example, they identify and name the following objects and situations:

ESCHER (n.)

One of those push taps installed in public washrooms enabling the user to wash their trousers (sic) without actually getting into the basin.

p.49

FRAMLINGHAM (n.)

A kind of burglar alarm in common usage. It is cunningly designed so that it can ring at full volume in the street without apparently disturbing anyone.

p.53

HADZOR (n.)

A sharp instrument placed in the washing-up bowl which makes it easier to cut yourself.

p.65

TORLUNDY (n.)

Narrow but thickly grimed strip of floor between the fridge and the sink unit in the kitchen of a rented flat.

p.136

78 Idiot and parasite

Michael (1997) has addressed these 'little problems' and devised technological solutions (as well as finding novel innovations and converting them into the named definitions of little problems in the style of the Meaning of Liff). So, for example, he has proposed that Torlundy can be tackled with Dirt Catch Strips that have an adhesive and disinfectant-coated surface and can be cut to measure so that they fit any space between kitchen appliances and cabinets.

Clearly, there are many such unnamed, semi-attuned-to and disconcerting elements that are interstitial but constituent parts of the events of everyday life, including research events. With regard to the latter, we could point to the ritual of finding places to put bags and coats at the beginning of a focus group, the institutional coffee table around which researcher and participants sit and which is routinely just too low to reach comfortably, the institutional coffee itself. As elements that feed into research events, once identified and attuned to, they allow us to speculate on the character of that research event – to begin to articulate interesting problems about its eventuation. Is the research event really about the stated research question at stake, or does it become an event primarily marked by attempts to regain, subtly and unobtrusively, bodily comfort, or else discipline corporeal discomforts and disconcertments?

Now, this might look like another self-indulgence: researching the research process, where it is the most 'trivial' aspects of the research process (e.g. low coffee tables, and the shuffling of coats and bags) that are subject to scrutiny. However, the point is that we don't know what is 'trivial': a low institutional table might materially and semiotically 'signal' all sorts of things that impact how the way the research question at stake comes to be practically enacted over the course the research event. I am not suggesting that this be a concern that is integrated into every research event design, or that can be exhaustive in its attunement to, and identification of, interstitial, barely noticeable but disconcerting little problems. Rather, the aim is to sensitize us to the many ways in which others (participants) are sensitized to, and disconcerted by, the research events of which they become a part, and to prompt the asking of potentially interesting questions about what those research events might 'mean', how they are ordered and disordered, and what pre-propositions they might enable.

In the next chapter, this mutuality of disconcertment and attunement is further explored, not least in relation to the way that an overtly speculative research event can be 'rejected'. There, we turn to the proactively idiotic.

5
SPECULATION
Fabulating and fabricating the idiot

Introduction

A few years ago, while resident in Australia, I was working at my desk, in my apartment, in my apartment block in Kings Cross, a suburb of Sydney. I don't recall what I was working on, though I do remember I was increasingly anxious about a specific chapter on design and disruption I was committed to writing. I had been working at the intersection of design and the social sciences for a few years, and novel ideas were becoming harder to come by: I couldn't think of anything interesting to write on, at least without repeating myself (again). Probably as yet another displacement activity, I went to iTunes on my computer to play some music. This would be relayed through my Damson Cisor BT5 Resonating Bluetooth Speaker. However, the speaker started playing something different, a piece of squeaky but pleasant ambient music that was nothing like the music iTunes was saying it was playing (almost certainly 1980s new wave). My initial thought was that the speaker was picking up music from another device belonging to another resident in the apartment block. I didn't dwell too long on this explanation as, from the little I knew about Bluetooth, it was highly unlikely that a connection could be made to my speaker through the various floors and walls between my apartment and the others. I started shuffling the various documents on my desk and found my iPhone hidden under a book or two. This, it turned out, was the culprit: the iPhone had connected to the speaker ahead of my laptop (presumably when I switched on the speaker to connect to my computer). What struck, and partly riled, me at the time, was that these devices had autonomously determined to connect together, in the process confusing me and inspiring a mildly paranoid vision in which my speaker was hijacked by another resident's computer or phone or tablet (see Michael, 2016c).

DOI: 10.4324/9781351133555-5

This minor, and otherwise ridiculous and forgettable, incident turned out to be the inspiration for writing the chapter I was struggling with. The design of these devices and their operation comprised a species of sociotechnical conspiracy that by-passed my situated agency: together, they had 'misbehaved'.

Arguably, here was an instance of something akin to idiocy (and indeed parasitism) in the technical sense discussed in the previous chapter. Stepping back from this collective idiocy, I began to speculate on how we might understand it: that is, to – revise its meaning in a more speculative mode. In keeping with this, I went on to imagine that this 'misbehaviour' opened up an opportunity for thinking about the potential sociotechnical relations in my apartment building. Perhaps, had I followed up on the mistaken belief that my speaker had been 'hijacked' by someone else's Bluetooth device, had I discovered my mistake and offered subsequent apologies, a different set of relations might have emerged among the occupants of the building. Instead of the more or less resolute anonymity practised in the apartment block, what might emerge is potentially a new sort of technosociality (see Chapter 4) – an alternative sociality partly mediated by, and entangled with, our technologies (and their in/discipline).

Additionally, I went on to speculate, maybe the idiocy of the technologies and their inter-relations could be developed and deployed more proactively. By deliberately introducing an idiotic device, or an idiotic coterie of devices, into a particular setting or situation, could that idiocy provide an opportunity for rethinking and reconfiguring that setting or situation? Could such an idiotic system disconcert and lure its users into not only rethinking their circumstances but also affectively re-attuning themselves to those circumstances, and deriving new patterns of relationships and practices, that is, pre-propositions that reflected an emergent technosociality?

This latter might seem rather fanciful (not least in the light of the ethical challenges it throws up). Nevertheless, it does serve to dramatize the two general modes of speculation that I want to discuss in this chapter. On the one hand, I told a story of how one can narratively speculate about the re-configuration of the technosociality of an apartment block. The research event becomes a locale for the nurturing, emergence and circulation of idiotic new stories (of various kinds) and their pre-propositions. On the other hand, the research event can also be the site into which idiotic artefacts and activities can be proactively designed and introduced as a means for enabling participants and practitioners (researchers included) to query what it is we think we are busy doing, and to open up inventive problems (with their attendant pre-propositions). If, especially following Donna Haraway (2015, 2016), we call the former speculative fabulation, we can call the latter speculative fabrication. As we shall see, these are not as distinct as might first appear.

This chapter is therefore concerned with how versions of idiocy can be proactively interjected into the research event as a means of opening up its parameters, of exploring its status as 'research', and enabling the emergence of more inventive problems. We begin with a consideration of the creative role of fabulation, broadly understood, within the research event. Here, we will see how fabulation and more broadly storying and narrativizing can play several roles in the research event. There is then an extended account of speculative fabrication as a way of idiotically structuring the research event. Here, I trace a number of ways in which idiotic objects and events can be designed as key elements in a research event. Focusing especially on 'speculative design', I discuss how this tradition of work provides techniques for generating what Massumi (2011) has called 'semblance', an aesthetic space of potentiality in which new ways of grasping commonplace concepts and practices can emerge. As we shall see, in both the cases of fabulation and fabrication (and their interweaving), there is nothing straightforward to these processes of speculative intervention; there are no guarantees that the speculative research event opens up potentialities, enables the framing of inventive problems or facilitates the emergence of novel pre-propositions. On this score, there is also an examination of the failure of such idiotic interjections and the roles they can play.

Speculative fabulation

If fabulation connotes, among other things, storytelling – the crafting and telling of fables – of one sort or another, social scientists are of course used to detecting and deploying fables, or, more specifically, narratives, in their analysis and production of various writings. There are plenty of examples of the analysis of the role of stories in a range of social events, including everyday life (e.g. the ways in which mundane objects serve in the narration of family life, Miller, 2009) and science (e.g. in debates over embryo research, Mulkay, 1997), and there are plenty of resources that lay out techniques for the derivation and analysis of narratives (e.g. Reissman, 2008; Elliott, 2005). As Hyvärinen (2016) summarizes, we can count 'three existing alternatives of narrative sociology: that is, sociological analysis of collected narrative texts, storytelling sociology, and the analysis of narrative realities and narrative genres' (p.39). The emphasis here is on narrative as a means of deriving or portraying someone's (a lay person, a practitioner, a social scientist) more or less well-demarcated reality.

Further, in the present instance, fabulation is treated as a process whereby 'fabulous' narratives are encouraged to surface within, or are even be introduced into, the research event in order to facilitate novel pre-propositions. In this respect, even if we take fabulation as a subgenre of narrative, or more broadly of writing, or even more broadly of representation, it is characterized by the potential artistic characteristics of future orientation, incompletion and invitation. As Bochner and Ellis (2003) put it:

> [t]he product of research, whether an article, a graph, a poem, a story, a play, a dance, or a painting, ... [is] not a closed statement but an open question; not a way of declaring 'this is how it is' but a means of inviting others to consider what it (or they) could become.
>
> *p.507*

Before directly addressing fabulation, there are few more distinctions to draw. For instance, there is the differentiation of fabulation from expectation. We have already touched on expectations in Chapter 4. There we suggested that the attempt to engage publics about the expectations of stem cell research innovation, and related political processes, that were embodied in the Landscape of Expectations installation (Horst and Michael, 2011; see below), might appear 'fabulous' – even fantastical – to some groups. There are several social scientific perspectives on the enactment of futures (e.g. Anderson, 2010; Adams et al., 2009), but for the present discussion, we draw on the sociology of expectations (e.g. Brown and Michael, 2003; Borup et al., 2006). Central to this approach is the argument that expectations, which *prima facie* are narratives about real possibilities (solutions, innovations), can also be seen to be 'fabulous'. This can be the case when expectations are grasped as more or less hopeful or promissory projections that function as a means of affecting relevant institutions in the present which will thereby affect the future. Sometimes these projections are regarded as unrealistic 'hype' that, if successfully and persuasively deployed, can nevertheless serve to garner various resources (funds, regulatory leniency or support, community enthusiasm). However, it is not always easy to differentiate expectations from fabulations, hope from hype (see Brown, 2003), not least as both are entangled with prospective relationalities. Having noted this, expectations tend to depict and promise well-delineated futures whereas fabulations are, arguably, (self-)problematizing. By this, I mean that fabulations wear their constructedness on their sleeve, as it were: they incorporate their own problematic status, and as such do not fix a future, nor a present, but open up the possibility of crafting multiple possible futures (any specified future is thus contingent and encourages critique and a counter-creativity). By comparison, expectations, as noted previously, close down present actions – certain actions need to be followed if the expected future is to be realized.

It is also important, albeit briefly, to address the relationship between fabulation and utopian (otherwise known as transcendental – see Geuss, 1981; Held, 1980) critique. The latter can presuppose an ideal state of affairs that has been thwarted by existing conditions (of capitalism, patriarchy, neoliberalism, anthropocene, etc.) which can serve as a bedrock from which to critique those conditions. Additionally, as Bauman (1976) notes, utopias can also have an impact on the unfolding of history by, for example, inspiring social movements. For Levitas (2013), utopia is a method whereby sociology is itself reworked to at once encompass the nonhuman, the 'natural' and the material, and engage with a normative dimension that explores what it means to be human. In keeping with the general tenor of this volume, Levitas' framing of utopia as method eschews the version of sociology as an objective form of knowledge, and utopia as 'mere' speculation', and instead argues that utopias are a 'repressed, already existing, form of knowledge about possible futures' (Levitas, 2013, p.xv). In many ways, this book is about enabling the expression of those futures. However, while Levitas wants to engage in a sort of analytic archaeology that excavates those possible futures by seeking them out in diverse social and political practices, the various techniques discussed in this volume resist the temptation to demarcate futures as such, but rather to resource participants and practitioners with some tools for an exploration of potentialities. Additionally, sociology, in Levitas' utopian reimagining, is a creative practice 'building on the strengths of the discipline which include its focus on institutions, its systemic holism, its attention to subjects and agents as well as structures and processes' (p.149). Such visions of the future – which Levitas takes to be part of 'a process which is necessarily provisional, reflexive and dialogic' (p.149) – can certainly resource the ways in which people open up possibilities, even if some of the futures that are currently imagined reside in what Tsing (2014, 2015) calls 'blasted landscapes', or the anthropocene, or Haraway's (2015, 2016) Chthulucene (see below). The point of contrast here, though this is by no means definitive, is that utopian critique can entail the demarcation of whole future societies, whereas speculative fabulation perhaps is better understood as providing some narrative means for allowing such holistic visions to emerge piecemeal.

If the above-mentioned comparisons sketch outlines between the speculative, the utopian and the expectational, we can now turn to how we might 'operationalize' fabulation. Echoing Hyvarinen's (2016) tripartite division of narrative sociology, three non-mutually exclusive and non-exhaustive options come to mind: investigations into how fabulation is 'embodied' in, or enacted through, existing cultural artefacts and practices; explorations of how fabulation is disseminated or 'transmitted' through scholarly and engaged works and practices; and fabulation as a part – a prompt and/or a product – of participant engagement.

Detecting fabulation

As an example of the first option, we can look, albeit briefly, to *Glitterworlds* by Rebecca Coleman (2020). In Coleman's complex re-articulation that extends glitter's meanings beyond critical environmental or medical discourses, she discusses the variegated roles glitter can play through an analysis of the films of *Glitter* and *Precious*. Drawing in part on Nyong'o's (2019) work, Coleman puts it thus:

> A prevalent way in which fabulation has been theorised is as the creation of an alternative future; indeed, in this book I have discussed and developed it in this way. The examples of *Glitter* and *Precious* complicate this understanding of fabulation by showing how the futures fabricated through fabulation may be not so much alternative or different as seeking to grasp and ground themselves in what is already possible or normal for many … they both exist and do not yet exist, they are fantasies that are part of 'real life', blurring the boundaries between the two.
>
> *p.123*

Coleman also detects fabulation in the practice of glitter-bombing in which, for instance, 'LGBTQ★ activists, protesting against homophobic and anti-choice ideas and policies, attended public events where the (politicians) were appearing and glitter-bombed them, throwing or sprinkling glitter over them. They often videoed the incidents and circulated them on social media' (p.125). Coleman picks up on the ways in which glitter-bombing is, on the one hand, a means to bringing political attention to LGBTQ* issues and concerns and facilitating political change, and on the other, 'a mode of fabulation in its creation of "a people to come"' (p.137).

The example of glitter-bombing bears some resemblance to the example of the 'Destroying iPhones' YouTube genre discussed as a 'seeking out the idiot' in Chapter 4. After all, both entail an overt lack of 'seriousness' (from certain perspectives) while inviting novel pre-propositions to be glimpsed. On one level, then, they comprise feral (research) events out of which can emerge more inventive problems. For instance, how can new forms of spectacle resource new modes of, respectively, political and epistemic practice?

Circulating fabulation

Clearly, in the cases discussed earlier, a particular form of critical and creative scholarship has been mobilized to crystallize the speculative possibilities of particular cultural artefacts and practices. But social scientists also compose their own fabulations. In some ways, this can be tied to a tradition of narrativization in a discipline such as sociology. As Watson (2016, 2021) has summarized, the use of fiction has long been a means by which sociologists have attempted to disseminate sociological insights, to engage with publics in ways that better convey, and render more accessible, core sociological ideas. But additionally, dissemination can also attend to the prospective and the possible, involve speculations on the not-as-yet whether through poetry, instructional manuals, science fiction novels, speculative documentaries, digital games design and playing (see, for example, Jungnickel, 2020; Salazar et al., 2017). In all these cases, the broad aim is to enable access to other ways of grasping – understanding and imagining – states of affairs that are potentialities, which implicate alternative sociomaterial relations, that invite more inventive problems with their emergent pre-propositions.

As an example, we can turn to the work of Haraway (2016). In her *Staying with the Trouble*, we are presented with an argument for speculative fabulation – a complex and collective process of 'participat(ing) in a kind of genre fiction committed to strengthening ways to propose near futures, possible futures, and implausible but real nows' (p.136). Such social, semiotic and material practices are grounded in, and resourced by, a 'rich terran muddle' (p.53) characterized by tentacularity, laterality, heterogeneity, multispecies becoming and captured in the figure of 'a buzzing, stinging, sucking swarm' – a compost pile in which humans are thoroughly immersed (p.55). What does speculative fabulation afford? It is a means – a lure – that enables the

> proposing (of) the Chthulucene as a needed third story … (that) unlike either the Anthropocene or the Capitalocene … is made up of ongoing multispecies

stories and practices of becoming-with in times that remain at stake, in precarious times, in which the world is not finished …

p.55

Accordingly, there is a contrast with

the dominant dramas of Anthropocene and Capitalocene discourse, (insofar as) human beings are not the only important actors in the Chthulucene … human beings are with and of the earth, and the biotic and abiotic powers of this earth are the main story.

p.55

Here, Haraway, in her contrast between her Chthulucene and the more familiar Anthropocene and the Capitalocene, moves away from the 'too-big players and too-big stories of Capital and Anthropos' (p.55). These trigger 'apocalyptic panics and even odder disengaged denunciations … cynicism, defeatism, and self-certain and self-fulfilling predictions, like the "game over, too late" discourse …' (p.55–56). Instead, Haraway counterposes an engagement with the specific complexities and dynamics of the more-than-human (say coral and lichen symbionts): in this way, we might be brought into 'the storied tissues of the thickly present Chthulucene, where it remains possible – just barely – to play a much better SF game, in nonarrogant collaboration with all those in the muddle' (p.56). This is also a process of making odd kin with others who are more than ancestral or genealogical, who might be neither individuals nor humans but are nevertheless persons (Haraway, 2015). In this composing of kinship connections, there is both a 'join(ing of) forces to reconstitute refuges, to make possible partial and robust biological-cultural-political-technological recuperation and recomposition, which must include mourning of irreversible losses' (Haraway, 2016, p.101).

The speculative fabulation that (along with others) Haraway so expertly muddles – The Camille Stories: Children of the Compost – narrates a potential unfolding of the Chthulucene into the 24th century. It powerfully and troublingly conjures a biological–cultural–political–technological muddle that painfully and joyously entails 'the layered, curious practice of becoming-with others for a habitable flourishing world' (p.168). To reiterate, this fabulation is a lure – a speculative opening up of potentialities that are more hopeful than those too-easily associated with the Anthropocene and the Capitalocene (see also, Wilkie et al., 2017). Were we to abstract from Haraway's Chthulucene, we might say – crudely – that it is marked by naturecultures whose spatiality comprises topological, heterogeneous involutions that temporally unfold with increasingly nurtured complexity that, in turn, reflects both loss of species and habitat but also inflects with the reconstitution of naturecultural refuges and a proliferation of kin-making.

To the extent that The Camille Stories lure those outside of academia, they are a speculative fabulation that is also tied to the process of dissemination or 'transmission' wherein scholarly works and practices (understood in the widest sense to include various experiments with form) are distributed beyond academia. As Jungnickel (2020) notes transmission is not distinct from the process of research: 'Transmissions (the book) … implies that the formats and conventions involved in making and sharing knowledge cannot be clearly separated' (p.3). The forms of representation and enactment to which, within our (inter)disciplinary traditions, we are most bound, affect what is 'sayable' and 'doable', as do, relatedly, the audiences to which we most usually address ourselves (e.g. Myers, 1989). Across various works (e.g. Back and Puwar, 2012; Jungnickel, 2020; Salazar et al., 2017), there is advocated, in one way or another, an expansion of relations between making and sharing. In terms of the research event, this implies a reconsideration of the elements ingredient to the opening up of the possible. New audiences (and collaborators), new literary and other forms of expression and enactment (e.g. exhibitions, installations, curations, performances) can be part of an 'idiotic impetus' towards pausing and rethinking the presuppositions that underpin the research event, and orienting to the not-as-yet. We shall return to such matters in Chapters 6 and 7 where we discuss, respectively, the research event in relation to interdisciplinarity, and 'analysis' in relation to 'dissemination'.

Interjecting fabulations

Finally, in this section, we can turn to the option of asking and enabling research participants to fabulate – to sketch a future or a scenario that embodies new patterns of pre-propositions. There are various activities through which such participant fabulation can be enabled, for instance, participatory animation (D'Onofrio, 2017), playing (Hjorth and Richardson, 2020) and participatory design (Le Dantec and DiSalvo, 2013). For present purposes, the focus is on more 'literary' techniques wherein texts are requested from participants in response to an imaginative exercise.

In the design-social science research project 'Sustainability Invention and Energy Demand Reduction: Co-Designing Communities and Practice' (see Boucher et al., 2018), cultural probes were used in order to derive material that would contribute to the broader research process and its exploration of the role of community, information, and the future in shaping energy demand reduction. Cultural probes (e.g. Boehner et al., 2012; see below) set their users strange tasks, in the present case, this might be writing an obituary for a favourite appliance, or filling out the speech bubbles in a dialogue between objects, or adding headlines about the future in fabricated newspapers and magazines, or adding coloured stamps and annotations to a plan of a house to indicate emotion experiences. In all these cases, people have the opportunity to write down their thoughts – to speculate – on future possibilities. These might range across technological innovations, political changes and interpersonal shifts.

If cultural probes serve as interjections of the idiotic, they do not necessarily yield positive speculation. While they might open up possibilities, these need not be especially focused on the prospective (responses might be rather limited in their outlook) and might even be quite retrograde. This is perhaps not unsurprising given that not all people take kindly to the potentiality of such idiocy – some indeed find it threatening (Connolly, 2011; see below). As we shall see, a degree of supplementary work needs to be conducted by researchers in order to make an idiotic intervention 'acceptable' as well as 'graspable'. An example of spurious speculation can be found in another study (Lupton and Michael, 2017; Michael and Lupton, 2016) in which participants engaged in a 'Personal Data Machine' activity, in which, as pairs, they were asked to design data-gathering devices. One part of the task involved participants designing, and reflecting upon, a personal data machine to gather data on others. Participants were encouraged to use their imaginations in this task, not least through simultaneous exposure to a slideshow that displayed a sequence of technologies that innovatively or speculatively gathered and presented data. Examples of participant-produced and narrated personal data machines included devices that could detect others' lies, track the activities of commercial competitors, reveal workmates' salaries, scan potential partners to determine assets or criminal record, measure workers' geolocation and productivity. If these proposals could be counted speculative, they were of a particular delimited sort which were sometimes dispiritingly invasive. The point here is that that there are no guaranties that such speculative methods will open up new, promising pre-propositions, as opposed to reproduce and reinforce the worst of existing practices. The additional point is that work needs to be done to enable the research event to unfold towards potentialities that are novel, that allow for inventive problem making. Such work, as we shall see below, entails a demarcation of the ingredients that compose the research event, for example, the choice of participants, the character of the task or the storying of the 'idiotic' device that aims to prompt speculation.

In the next section, many of the themes above are taken up and elaborated through a discussion of one particular mode of speculative fabrication, namely speculative design.

Speculative fabrication and design

In this section, I treat speculative fabrication as a counterpart to speculative fabulation. In particular, I focus on a tradition of speculative design that, where it has been combined with social science, has been potentially productive in opening up the research event by virtue of interjecting forms of idiocy. As we shall also see this has not been straightforward, and we will need to address the ways in which the idiotic is modulated in order to be productive, to offer promise as opposed to pose threat. In this section, then, there is a preliminary account of speculative design which situates it both anecdotally and among other cognate traditions of design (each of which have a strong social scientific bent). This will be followed with an extended example of speculative design as a way of charting some of techniques that are possible, but also exploring the compromises that are enacted along the way if these designerly idiotic interjections are to 'work'. As ever, this is just one tradition of speculative fabrication, and there are others that draw on different artistic and craft practices including museum-based exercises and displays (e.g. Last, 2014; Raven and Stripple, 2021), various artistic activities (e.g. Gabrys and Yusoff, 2012; Leavy, 2015), craft-based workshops (e.g. Lindstrom and Stahl, 2020; Coleman, 2020); and hacking and makerspaces (e.g. Davies, 2018; Kelty, 2018). The aim is not to privilege speculative design over any of these other sorts of speculative enterprise – each has its advantages and disadvantages (and we will certainly trace some of the challenges faced, as well as benefits afforded, by speculative design).

Encountering speculative design

I chanced upon speculative design through Toby Kerridge's Biojewellery project which was presented to me as an instance of Public Engagement with Science and Technology (PEST). This involved the extraction of bone cells taken from the jaws of couples who were having their wisdom teeth removed. The cells were then cultured on a bioactive scaffold and subsequently made into rings with the addition of precious metals. The rings were eventually exchanged between the members of each couple (Thompson et al., n.d.). Various empirical materials that were generated by the project were put on display at a number of international venues and events, and the project was further disseminated through several media. What particularly struck me, over and above a visceral uneasiness towards the very idea of Biojewellery, was that little attempt was made to appraise, let alone measure, how the public regarded Biojewellery and its broader implications. Unlike typical social scientific practice, the viewpoints of the public remained largely untapped; from the perspective of a science studies approach to public engagement, the public's views were, disappointingly, barely recorded and certainly not subjected to sustained analysis. I struggled to grasp both the substance of the Biojewellery project and the claim that it was an example of PEST. It was, put baldly but technically, idiotic. However, given that it was taken seriously by the designers, it was also intriguing – one might say, it made me hesitate. What was serious about Biojewellery that I could not see from my sociological and science and technology studies (STS) perspective?

After the Biojewellery project, Kerridge became a key researcher on Material Beliefs (see Beaver et al., 2009), a project which aimed 'To create a range of deliverables that provide a broad audience with a rich set of insights into the potential of engineering research'. As with the Biojewellery project, Material Beliefs was invested in engaging with the public. To 'communicate and democratise recent innovation in UK engineering' meant 'bring(ing) to life the detail and fascination of engineering in the imaginative worlds of an audience of end-users' (Beaver et al., 2009, p.13). Initial collaborations with engineers were supplemented with engagement events with publics of various kinds who provided 'alternative perspectives to fuel design concepts' (Beaver et al., 2009, p.45).

Out of this activity, four sets of design prototype were developed of which only one is discussed here. The Neuroscope was 'an interactive device (that) interact(s) with the cell culture from the home'. Accordingly, the user looks into the conical flask-shaped Neuroscope to 'see (a) virtual representation, which is updating in real time, because the (Neuroscope) is networked to the cell culture in the lab'. Interacting with the Neuroscope resulted in 'sending signals to the cell culture, which then will feedback into the virtual environment, so there is a loop between what you do with the Neuroscope and the cell culture' (Beaver et al., 2009, p.104). Once more, as a speculative prototype, it was designed and deployed to serve no directly practical purpose. Idiotically, it drew an oblique and uncomfortable connection between biomedicine and publics insofar as it gestured towards such concerns as the boundaries between, on the one hand, the domestic and the entertaining, and, on the other, the technoscientific and the epistemic. In this respect, it gave cause to pause insofar as it troubled STS's usual perspective on PEST, opening up the space for inventive problem-making, particularly with regard to the demarcations of the 'laboratory' and the 'domestic'.

Taken together with other examples of speculative design such as threshold devices the 'plane tracker' and the 'local barometer' (Gaver et al., 2008), and the drift table (Gaver et al., 2004), this opening up of more interesting questions for STS and PEST could be specified in more detail (see also Michael, 2012a, 2012b).

- Unlike STS and PEST, the speculative designs addressed no overt controversies (around, say, disputed technological innovations) but generated odd opaque but complex objects that could be playfully explored by members of the public. Did STS and PEST really address technoscientific developments in the most productive way? What additionally could be meant by 'productive'?
- In contrast to STS and PEST with their social scientific impetus towards systematic 'data-gathering', in speculative design, it appeared that, despite the opportunities afforded public users for discussion of the designs, 'data-gathering' appeared to be an afterthought (though see below regarding probes), and certainly 'lacked' systematicity. This raises questions: what counts as the 'role' of public engagement – data gathering or the immediate and local impact of the designs? What are the disjunctions between the experiences of the researchers (as data gatherers) and participants (as social actors who go on to discuss their research experiences with friends and family)?
- As a corollary, to the extent that public views of the speculative design were collected, these were not used as data from which to abstract broader lessons that could have 'impact', that could be presented as useful resources for stakeholders, not least policymakers. What is assumed as being 'useful' or 'impactful' about social research in STS and PEST? Who can count as stakeholders and what presuppositions underlie this category?
- STS and PEST often focus on publics in terms of their potential citizenliness and on how their views about a particular technoscientific or biomedical controversy might be expressed and relayed to policymakers or politicians. By contrast, the speculative designers mentioned earlier are not especially concerned with this process, or their role as an intermediary that collects and conveys the public's citizenly perspective. This 'idiotic' disinterest throws into disarray what

might count as a citizen and a political process: is the STS and PEST approach to citizenship really a good or effective way of 'gathering' and 'mediating' public perceptions? What model of the citizen is in play in this social scientific research practice and institutional orientation? What other social conduits, other modes of communication, can engage the political (see Mouffe, 2005)?
- Relatedly, if STS and PEST scholars perform as spokespersons for the public, the designers seemed to refuse this role. Apparently, it was not their academic 'duty' to support the democratic process (or a version of it) by enabling and circulating the public voice. What does this say about the responsibilities of the academic, not least when the public voice is one which has to some degree been shaped through the academics' empirical techniques (Felt and Fochler, 2010; Lezaun and Soneryd, 2007)?

These initial encounters with speculative design comprise my own encounter with what may be called a 'disciplinary idiot'. Here was a research event in the expanded sense that embraced preliminary conversations and discussions with colleagues from a different discipline around a seemingly shared interest (public engagement). What emerged was incomprehension with regard to how the designers' 'public engagement' could ever possibly be counted as such (from within the perspective and practices of STS and PEST). What this introduced was a hesitancy – an affective response that troubled my usual assumptions and eventually allowed for a posing of more inventive problems with their emergent pre-propositions that reconfigured such conceptual staples as 'controversy', 'knowledge', 'public', 'citizenship' and 'researcher'.

More broadly, this is a case of how 'interdisciplinarity' can enter into the research event. It brings into relief a few of the issues that follow in the train of 'collaboration' across (and within) disciplines. These issues will be multiplied and elaborated in the next chapter.

Speculative design and some partial others

Above, I briefly situated speculative design in relation to other speculative research practices, including fabulation. In this section, I look at other versions of design that also have a speculative dimension. Traditional forms of design are fundamentally concerned with designing and developing products that fulfil some function or solve some problem. Many of these issues might be rather 'proximal' in the sense of being of immediate, utilitarian and identifiable concern, whereas others might be altogether more 'distal', projective and transformative (that is, generative of designs that aim for, say, future social or environmental justice – see, for example, Papaneck, 1984). By contrast, speculative design, as we have noted previously and will detail further seems not so interested in this utilitarian or functional characteristic, even where this has utopian undertones.

In the case of participatory design, in which users are enrolled to help in the specification of the problem at stake and in the evolution of a design solution (e.g.

Ehn, 1988), it is in relatively recent iterations of that tradition that a more speculative dimension has emerged. In particular, the process of working with participants to specify and implement designs is conducted in order to open up the questions and issues at stake. As Binder et al. (2015, p.163) frame it participatory design, or what they call democratic design experiments, become engagements through which '"the possible" becomes tangible, formable and within reach of engaged yet diverse citizens'. In a similar vein, La Dantec and DiSalvo (2013) have argued for a version of participatory design in which there is

> broadening (of) the view of what counts as innovation, moving away from a technocratic view of innovation toward one that includes social innovation: innovation that arises out of social interactions and action that arises from the constitution of a public … (as such, there is a) … federating (of) individuals in the discovery of unknown issues.
>
> *p.247*

In these latter versions of participatory design, the divergence from speculative design is that speculation comes not so much in response to the prototype, but within the practical processes by which the prototype comes to be developed. In this respect, the designer is just another participant in the collective design process, as opposed to the 'synthesist' of various views (partly derived from probe returns, but also other sources of materials such as design traditions and popular culture – for further discussion of the implications of this way of working for analysis, see Chapter 7).

Another cognate design tradition is that of critical design (Dunne, 2005; Dunne and Raby, 2001) in which potential technological futures are sketched and used as a basis for design prototypes that serve to critique or problematize those futures. For example, how might robots with a range of emotions trouble projections of seamless digital futures (e.g. the idealizations of the smart home). Though more recent thinking on critical design has crystallized the role of the speculative (Dunne and Raby, 2013), there remains at least two major differences with speculative design. First, critical design's primary point of contact with potential users of its prototypes is the gallery, museum or exhibition. The public's encounter with the prototype is primarily representational insofar as it is by and large 'observational'. By contrast, speculative designs are meant to be 'used' – there is a practical engagement in which participants draw on the designs in their everyday routines. As such participants usually cohabit with the prototypes for a period of time, during which the designers pay ethnographic visits to the participants in order to derive a sense of how, and the extent to which, the prototypes have affected their human cohabitees. The second difference lies in the temporal framing of the prototype. In the case of the critical design, more or less discrete, well-delineated futures are established against which the designs are counter-indications: they point towards alternative futures. By contrast, speculative design does not enter into such future projection – the focus is much more on immediate concerns such as, for instance, the experiences and sociomaterializations of 'home', or neighbourhood, or community: speculative prototypes can be understood as enabling a speculative response to these in which the future remains open.

The demarcations drawn in the foregoing serve to pick out what is distinctive about speculative design. This could perhaps best be summarized as the proactive interjection of the idiotic into everyday life as a way of prompting an opening up of potential ideas, visions, practices, understandings and affects. In what follows, we consider in more detail the specifics of how this is accomplished but also compromised. The broader aim is to examine how engaging empirically with the prospective is a fraught as well as productive process.

Speculative design as social science method

Let me start with a proviso, designers themselves do not necessarily recognize the version of speculative design elaborated here. After all, they are not social scientists and much of their work is directed towards their own academic and practitioner community of designers of various sorts. Having said that, the present account is concerned with how speculative design can be put to use as a speculative social science method that serves less in the representation of this or that social (or, better still, sociomaterial) phenomenon or event, but as a performative engagement with the world that opens us up to its potentialities. As a playful – idiotic – intervention, speculative design can be said to embody the perspective that social scientific methodology is partially constitutive of its object of study. But further, it also points towards the ways in which that world is partially constitutive of the research, the researcher and the research event. This is not unique to speculative design – the constitution of a more open object of study is something shared with several other forms of engagement (see previous discussion).

One comparator – social scientific – tradition that has not been mentioned thus far is Action Research. It is particularly helpful in highlighting once more the more playful dimensions of speculative design when understood as social scientific research. Action Research comes in several guises (see Reason and Bradbury, 2001, for numerous exemplars; also Lewin, 1946; Bargal, 2006) but it can be generically characterized in the following terms: 'social research carried out by a team that encompasses professional action researchers and the members of an organization, community, or network ("stakeholders") who are seeking to improve the participants' situation' (Greenwood and Levin, 2007, p.3). This approach can involve objects and practices whereby social scientists and lay participants work together to specify relevant problems and identify potential solutions. In many respects, there are resonances with participatory design; however, the problem–solution orientation possesses neither the playful – ludic, idiotic – ethos of speculative design, nor its more open sensibility to emergent, inventive problems.

Now, speculative design can be set out as a number of phases. Crudely (because these phases can blend into each other, and have intervening steps), these can be listed as: participants are engaged (through site visits and/or through cultural probes); probe returns are considered and along with other materials used as a basis for developing a brief for a prototype; the design, development and testing of the prototype; the deployment of the prototype to users (individuals, households, communities); ethnographic engagement with users which might also include filming and quasi-documentary making (see, for details, Boucher et al., 2018; Gaver et al., 2007, 2008, 2011). For immediate purposes, I will focus on the cultural probes (shortened to probes) and the prototypes as speculative devices.

In order to grasp how these design artefacts work as speculative devices, we can draw on the notion of semblance. Following Massumi (2011), the aesthetics of artefacts (and, relatedly, events) as well as that of works of art, insofar as they do not quite 'make sense', can trigger expanded affects, both in terms of how one is affected and how one can be affective. Put in terms of the research event, the idiotic design probe or prototype do not attain ready satisfaction when concrescing with the user. The uncertainty, opaqueness and playfulness initially embodied in the design artefact open up potentialities for the user, both in how they respond to it and how they subsequently make use of it (although this can include rejection – see below).

Probes, as we have seen, invite users to engage in strange, afunctional tasks. They are not expected to yield representations or realistic depictions of a particular situation, phenomenon or event (such as energy, or the home). As Boehner et al. (2012) note, probes are not expected to expose 'what is'; rather they engage with 'what might be'. Moreover, they are not meant to generate a corpus of data to be analysed systematically, but to yield materials that serve as inspiration for the design brief to come. In this sense, as we shall elaborate in Chapter 7, probe returns can themselves be used semblamatically (also see Michael et al., 2018).

Individual probes have usually been deployed as part of a small collection of probes (and their respective instructions). Within such a probe pack might be counted a disposable camera whose instructions invite the user to photograph, for example, the spiritual centre of their dwelling. Or there might be included a 'Listening Glass' – a nondescript drinking glass which volunteers are asked to press against surfaces in the home in order to listen to and document the strange or curious noises 'made' by the house. Or there might be a sheet of paper asking the volunteer to describe a 'sense of energy' – the pain of energy, the smell of energy, the feel of energy, etc. – as encountered in the different rooms of the home. In all these cases, the probes can disjunctively open up the meanings of the home by providing the user with the opportunity to experience it in a potentially novel way. The expectation with probe packs is that the individual items within will not appeal to all participants, so returns are not envisaged to be uniform – this is made clear so that users know that they can return as many or as few probes as they wish, and at their own pace. It follows that comparability across volunteers is not an issue. Instead of the usual methodological injunctions to ensure that participants are asked, and answer, all the same questions on an interview schedule, the choice of probes is left up to the volunteers. This reflects the fact that the aim is not systematically to chart the similarities and differences within a sample, but to collect materials that individually or collectively open up analytic and synthetic possibilities.

Probe packs have usually been posted to volunteers, or, where they are printed paper probes, have been available for download from the project website, or sent via email. However, probes can also be deployed collectively as part of a research workshop. Here I consider a project I was involved with – 'Sustainability Invention and Energy-demand Reduction: Co-Designing Communities and Practice to (shortened to ECDC) which was funded under Research Councils United Kingdom (RCUK) Energy Programme (there were six other projects also funded). The rationale underpinning the project focused on the ways in which individuals and communities use, understand and manage energy: this would be fed into UK initiatives to fulfil government targets around energy reduction and climate change (see Boucher et al., 2018; Michael et al., 2018).

Initially, the ECDC team made contact with and visited several UK energy communities involved in various projects of energy- demand reduction. The subsequent ECDC probe workshop served a number of purposes: for example, it was an opportunity for participants (drawn from the different energy communities and from relevant policy-oriented constituencies) to meet each other and the researchers, and it functioned as a setting in which the researchers could derive a sense of the communities' relations to one another and to government initiatives (ECDC included). However, the workshop was primarily concerned with deriving various materials that would be used in the design of the prototype – what ultimately would become the Energy Babble – that would eventually be implemented across the energy communities. The workshop involved three communal exercises that were aimed at speculatively exploring three broad themes – community, the future and energy. In all cases, participants were divided into mixed groups composed of members from different communities and constituencies.

In the first activity, participants were asked to complete a large minimally specified map in order to depict a composite community space. This was done by directly drawing onto the map, adding a variety of pre-printed more-or-less pertinent stickers (these included buildings, vehicles, plants and animals, but also guns and alien spacecraft) and annotating with post-it notes. The objective was to gain insight into the ways in which 'community' could be enacted but also reconfigured in relation to relatively unfamiliar co-participants and imagery. In the second task, mixed participant groups were provided with the front pages of made-up papers (that ranged across broadsheet, tabloid and community newspapers) and periodicals (including science popularization and architecture journals). Each front page contained photos, sometimes diagrams and some suggestive text (e.g. 'breakthrough' for the popular science journal; 'UN declares' for the broadsheet). The participants were invited, in light of UK government targets for renewable energy, to fill out the headlines and add other text in the available sections. Here, the aim was to prompt participants to imagine possible energy futures. The final exercise involved providing participants with a number of plans and diagrams of standard UK dwellings and asking them to use variously coloured stamps and pens to indicate 'the energy intensity' around the home. The hope was that this would enable participants to explore their domestic experience of, and emotions towards, energy and energy use. After each exercise, participants shared their responses to the probe tasks. As mentioned, these responses were later fed into the process of developing the prototype and were also subject to analysis (see Chapter 7).

All three exercises were designed with what might considered a modicum of 'semblance'. They were all 'recognizable' in the sense of that they 'made sense' in relation to community and energy demand reduction – key factors in the overarching research programme and in the participants' everyday lives. However, there were a number of features in each exercise that didn't quite make sense. For example, the seeming irrelevance of some the stickers in the community map task, or the photograph of a pumpkin-shaped structure on the cover of the architectural magazine were, at least to a degree, odd enough to prompt a troubling of the usual enactments of 'community' and 'energy future'.

Let us now consider the speculative prototype as an idiotic method. Before that, it is worth noting that while in the case of ECDC, probes and prototypes comprised two phases wherein the former contributed to the latter, they can nevertheless be separated and stand-alone. The Lupton and Michael (2017) study mentioned previously, for instance, involved a probe workshop that was not a precursor to the development of a prototype; and the work of Dunne and Raby (2013) can generate prototypes without recourse to user engagement (via probes, for instance).

Prototypes are highly finished (that is, well-constructed, aesthetically pleasing, functionally polished, materially refined) devices which, as with the probes, are designed to be playful, opaque, provocative and afunctional. Within a broad, often indistinct, field of interest such as the 'home' or 'energy', they are designed to propose a range of interpretations and activities that are not always straightforward and routinely surprise the designers themselves. From the perspective of social science, the hope is that the prototypes are generative of novel and inventive re-problematizations, that they prompt new pre-propositions.

As an initial example, we can draw on Gaver et al.'s (2008) 'threshold devices'. These involved collecting information from the home's surroundings in odd ways that might prompt a rethinking of how the home feeds into and emerges out of its connections to those surroundings. These connections are themselves open to such rethinking and can take on emotional, utilitarian, political, economic, cultural or aesthetic qualities. Focusing on the 'Local Barometer' prototype, this involved six small devices, each brightly coloured, each integrating a little screen, each displaying local information. The information – scrolling images and text – derived from an online website to which classified advertisements could be posted. 'Small ads' were selected on the basis of an anemometer's readings. Thus wind direction and speed determined where the ads came from – how far away and in what direction. The thought behind the Local Barometer was that this odd – one might say, semblamatic – flow of commercial information that was carried into the home on the wind, as it were, would facilitate a different sort of engagement with the home's relation to its more or less distant neighbourhoods.

Ethnographic visits with the user threw up a number of insights: the ads began to shift in their meaning from 'invasive' to 'surprising'; local areas were seen as more complex – the ads reinforcing and contradicting their reputation. Indeed, the ads' origin began to serve as a means for reading the weather. In the present volume's terminology, pre-propositions were being suggested, relations and prospects were being enacted that questioned, for instance, the notion of 'neighbourhood' now emerging as a variable and heterogeneous concoction of (the relationalities between) reputation, artefacts, people, weather, electromagnetic waves, space and so on and so forth.

Turning to another example, ECDC's Energy Babble (see Boucher et al., 2018) aimed at a more collective engagement with energy communities. Without going into the technical detail, the Energy Babble was an aesthetically intriguing object made up of a cream-yellow rectangular body with an off-centre quasi-dome (all injection moulded) which housed a speaker. The dome was surrounded by two blown-glass sections that opened upwards as a funnel. A bright yellow knob (that controlled various functions) sat to one side of the dome, and a microphone handset was attached to the main body via a thick bright yellow spiralized cable. The impression was of a well-finished object that combined aspects of an old-fashioned telephone and laboratory glassware.

Twenty-one Energy Babbles were distributed to the previously contacted energy communities, and these were situated both in individual homes and communal spaces. The 'babble' part of the Energy Babble entailed a stream of talk that drew on online feeds, Twitter accounts and URLs each of which was sampled and scraped because they related, in one way or another, to energy, and energy demand reduction. This content was supplemented by contributions – via the microphone – from the volunteer users. These disparate inputs were subsequently processed in order to produce more mangled versions – babble – that were broadcast as a message preceded by a jingle. The content included news on energy and environmental matters, but also other unrelated topics. Oftentimes, the various processes applied in the collecting and manipulation of inputs yielded babble output that did not quite make sense.

The responses of the various users were, by and large, instrumental – rather than drawing on the Energy Babble as a means of questioning the meanings of 'energy', 'community' or 'future' or 'information', the primary focus was on the uses to which the Babble could be put. In the main, these uses concerned how it might function to enable energy saving, that is, serve in the communication of relevant knowledges and practices. In this respect, many users bemoaned the fact that it didn't contribute directly to energy saving as it failed to relay any useful information. Others enjoyed the visual and aural aesthetics of the Babble; and for others still the Babble was seen as a marketing opportunity, deployed to what amounted to a 'sales tool', the novelty of which – the fact that the user couldn't know what they would hear next – could serve as a part of 'outreach' initiatives, that might entice people into taking a more active part in their energy communities. In yet other cases, its perceived uses seemed more tangential to the design intent behind the Babble: it could be used, for instance, as a model application of the recently released Raspberry Pi do-it-yourself computer. Wilkie and Michael (2018) suggest that despite these instrumentalized views of the Energy Babble, there can nevertheless be detected speculative indications of more inventive problems. Thus, other issues and connections mentioned by the participants, such as the links evoked between local community energy demand reduction and international poverty, or the process by which the Babble entered into and was differentially situated with in the energy community, suggest that the parameters of 'community' can be opened up. Thus, it can be asked: what are the internal dynamics, fractures and hierarchies of an energy community? What are the boundaries of an energy community and its interests and activities? Are there ways of regarding the Energy Babble research event in terms of an expansion of pre-propositions that re-envisions an 'energy community' such that it encompasses this internal 'multiplicity' and external porosity?

However, perhaps we should not be so surprised by the instrumentalizing views of the energy community participants. After all, the very raison d'etre of energy communities is bound up with finding concrete ways of achieving and modelling energy demand reduction. They are in competition with one another (and, in their view, with academic researchers) for scarce government resources, competition in which they must persuasively establish the utility and viability of their energy demand reduction proposals. If this 'pre-disposition' was an ingredient within the Babble research event, to some extent it was reinforced by the activities of the researchers themselves as they went about introducing the Babble to, and installing it within, the energy communities. While the oddness of the Babble was certainly discussed by the researchers, this was diluted with comments that stressed its functionality. In other words, there was an enactment of the Babble that was ambiguously speculative and instrumental. Thus, the Babble was performed as both odd and curious, but as also having utility: simultaneously, it came both to intrigue and to reassure, to open up and to close down the potential relationships with energy, community and the future.

This suggests that insofar as the Energy Babble device was designed to play an idiotic role in the research event, this was not straightforward. Its idiocy was, on the one hand, diffused by its energy community users and, on the other, tempered by the ambiguity which the researchers ascribed to it. This is suggestive of a broader set of issues about the use of the idiotic – and, indeed, any similar methodological provocation – as a way of opening up the research event, of rendering it more speculative.

Threat, promise and the idiot

As we have repeatedly seen, the figure of the idiot is disruptive in that it makes no sense (within the confines of a particular point of view): it obliges a hesitation with regard to that point of view, an inkling that perhaps we are not in possession of the meaning of what we know. The idiot is a sort of promise that there is something more to be said and seen, to be known and practised, to be speculated. But this is an idiot that is relatively mild – domesticated, even – in its otherness and its senselessness. The idiot, after all, can be far more threatening: in everyday life idiocy takes several forms – it can be uncontrolled and undisciplined and it can pose a threat because it puts others at risk, even if only accidently or unconsciously. Or it can pose a threat by virtue expressing its otherness not as with the gentle Prince Myshkin or the monotonic Bartleby, but through insult, intimidation and violence. But even the gentler forms idiocy, embodied in the speculative prototype, say, can constitute a disabling threat. Put otherwise, though they are antonyms, there is a fine balance to be struck between the threat and the promise of the idiot.

By way of illustration, let us consider another speculative prototype, the Home Health Monitor (Gaver et al., 2009). At base, this prototype involved a number of sensors that were fitted throughout the chosen home in order to monitor the frequency of several physical occurrences (e.g. a door's opening or closing within a particular timeframe, whether a settee was sat upon or not, etc.). Such types of event were used by the designers as indicators of a particular social state of affairs: intimacy, privacy, cleaning. The records derived from this monitoring were used to generate aphorisms, photographs, diagrams of the daily measures. The intent here was that these rather strange – idiotic – outputs would prompt a playful engagement with the 'health' of the home: one might have expected a 'ludic' response in which the meaning of the home, what might be meant by 'home health' might be explored more speculatively. As it turned out, the volunteers became more concerned about the extent to which the output measures were credible and correct. For the designers, there was a lack of 'appropriate' engagement that could be generally attributed to Home Health Monitor's shortcomings: the experiences it offered failed to be sufficiently meaningful. This was especially disappointing given that this design was a revised version of the Home Health Horoscope (whose outputs were horoscopes) whose failure to precipitate playful engagement manifested in a questioning of the designers' research agenda.

So, these prototypes' lack of success can be put down to their deficiencies (and there were several identified by Gaver and his colleagues). In the end, the prototypes were regarded by participants more as a technical or social problem to be solved. But we might also consider the participants themselves here, not least as they emerged from their initial and continuing relations and interactions with the designers. Connolly suggests that confronted by such potential openness – by what he calls the 'world of becoming', or by what Massumi might call semblance – the experience is one of threat, and people resort to 'conventional wisdom or power' (Connolly, 2011, p.159).

But let us take a step back here and recall that with regard to the Energy Babble, in order to make it seem less alien, less threatening, it was introduced as having instrumental or functional value. In the process, its promise as a speculative design was arguably diluted. Something similar might have happened with the Home Health Monitor. The broader point is that any modulation between the threat and the promise of the idiot can be derailed. In seeking to make the idiot more 'accessible', in reducing its possible threat, its promise is dissipated – its utility, for example, is emphasized and it becomes instrumentalized at the expense of its otherworldliness.

Another way of thinking about this is in terms of care: the designers are attempting to be careful and caring with regard to the participants and the prototype in the context of the latter's immediate deployment: they render the prototype more palatable, more attuned to the sensibilities of its users. In the process, longer term cares about the relevant issues (say, the productive possibilities entailed in 'home health', or the potentialities of rethinking the interconnections of energy, information, community and future) can become blurred. Having noted this, care makes an appearance in other ways. Above, it was noted that prototypes can be highly finished – they are put together well, they are aesthetically pleasing to the eye and hand, they convey refinement and craft. These qualities also signify care – and respect – in that they enact the application of hard work, exacting technique, robust skill for the benefit of users. Needless to say, such care also speaks to the designer community (insofar as it embodies and enacts practitioner standards of functional elegance, build quality, aesthetics, etc.), but it can also serve to draw participants 'in' as it were – to encourage them to take a chance with a seemingly discombobulating prototype in which so much time, effort, expertise and artistry have been invested. Having noted this, such high finishing also has its downsides in that it might obscure the internal workings and the assumptions and contingencies built into the prototype, thereby triggering a different sort of sense of threat. Once more care can backfire, and become 'un-caring'.

In summary, this section has attempted to clarify how the deployment of an idiotic artefact (or intervention or activity for that matter) as a prompt to opening up the research event is by no means straightforward. The pre-propositions that emerge from the research event can be 'retrograde', reinforcing existing relationalities. A balance between threat and promise thus needs to be struck – or rather a complex and convoluted balancing act is required in which care of the idiot and participants, and the care of such care as it were, need to be carefully practised. This point is taken up in the next chapter.

Concluding remark

At the beginning of the section on speculative design, my early encounters with it were couched in terms of being confronted with a disciplinary idiot. The claims being made that the research involved in the Biojewellery project concerned PEST made no sense to me – at least in relation to my particular social scientific grasp of this field. This is not an uncommon experience: initial, and extended, interactions with practitioners of – even collaborators from – a different academic discipline can be confusing, frustrating, aggravating, 'idiotic'. Given that there seems to be a broad institutional privileging of interdisciplinarity, research dealings with colleagues from divergent disciplines are fast becoming not so much commonplace as unavoidable. Under such circumstances, researchers will have to find ways of managing their mutual 'idiocies', as it were. That is to say, as some of the dynamics described in this chapter imply, means of balancing the convolutions of threat and promise will need to be found. The next chapter addresses the research event in terms of interdisciplinarity and explores how contemporary social scientific research practice is increasingly entangled in delicate and tricky interdisciplinary relations. As we shall see, care (in its various guises) in and of such relations is key if they are to yield promising pre-propositions.

6
INTERDISCIPLINARITY AND PRACTICE
We are all practitioners ...

Introduction

We had been awarded a very large grant to use design and social scientific methods in order to explore the ways in which 'community' might work to shape how people used energy, and specifically how they attempted to reduce their energy consumption. The process of writing the grant had been hectic (we had little time), but it had been relatively painless in the sense that I coordinated the writing, as my collaborators fed me with text that I could weave into a reasonably coherent interdisciplinary application. This belied the underlying disciplinary tensions that would surface at several points later on, once the project was underway and in the writing up 'phases'.

The first manifestation of disciplinary difference was at the point when we were interviewing for a designer colleague – specifically a maker, someone who could design and make actual stuff. We had a good a selection of candidates and the interviews generally went very well. I remember that during our deliberations there was the usual shifting and nuancing of criteria but, despite some misgivings, we arrived at an agreed choice. I went home happy with a good day's work. Early the next morning I received a phone call asking me to come to a meeting with the designers. They had had further discussions among themselves and a different candidate was now favoured. What irked me was that this was the candidate against whom I had argued most strongly, mainly on the grounds that I was uncomfortable with what I, in retrospect mistakenly, perceived as the political implications of their designs. Fortunately, I mustered the good sense to defer to the designers: after all, they would have to work with the appointee most closely and they were the ones best situated to judge the quality of the making. In reflecting on my initial resistance to the candidate, I can point to the fact that I was using discipline-derived criteria of accomplishment: I was assessing the work presented in the portfolio on the basis

DOI: 10.4324/9781351133555-6

of its supposed social scientific virtues (which on reflection were not a little crude). As it turned out, the eventual appointee could not have been a better colleague whose contribution to the project was outstanding.

One might say that this was good interdisciplinarity in action in the sense that different disciplinary sensibilities were resolved. The resolution was partly grounded in the recognition of my colleagues' expertise and experience, my embryonic intuitions concerning the exigencies and practicalities of the project, but also in my commitment to our friendship and our continued working relations. This chapter is concerned with the ways in which disciplinarity and its various hybridizations affect the research event. As such this chapter examines disciplinarity and some of the varieties of interdisciplinarity, and the types of heterogeneous relations that are central to more or less 'successful' interdisciplinary enactments. However, it also departs from – or perhaps expands on – the notion of disciplinarity. In this respect, drawing on the ideas of practice and practitioners, we aim fruitfully to muddy the differences between researchers and participants.

In what follows, after a discussion of the relation between disciplinarity and the research event, we sketch a number of concepts to help us think through how a research event might usefully encompass its heterogeneous elements. More specifically, we offer the concepts of composition, comprehension, compromise, compassion and composting, as a way of luring the researcher into thinking afresh about how they go about usefully engaging in, being engaged by, the divergent prehensions that make up the research event.

Disciplinarity and the research event

Before we turn to interdisciplinarity and its variants, we should perhaps pay a little attention to disciplines and what they are. This is not always easy as the enactment of disciplinarity often embraces practices, activities, knowledges that at some level do not seem to 'cohere' intellectually. This is the case especially in those disciplines which straddle the social and natural sciences, and sometimes the humanities (e.g. Geography, Psychology, Anthropology – for a more nuanced categorization [see Blume, 1990]). But then, disciplines can likely be best understood as historical fabrications within institutions, and across university and education systems, and even beyond, embroiled within political and economic contingencies. Disciplinary boundaries emerge and are shaped and sustained by design and circumstance. These traverse such factors as, for example, the emergence of new technologies and methods, modes of professionalization (training, associations, journals), institutional differentiation, funder-led research prioritization and resource allocation, and ever-increasing and ever more elaborated forms of audit such as research and teaching quality assessment (for accounts, each with their own disciplinary flavour, of the processes of disciplinary differentiation and emergence see, for example, Abbott, 2001a; Horigan, 1988; Whitely, 2000).

Cross-cutting the disciplines are the mounting pressures towards interdisciplinarity. It would not be far-fetched to say that the expressed need for interdisciplinarity has taken on a status that is akin to that of mantra (see Shove and Wouters, 2005; Callard and Fitzgerald, 2015; Weingart, 2000). As various authors have noted, this is by no means straightforward. For example, interdisciplinarity can be source of disciplinarity as disciplines emerge out of the combinations and differentiations of prior disciplines, and this again can be driven by a range of factors (e.g. a surplus of physics PhDs who move into biology to create the new discipline of biophysics – see, for examples, Lemaine et al., 1976). Or interdisciplinarity can serve in the reinforcement of existing disciplinary distinctions and hierarchies as 'softer' disciplines are marginalized and the voice of their practitioners sidelined or subordinated (Frickel et al., 2017; Garforth and Kerr, 2011).

The simple point is that the relations between disciplinarity and interdisciplinarity are convoluted, and it might not always be easy to tell these apart. As will be suggested below, for the purposes of the present discussion, it might be more fruitful to address not the disciplinarity of collaborators, but their commitments, practices and experiences and how these might lead to particular sorts of possibility (whether that be productive or not). As Callard and Fitzgerald (2015) summarize, it might be advantageous to 'retire formulations of interdisciplinarity that delineate sets of expertise from the outset' (p.32). If Callard and Fitzgerald are advocating a pragmatic reorientation away from disciplines towards other scales (including personal and practical ones), from the present perspective, we are simply avoiding Whitehead's fallacy of misplaced concreteness. That is to say, we do not assume that disciplines are determinative of people's practices, positions or interventions. Indeed, within our framing of the research event, this would be unusual given the assumed possibility that people are co-emergent in the process of the research event. As Barry and Born (2013b) note, while interdisciplinary collaboration can be affected by a range of factors internal and external to disciplines (see below), a certain autonomy can manifest in the unfolding of the research event which can generate unexpected novel conceptual, empirical and relational possibilities (in what they call the 'logic of ontology').

One implication is that it also becomes problematic to differentiate between different forms of disciplinary intersection. Formal typologizations of inter-, cross-, trans-, and multidisciplinarity (see, for example, Thompson Klein, 2000; Klein, 2010; Toomey et al., 2015; also Weingart and Stehr, 2000) might be useful insofar as they demarcate different categories of disciplinary intersection but, depending on the particular research event in its concreteness, disciplinary intersections might well take unforeseen and unusual forms. Such typologies might be more valuable as a means of enacting research intersections for the purposes of satisfying a particular aspect of the research event (for example, to fit in with funding criteria, or to appeal to particular academic and user audiences). While it might be helpful (despite varying definitions) to distinguish between multidisciplinarity (e.g. brings together and juxtaposes knowledges from diverse disciplines), interdisciplinarity (e.g. aims for a coherent knowledge derived from the integration of knowledges from different disciplines) and transdisciplinarity (e.g. entails a more radical integration in which practitioners take on the skills and knowledges of their other-disciplinary

104 Interdisciplinarity and practice

collaborators thereby blurring disciplinary boundaries), interdisciplinarity will nevertheless be used as a catch-all to indicate the intersection of disciplines, or, more precisely, the practical collaborations of practitioners who bring different skills, knowledges, commitments and concerns into the research event.

As signalled earlier, it seems reasonable to assume that there will be influences on interdisciplinary practices that derive from events, at a more or less distant 'remove' from the research event itself. In other words, elements that might appear peripheral to the doing of interdisciplinarity nonetheless play a role in shaping it. Thus, calls for interdisciplinarity have become part of a default research strategy of many institutions which is itself a response to a number of other, albeit contentious, eventuations. For instance, a very partial list of these eventuations might include: the increasing awareness of the sheer complexity of problems (such as environmental issues) that are being faced (e.g. Nowotny et al., 2001) and which require the input of multiple forms of expertise; the political and economic desire to translate laboratory research results into 'real world' (e.g. clinical) utility (e.g. Wainwright et al., 2006); the 'need' to ensure the broader user viability or to affirm the public accountability of a piece of research (Barry et al., 2008; Barry and Born, 2013b); or, related to all of the above, the competition among research institutions to portray the excellence of their research programmes (for example, in terms of 'comprehensiveness' or 'impact' or some other metric that can feed into the various league tables by which universities promote themselves). To reiterate, these and other factors combine to afford interdisciplinarity the prominence it presently enjoys.

One implication of the integration of interdisciplinarity into research strategies is that it becomes, as Shove and Wouters (2005) note, a mode of disciplining researchers; that is to say, interdisciplinarity serves in the reorientation of research endeavour in particular directions, and in the shaping of research practice into particular forms (e.g. seeking large-scale grants from prestigious funders). However, as Callard and Fitzgerald (2015) note, for certain fields and substantive topics (such as, broadly speaking, the relations between environmental and psychological conditions), cutting across medical and social science might be a highly fruitful research strategy. They suggest that this general interest need not be formulated as a discrete research question at outset: rather the desire to straddle and trouble disciplines might eventually – even 'organically' – yield a viable research question (along with its research community). Here, the top-down, institutionally led interdisciplinarity can indeed facilitate bottom-up interdisciplinary initiative and invention.

Needless to say, there are also countervailing eventuations that make the passage of interdisciplinary rather less smooth than some of the foregoing might suggest. For all the ostensible support interdisciplinarity attracts, people are not always willing or equipped to engage sympathetically with it. On research committees or in editorial meetings, it is not difficult to find oneself, or to witness others, retrenching within home disciplines and arguing against the validity of other disciplines' methodological, epistemological or empirical framing. This is not unexpected – after all, many of us have been 'trained' to do 'being rigorous' in specific disciplinary ways. Despite our best efforts to treat interdisciplinarity work (whether proposals or potential publications) within their own terms of reference, sometimes old habits in the form of disciplinary standards can reassert themselves (see McLeish and McLeish, 2016). Put otherwise, even where there is sympathy-in-principle towards interdisciplinarity (Forster 2003), this is likely to be enacted from the perspective of a home 'discipline' (in an extended sense to include social and cultural as well as epistemic allegiances). The upshot of all this is that interdisciplinary proposals or papers might be judged to be diluted or corrupted versions of good (disciplinary) research. Having noted this, once more we cannot assume that these commitments are determinative: the engagement with other disciplines is also a potential occasion for revision and reformulation, for emergence.

This suggests that in contrast to much of the writing on interdisciplinarity that takes a 'view from nowhere' perspective (Haraway, 1995), as with any epistemic and epistemological account, we need to see claims around interdisciplinarity as situated, that is, partly reflective of various commitments (to disciplines, programmes of research and research policy, institutions, etc.). Needless to say, the present account reflects, at the very least, the partial view from my own ostensibly relatively 'senior' institutional positioning and my own home (multi-)discipline of Science and Technology Studies.

In sum, this section has touched on some of the issues that arise when one considers interdisciplinarity as, effectively, a panoply of ingredients that feed into a research event. Along the way, there have been indications that the research event needs to be further expanded to encompass a broader variety of constituents (or prehensions). We have touched upon the extended relationalities of research that range from the cultural differentiations of disciplines, through institutional and sectoral pressures, to global dynamics of knowledge production. These can be disaggregated into a cast of more or less local elements that include (the documents and meetings that mediate) the governmental framing of programmes of research, the distribution of resources across faculties, disciplines and departments, the patterning of invitations to disciplinary practitioners to participate in collaborative initiatives, and so on and so forth. Adding to the extended cast-list of elements that contribute to the composition of the 'interdisciplinary' research event, we could touch upon forms of practice that address the financial and regulatory elements of research, and, in the process, we can take note of how research entails a variety of largely neglected practitioners (e.g. finance professionals, human resource administrators, technicians and inspectors – see Davies et al., 2018). Or we could attend to the ways in which interdisciplinary collaborations do not just reflect, and inflect with, disciplinary hierarchies, but also levels of seniority: early career, postdoctoral and postgraduate researchers are all likely to be more invested in a research project than senior colleagues for whom this might be a small part of a larger research programme (Fukushima, 2018; Michael, 2018a).

There is much more that could be said about interdisciplinarity and the ways in which it comes to be composed (and as noted, the commentaries on interdisciplinarity are fast accumulating). For present purposes, it suffices to say that interdisciplinarity, as treated here, can serve to throw into relief the nexus of relations and practices that feed into a research event, and the complexity, extensiveness, precarity and creativity of such relations. As Celia Lury (2018) has suggested, in order to grasp these convolutions and involutions of interdisciplinarity, perhaps we should seek better motifs (or prepositions as Serres would have it – see previous discussions) such as rendering, or folding or recursion, or topology (also see Callard and Fitzgerald, 2015). In what follows, a range of suggestions are presented that are meant as triggers or lures – certainly not guides – for thinking about the contingencies and the unruliness of interdisciplinary work. In addition to composition, these are comprehension, compassion, compromise and composting. As we shall see, these notions take us down some familiar conceptual roads even if these are treated in perhaps unfamiliar fashion. However, before we proceed, we need to return to some of the broader implications of the troubling of the very notions of discipline and interdisciplinarity, not least when counterposed to the term practice and practitioner.

We are all practitioners …

In reflecting on some of the difficulties that arose in their collaborations with bioscientists, Callard and Fitzgerald (2015) suggest that, for all the frustrations and tensions, these moments of disparity are also data insofar as they enable collaboration and collaborative processes to be subject to critical reflection and analysis. Another – perhaps more contentious – way of putting this is that collaborators become part of the study. This is not to say that they are the 'objects' of study, but that they and their practices are subject to some form of social scientific analysis. Conversely, even if it is not formally social scientific, those collaborators – who might well be scientists – will doubtless be analysing the practices displayed and accounts given by their social scientific counterparts. The point is that the collaboration itself becomes a research event which is eventuated in different ways that reflect the divergent commitments, practices and exigencies faced by the various participants, or, rather, practitioners.

Now, in light of the foregoing, another observation can be offered. What we are witness to in the above framing of interdisciplinary interrelations is a more or less subtle shift: beyond the strictly 'academic' or 'disciplinary', the emphasis has gravitated towards a sense that participants engage in a multiplicity of practices that are, to be sure, 'relevant' to the topic of investigation, but also pertinent to the process of collaboration. That is to say, we have practitioners who practice in ways that straddle the epistemic and epistemological, but also the social and the political simultaneously. This, of course, has long been a basic observation of Science and Technology Studies (e.g. Latour, 1987). How they practice, how they contribute to the research can have a major impact on the nature of that event, not only in terms of what is being investigated and how, but also whether it is a research event *per se*. As we have seen in our discussions of the 'idiot', practices can derail the common world (see below) that was more or less consensually assumed to frame the research event.

An additional issue also needs to be raised: who can be a practitioner within a research event? So far in this discussion we have focused primarily on academic disciplinary practitioners. Yet, even in the 'harder sciences', potential contributors to a research event can potentially be drawn from any relevant walk of life. Clearly, there is much weight being carried by the term 'relevant' here (Savransky, 2016). As various scholars in Science and Technology Studies have contended and contested, who can have a say in the doing of research – that is, who, has relevance – is itself open to discussion (for a famous version of this debate see, for example, Collins and Evans, 2002; Wynne, 2003). Relevant questions with regard to relevance can concern: the resourcing of research (is it sufficiently potentially valuable to warrant funding?); the methodological conduct of research (is this the right way to study the effect of, say, this medical intervention on this target population?); the formulation of the research question (does this biotechnological research agenda best serve the articulation of this health issue?); the right to deploy knowledge derived from research – or practically translate such knowledge into intervention – (are these engineers the best people to seek solutions for these environmental problems?). In all this, who (and what) is relevant to a research event is always – at least in principle – up for debate, and as such, so is the research event itself. And the impetus for debate might come from many sources: other accredited experts, policy makers and politicians, spokespersons for interested parties such as non-governmental organizations and charities, members of the lay public and so on and so forth.

Put crudely, practitioners are diverse. The same point applies no less to a social scientific research event. And brought into relief in this latter setting is that those who might dispute the funding of the research, the research question, the methodology, the implications and applications of any findings (not to say their 'validity' – see Chapter 7) might be the very people who are the participants in the study. They too are practitioners both in the general sense of being engaged in, and immersed within, practices (e.g. Schatzki et al., 2001; Shove et al., 2012) but also in the more specific sense of having a sort of practical expertise that is relevant to the research event at hand. And of course, that 'relevance' might turn out to yield a reconfiguration and redefinition of that research event, in other words, it opens up unexpected pre-propositions. On the basis of these points, it seems only appropriate to replace the notion of participant with a term such as practitioner.

Now, one way of approaching this patterning of divergent – academic and non-academic – practices within a research event is via Isabelle Stengers' linked concepts of cosmopolitics and ecology of practices. It is to these we now turn.

Composition

In this section, we consider how the interdisciplinary – or rather the inter-practitioner –research event is composed, put together. Let us begin with Latour's account of compositionism. For Latour, reality is multiplicitous, a pluriverse (Latour, 2004a, 2005) or a multinaturalism (Latour, 2011). It manifests itself as diverse forms in which a heterogeneous array of components (ranging across the human and the nonhuman) are combined, or composed. In this respect, Latour's schema is not dissimilar to Whitehead's (1978) with his model of the concrescence of prehensions that produce an actual entity or occasion. Latour (2010b) calls this compositionism: the bringing together of different elements which entails reflections on those elements (which have themselves been composed) and on the manner of their bringing together. If 'compositionism urges us to accept that everything is composed. The issue now becomes one of asking "what is *well* and what is *badly* constructed (or composed)"' (p.478)? Of course, what counts as 'well' and 'badly' is something that is open to contestation. Indeed, Latour sees this as integral to compositionism. To compose thus involves a chronic circumspection in which it is important to take into account, as he writes, 'meanings of the word, including to compose with, that is to compromise, to care, to move slowly, with caution and precaution' (p.487). Out of this circumspect process of composition, which entails collective reflection upon that process of composition – of gathering and combining diverse elements that make up an event (in the present case a research event) – Latour suggests that a 'common world' emerges, that is, a space shared by the participants in the research event. As we shall see, this is not as straightforward as might appear.

For Latour, this process of composition is intimately tied to the notion of 'cosmopolitics'– an idea that addresses the bringing together of different practitioners and practices that combine to make an event. In Latour's case, the event is oriented towards what he calls 'matters of concern' (in our case this takes the form of the research event, of course). Accordingly, the issue at stake in arguments over the reality of some matter of fact typically entails disparate positions (not least, claims to facts) that make that issue an issue (i.e. contestable) in the first place. Part of the usual process of contestation is critique or interrogation in which the preconditions behind a position are revealed and thus that position is undermined ('you are arguing this point because these factors of which you are unaware have made you argue so'). However, for Latour (2004b), such critique itself rests on statements of facts which can themselves be subjected to like critique ('you identify these factor because of these other factors of which you are unaware'). Rather, he argues for a remodelling of the critic (and we are all potential critics!) as one engaged in the process by which positions and relations between positions are assembled. In other words, within the setting of an interdisciplinary (or inter-practitioner) research event, the aim is to foster mutual comprehension of how disparate viewpoints and related practices are assembled.

To be sure, the foregoing has been a rather abstracted discussion. We can turn to Stengers' work on cosmopolitics and the ecology of practices to unpack further the present perspective. After all, Stengers has been a major influence on the work of Latour. What Stengers' emphasizes is that cosmopolitics occasions 'a space for hesitation' (2005a, p.995). In other words, it is important to introduce means by which to facilitate a slowing down (not to jump too hastily to a view of others' viewpoints and practices). In this respect, Stengers (2005b) speaks of staging, of art and artifice through which practitioners – who might otherwise be marginalized – are enabled to make their presence felt along with every other practitioner. However, this sensibility does not mean that the process is seamless, for what counts as an appropriate way of making a presence felt, of having voice, is multiple. In Stengers' cosmopolitical schema, in her ecology of practices, there are no shared criteria by which different practitioners' contributions can be directly measured: comparisons are never simple as the parameters by which the comparison is drawn are themselves contestable (this echoes the point that interdisciplinarity is grasped from within a disciplinary perspective). That means that any decision about the meaning or outcome of the event needs to be thoroughgoingly and slowly examined and re-examined. As such practitioners make themselves present in 'a mode that makes the decision as decision as difficult as possible, that precludes any shortcut or simplification, any differentiation a priori between that which counts and that which does not' (Stengers, 2005a, p.1003). In relation to the research event, the 'decision' can involve a finding, an interpretation, a relation or a potentiality.

In sum, the notions of cosmopolitics, ecology of practices and composition suggest that the research event needs to be slow, circumspect, staged and artful. At its simplest, this implies that the researcher(s) need to resist the temptation of applying categories (blithely as opposed to circumspectly, critically or creatively) and presupposing relationalities (for example, hierarchies among disciplines, relations of power between 'researcher' and 'researched', or pre-existing interests that animate the 'researched'). Sure enough, the outcome of this is by no means guaranteed: a resolution where practitioners reach agreement must necessarily be treated with caution. Perhaps it behoves us to apply more modest aspirations – of drawing out of the research event more interesting questions, or more inventive problems to address, in which the researchers' initial framings are reconfigured.

The obvious question that arises in light of the foregoing is: how does one 'do' a cosmopolitical research event which embraces the contested differences among practitioners? As mentioned, the aim is not to specify distinctive or discrete methods but rather to sketch an ethos that nuances composition. On this score, in what follows I present inter-related, for want of a better term, practical sensibilities: comprehension, compromise, compassion and composting. The purpose of the ensuing discussions is thus both more and less modest than a methodological recipe. Any practical recommendations are merely loose suggestions that – hopefully – open up a space for 'doing anew' or 'reflecting differently'. But the main purpose is to set out a terrain on which a broader discussion about how the multiple practices that make up a research event can 'grasped', even if how those multiple practices are formulated and what that grasping entails are chronically contestable, or better still, composable.

Comprehension

As serially noted previously, the research event unfolds through the coming together of disparate elements or what Whitehead calls prehensions. The notion of comprehension is a means of exploring this coming together: com – together, and prehensions – the heterogeneous components that concresce. There are a number of things to unpack from this very basic definition.

Most obviously, we might ask what counts as a prehension? In Whitehead's schema, to recall, prehensions range across the human and nonhuman, conscious and unconscious, microphysical and macrosocial. In terms of scale, in terms of consciousness, in terms of biological or physical or social category, anything can be a prehension. The one stipulation is that this 'anything' is concrete: it must actually be present in the process of concrescence, in the research event. Needless to say, social scientific practitioners, even in collaboration with natural scientific practitioners, cannot be aware of all the components present, nor their precise influence in the emergence of the research event. But the key point is that, of those elements that we seek to examine, we must ensure that their presence is concretely manifested. This means that we cannot presume uncritically the 'nature' of those components on the basis of pre-existing or familiar categories. To state again, we cannot fall into the 'fallacy of misplaced concreteness' (Whitehead, 1978) wherein abstracted categories are determinative of the character of elements that seemingly belong to those categories. In social science, this translates as a circumspection – a care – about how we enact others who ostensibly or putatively belong to a particular social grouping, whether that be cast along the lines of class, ethnicity, gender, expertise, etc. In the case of the interdisciplinary research event, this means not assuming that collaborators are wholly shaped by, most relevantly, their disciplinary or professional background. In other words, we always need to address those background elements in terms of their specificity as it unfolds in relation to the research event.

A simple example: in interviews, it has regularly been the case that people who are accredited experts (in, say, physics) will insist on their lack of expertise, and those who are self-confessedly inexpert, demonstrate deep and profound knowledge. Not only does this trouble differentiations between experts and non-experts, but also the very category of 'expertise' is put into doubt, or at least becomes deserving of more and specific local scrutiny. This is hardly surprising, such categories are deeply debateable (see previous discussion) but, and this is the point here, they are prehended in different ways within the specificities of the research event. More formally, we can rethink this point in terms of primary and secondary qualities. According to Whitehead (1978, 1933) and Halewood (2011), we should not presuppose that the elements of a research event possess an essence of some sort. These are primary qualities which come to be nuanced, shaped, reconfigured when other secondary qualities are added. So, there is a pre-existing essential category (reflecting an essence) say of class or gender, which might be affected when another category is applied (say geographical or historical). The same can be noted in relation to stuff: an object such as a bicycle has essential primary qualities (wheels, handlebars, peddles) to which can be added secondary qualities (colour, style): it thus becomes a red or blue bike, a road or an all-terrain bike. However, from the present perspective, the bike or class are always rendered in their specificity in which essence or primary quality is itself contingent or conditional. This is a middle-class individual from the northwest of England, this is a 'bike' according to an urban designer or a historian of technology. In other words, primary and secondary qualities collapse into one another when one considers prehensions in their particularity, as they enter into the research event.

This suggests that care needs to be taken not to 'reify' categories of prehensions – to grasp them through presupposed primary qualities. However, it is also important to be open to the possibility that such categories can nevertheless be influential: they can be referenced, enacted and attributed by participants in ways that shape the unfolding of the research event. The task, from the researcher's perspective, is to be attuned to such dynamics of 'abstraction' (see Chapter 7), dynamics in which they might well find themselves entangled (e.g. being attributed particular sorts of 'unwarranted' expertise). Relatedly, care clearly also needs to be taken when we engage with participants whose sociomaterial positionalities (e.g. status) might comparatively disempower or disadvantage them within the concrete specificities of the research event. We return to this latter issue in more detail in the 'Compassion' section, and its thorny relation to 'ethics' (and its complex associations with the processes of regulation and governance of social research).

While we have noted what sort of elements might be incorporated into the process of the research event, we also need to take note of – or at least retain a 'feeling' towards – that which is excluded. Elements make themselves 'felt' by their absence, after all. In the present case, this means that they do not fit in with the process of coming together or composition or concrescence within a research event. While this is a hardly a novel insight (see previous discussion of the other), how such processes of 'othering' are dealt with is important and will be later discussed in terms of compassion.

What prehension goes with what depends on the 'fit' – prehensions have 'experiences' of one another other (see Chapter 1) that emerge in the process of concrescence. Here, to reiterate, experience is not a characteristic of living creatures alone, but is generalized to all entities which 'feel' each other, affect one another and engage one with the other. In other words, experience signals the interactions among elements without prejudicing the form that those interactions might take (see the discussion on aesthetics and satisfaction in Chapter 3). At stake here is a version of comprehension which entails a fitting together of various elements that eventually reach a satisfaction, as Whitehead puts it, in which the event attains some sort of coherence or cogency (and subsequently becomes a prehension in other events). To clarify, this fitting together, by virtue of encompassing the multiplicity of experience, is thus not simply centred on comprehension in the sense of 'understanding' but also entails affects of all sorts. Further, the references to fitting together should not be understood as some sort of interlocking of pre-existing elements – rather, these elements become together in the unfolding and 'satisfaction' of the research event.

In the case of the research event, such cogency or satisfaction can take many forms: for example, it can be seen as a successful research event in which protocols were followed and useful data gathered. Or it can be seen as a failure in which method was derailed and any material collected had little seeming relevance to the research question as originally formulated. In this latter case, satisfaction might have been attained but it might not have been to the satisfaction of the researcher. However, and this is another dimension of comprehension (and indeed of Compromise – see next section), these two reckonings of the research event are interchangeable. As the research event is extended and elaborated, it might be seen that the methodologically 'successful' research simply produces more or less trite data and analysis, while the unsuccessful research event underpins the emergence of new, interesting questions.

To summarize this section, the concept of comprehension is put forward as a means to sensitize the researcher to a number of aspects of the research event as it comes together and unfolds. These include a feeling for the heterogeneity of the elements that make up the research event, including those that might be excluded; a steadfast orientation towards the concreteness of those elements and a resistance towards their being reduced to mere exemplars of an abstracted (social) category; a sense of what's included or excluded as a prehension forms part of broader 'aesthetic' process of combination which addresses 'what goes with what'; and an appreciation that this aesthetic need not be obviously 'consonant' as what counts as a 'good' or 'valuable' satisfaction might only become apparent subsequently. In what follows, we will explore some of these themes in more detail, not least in relation to the practices of the researcher.

Compromise

In our previous discussions of the idiot, one of its key characteristics is that that it poses some sort of threat to our research endeavour, or more strictly speaking, to the research event as conceptualized and enacted by the researcher. And yet, if we concede that there is something of the idiotic in all research events – if our co-practitioners (who might, as noted earlier, be co-researchers from other disciplines as well as participants, or what used to be called respondents) are doing and saying things that don't make much sense within our assumed framework of the research event, then it behoves us to slow down our thinking, to be less sure of our understanding of what is going on, and to be more speculative about our grasp of the research event. One way of approaching this practically is by focusing on what can be done together speculatively. Here, the notion of compromise might prove a useful prompt.

As noted previously, the term promise is an antonym of threat, and as such can serve in an effort to treat threat productively, not least, in that it might suggest the opening up of possibilities rather than their closing down. The notion of compromise, where the 'com' denotes 'together' or 'with', suggests a conjoint opening up. Etymologically, compromise thus connotes a putting (mise) forward (pro), together (com). Of course, this does not necessarily imply agreement let alone consensus, but a linked forward movement that is indicative of neither of uniformity nor colinearity of direction but nevertheless opens up possibilities for the unfolding of the research event. Crucially, there is nothing easy about this version of compromise – it is not a form of facile agreement that Stengers (2005b) warns against. After all, practitioners within a research event might be operating with divergent ontologies (Mol, 2002) which entail a range of prehensions (e.g. different institutional alliances, academic cultural traditions, epistemic cultures, formulations of the problem space, mundane working practices). Despite their differences, these practitioners (say, within a hospital) can nevertheless work together to move forward together.

Let me provide an example of the complexities of compromise. At the beginning of this chapter, I discussed how I deferred to the good sense of design colleagues in the selection of a 'maker' for our collaborative project. This deferral can be seen as a form of compromise – we put forward together – in the sense that there was a collective opening up of possibilities (see Michael, 2018c). However, this might be understood as a deferral not simply to others, but to a prospective future. A promise of what is to come, even if that remains rather vague – perhaps something like 'success' or 'productivity' that the once-disputed maker might afford. Another example might help clarify this point. In research conducted by Caragh Brosnan (Brosnan and Michael, 2014), members of the same research institution, while identifying as neuroscientists, worked in such different specialisms (crudely, located respectively in the laboratory or the clinic) that they differed in their very definitions of the 'neuro' and their understandings of the brain. Indeed, by and large, they rarely had collective research meetings that straddled disciplinary boundaries. Yet, this divide did not amount to an absolute separation. Rather, there was held in common a commitment to a future of collaboration (however that might manifest itself) – a promise of disciplinary calibration, as it were. As Brosnan and Michael note, this future was partially embodied in the research group leader, who being both a clinical and laboratory scientist, bestrode the two worlds of lab and clinic and signified the continued 'adhesion' of the different research groups, but also their future cohesion. In other words, the work of compromise in a future prospect is, as the above hints, symbolized in and by the research group leader. The point is that what counts as a compromise – a putting forward together is a complex matter and can be deferred to a collectively shared future moment, while enabling a putting forward that is adhesive (in the sense of a stickiness of connection across disparate actors) rather than cohesive (in the sense of an integrated movement towards a common purpose or goal).

Now, it is not difficult to imagine research events in which differences perceived by participants are subdued, that is, deferred to a future in which it is assumed that a common 'project' or endeavour or, indeed, common world to echo Latour, will emerge. Questions and objections (what is the point of this research? Couldn't the resources be put to more useful ends? You're asking the wrong questions) that are suspended might themselves be generative of interesting problems. Here is a mundane example of this pattern of compromise, at the level of the most basic form of interaction. The designers (in the aforementioned ECDC project) and I would meet to discuss the project (e.g. exploring design options, identifying social scientific readings, etc.) on a routine basis. These meetings were held around a long table in the large studio where the designers worked. During the meetings, there always seemed to be a lot of 'extraneous' activity – not only on the part of other designers in the studio (i.e. those not directly involved in our particular project), but also by members of the team. Colleagues would continually be getting up to enter another room – the kitchen/workshop – to get, or replenish, cups of tea; or they might go to their tables/workstations to do something or other that often seemed unrelated to the project; or they would begin to look up or discuss something online whose relevance to the meeting seemed spurious. I got rather frustrated – though kept this frustration under wraps – insofar as I felt that this was a dilution or dissipation of valuable collective discussion time. In the context of the present discussion, here was a formal difference (in terms of the process of conducting a meeting) that I took note of, but I didn't raise explicitly. Of course, I could have derogated this behaviour as an instance of a lack of professionalism.

However, over time, my compromise with this pattern allowed me to ask what might turn out to be an interesting question about the ways in which differences in architecture, and the traditions of scholarly practice, combine to shape what a 'productive meeting' might be. In general, sociologists tend to be housed in offices in ones and twos: they are generally isolated from their colleagues on a day-to-day basis. To be sure they bump into each other in corridors and in kitchens, and these are more or less treasured moments of communication. In this setting of comparatively few gatherings, it is not surprising that meetings take on a particularly weighty resonance. By contrast, designers occupying the common space of a studio are constantly in each other's presence, communicating with one another both explicitly and tacitly. Arguably, a research meeting does not have the elevated status it would for sociologists because many of the issues can be under discussion by virtue of the continuing flow of communication within the studio (for further discussion of the form and substance of the 'studio', see Farias and Wilkie, 2016).

This all suggests that compromise also needs to address the process of compromising: how do we put forward together a way of putting forward together. Indeed, to repeat Stengers' (2005b) point in her account of the ecology of practices (as a model for addressing the interactions and intersections of different practices and practitioners), one can never assume too much about the form of such interactions and intersections, because that would amount to importing another (procedural) practice that sits above the other practices. To reiterate, the very practice of compromise must itself be open to compromise: how practitioners go about their interactions is itself subject to a slowing down, a carefulness. This is discussed further when we turn to the prompt of 'Compassion' with its emphasis on the need for due care and attention towards the affective elements of collaboration.

So far in this discussion, the perspective on compromise has been primarily that of the 'researcher'. Much of the foregoing discussion in relation to practitioners (whether co-researchers or participants) has concerned the ways in which they might be productively understood in idiotic terms – that is, their difference or otherness is an opportunity to rethink the possibilities entailed in the research event. However, such idiocy is not always opaque (as we have seen idiocy can take many forms). Rather, there are plenty of hints as to how we as (particular types of) researchers are ourselves caught up in the projects and potentialities of others (again, whether as co-researchers or participants) – projects and potentialities that question the status of the 'research event'.

This further suggests that compromise also involves, at the very least, a recognition that researchers not only engage, but are engaged, and that this reflects the sometimes convoluted relations of power that play out in the unfolding of the 'research event'. For example, in interdisciplinary collaborations, the seemingly entrenched power differentials between social and natural scientists (e.g. Calvert, 2018) can often be undermined, or even reversed, when the demands on natural scientists to engage with public concerns (concerns that are mediated by social scientists) are taken into account. Or in the case of collaborations between social scientists and designers, there can be a shifting in relations of power through the lifetime of a project as making and theorization come to the fore in different phases.

With regard to researchers and research participants, much has been written about the many forms of status disparity that characterize their encounters. These disparities grounded in various hierarchies, however, need to be treated circumspectly. While these disparities may indeed impact the research event (e.g. the relative 'passivity' of a participant faced with a researcher assumed to be in possession of greater status see, from many examples, Fontana and Frey, 1994; Johnson, 2002), this is not always the case. As noted elsewhere (Michael, 2004b), these status differences can play out in unexpected ways. For instance, the co-presence of companion animals and technologies that remain 'undisciplined' within the event of research can serve – be deployed by the research participant – to overturn the meanings of that event, and the ostensible status differences. Similarly, the willingness to participate in a research event might be less about a contribution to the research, than an appropriation of that research as a means of repositioning by those research participants within other hierarchies. The energy communities that engaged in our Energy Babble (ECDC) project were in competition with other communities and their engagement sometimes seemed to be as much concerned with establishing their relative status as assisting in the project (Boucher et al., 2018; Wilkie and Michael, 2018). Here, then, the meaning of the research project was subordinated to a wider imperative of making oneself attractive to future funding by demonstrating collaboration with energy researchers. The broader point is that the researcher and the research might be component part of others' (participants', collaborators') compromises, where the putting forward together is oriented in unexpected ways (at least for the researcher). These, in part, reflect how the event of research (now transformed into something other than, or additional to, research) is reconfigured (by bringing in other local actors such as companion animals, or extending the 'research' event to actors such as competing energy communities). In sum, status differences cannot be assumed but must be treated carefully within the specificities of the compromising that seem to characterise a research event.

What should be apparent from this section is that compromise might serve as a prompt for scrutinizing how practitioner collaboration, whether with other-disciplinary scholars or participants, can unfold. As noted, an integral part of compromising is a reflection on the very promise of compromising. Such compromising, as hinted throughout the prior discussion, necessitates a degree of care: putting forward together requires a sensitivity to others, to their differences, to their counter-projects, to their complex sociomaterial relations to researcher and research event. It is to this process of care that we turn in the next section on compassion.

Compassion

We now turn more fully to the ethico-political aspects of the research event in its unfolding. Needless to say, the ethics of research is an enormous field of analysis, one that has become increasingly standardized and institutionalized, but also critiqued. We will certainly touch upon this later, however, as might be expected given the present notion of the research event, we treat ethics in their specificity as they enter into and are reconfigured in the process of the research event. On this score, we approach ethics through the lens of 'care' – as a reflexive and relational process that attempts to address the perspective of others, while also attempting to ensure that process remains open. As we shall see, this means exercising critique while acknowledging that the relationality entailed in that critique (that is, the particular object of criticism and the flow of communication that mediates that criticism) does not exhaust the relationalities that connect 'critic' and 'criticized'.

Now, in the context of the research event, it might appear that critic and criticized translate most readily into researcher and researched. However, as we emphasized in the foregoing, these personae hardly hold up to scrutiny: thinking through the research event means that practitioners and participants are not easily distinguishable as each goes about appropriating the 'research event' in ways that can usurp its meaning, ordering and status as 'research'. The researcher might well be a prehension in a participant's political or practical event. One upshot is that care and critique can be enacted by many of the co-participants in a research event. If the literature on care has tended to stress the role of the researcher or prime practitioner (e.g. a nurse; though not always, as Mol, 2008, documents – patients can care for their medics by making themselves available in particular ways), the present account attempts to examine the 'mutualities' of care, and a conjoining of critique, that compose a 'research event'. To this end, with its etymology of 'suffering with', the term 'compassion' is put forward as a tentative concept through which to attune to and examine how the mutualities entailed in the research event might play out. Here, to be clear, 'compassion' is extended beyond suffering to encompass a range of affects.

As we have noted throughout this text, the idea of the research event necessarily incorporates a multiplicity and heterogeneity of elements. These include not only those prehensions immediately relevant to the research event itself (people, social scientific techniques, forms of recording, sociomaterial settings), but also those that stand at some 'remove' (institutional and disciplinary expectations, political and ethical commitments, academic standards – though these are concretely present in the research event, embodied in the people, objects and techniques and realized in their specificity in the research event). When a research event is enacted, then, a whole range of concerns are addressed, or, in the terminology suggested previously, compassion maps onto a panoply of prehensions that extend far beyond the other research participants. Part of the process of doing being a researcher is to balance this array of relations. Thus, one must be duly 'ethically' diligent towards the research participants – inform them of their various 'rights' and of the ethical protections and enablements that have been put in place. Thus, one must be cognizant of the institutional demands placed on the researcher and research event so that one acts responsibly in relation to standards of ethics and to academic criteria of empirical research (design of interview schedules, individual questions, sampling, etc.). Thus, one must situate oneself within the ethico-political relations that animate the research – whether these be to illuminate 'proximal' or immediate dynamics of inequality, discrimination and disenfranchisement, and/or more 'distal' or diffuse patterns of disempowerment and empowerment.

This description of the multiple 'cares' that are enacted by the researcher in the research event, can also be grasped through a dichotomy which emphasizes different forms or logics of care. For Mol (2008), a 'logic of choice' is contrasted to the 'logic of care'. Within the general field of medical practice, in the 'logic of choice' the patient is enacted as a discrete individual who, as an empowered, responsible citizen, can exercise calculative decision-making to select among an array of pre-existing choices. This logic tends to break down when people are unable or unwilling to make choices, when the responsibility is less easy to apportion between practitioner and patient but rather circulates among them, and when treatment requires subtle practices of attunement rather than explicit choices. The 'logic of care' is designed to capture these ongoing, recursive interactions entailed in treatment practices. Mol's intention is to present a counterpoint to the privileged 'logic of choice' in order to show how this is mediated and modulated by what she calls the 'shared doctoring' intrinsic to the 'logic of care'. As she puts it

> Shared doctoring requires that everyone concerned should take each other's contributions seriously and at the same time attune to what bodies, machines, foodstuffs and other relevant entities are doing. Those who share doctoring must respect each other's experiences, while engaging in inventive, careful experiments ... they must change whatever it takes, including themselves. Shared doctoring requires us taking nothing for granted or as given ...
>
> Mol, 2008, p.65

If we replace the term 'doctoring' with 'studying', we can glimpse how Mol's perspective might broadly apply to the research event. The logic of choice applies in relation to how the research participants are asked to make certain choices about their participation in the research event: they are provided with a range of information that they are invited to consider in making their decision as to whether they participate in the research event or not. Thus, there is provided an accurate outline statement of the research and its purpose, there are reassurances that participation is always contingent and participants can exit the research event at any time without explanation, there are guarantees that they will remain anonymous, and that any data that they provide are confidential and kept securely, and so on and so forth. These are all familiar ethical criteria to anyone who has conducted social research in a university setting (e.g. Economic and Social Research Council, 2021; British Sociological Association, 2017). However, if ethics codifies a particular sort of caring for the participants, it is also supplemented by 'logics of care' through which an ethico-political shared studying takes place. Before going into this in more detail, it is worth noting that carefulness does not always bode well for the research event. There are complex circuits of assumption and presumption, reading and misreading that can play out. For instance, a researcher's research question can be stated in ways that while, on the one hand, seeming to be careful of the participant can end up generating problems: thus, the accurate outline statement of the research can nevertheless make the research appear trivial, or redundant, or self-indulgent (see Michael, 2015). However, conversely, the very same statement can make the research seem exciting, novel or intriguing. The point is that such a logic of choice is routinely mediated by a logic of care in which option choices are nuanced through forms of exchange – a joke, a smile, a shifted accent, even a little light teasing – that can affect, in one way or another, how choices are rendered.

Let us consider care – as a process of mutuality and iterability within the research event – a little more closely. Puig del la Bellacasa (2011, 2012, 2017) aims to draw attention to the role of care when dealing with areas of potential controversy or debate – what Latour (2004b) has called 'matters of concern'. She sees these as also 'matters of care' with the 'emphasis on care (that) signifies … an affective state, a material vital doing, and an ethico-political obligation' (2011, p.90). Accordingly, to engage with 'matters of care' is to recognize that one is caught up in affective circuits in which one affects, and is affected by, the matter at issue. This matter at issue is not, however, stable, let alone settled: it is entangled with and emerges through the very practices of researcher and the practices of others, whatever their relation to that matter at issue. In caring for a matter at issue, Puig tells us, we must also care for those others who also care for the matter at issue. However, this is not an undiscriminating caring: one should be caring about caring not least because care itself is not a singular or unitary activity. Indeed, it encompasses multiple relations, a range of valences and a recursivity that is neither straightforward nor always comfortable. Thus, in an example that Puig uses, to care for the environmental implications of energy-hungry sports utility vehicles or SUVs means also to take care of all those alternative accounts of the SUV (that, say, lay stress on status or safety).

Here, to practise care is to be ethico-politically sensitive insofar as one needs at once to engage with these alternative accounts (or practices), to be able to exercise criticism of others' views or actions while also being attuned to their and one's own complex situation or standpoint. Care also means accessing the affective circuits – or intimate entanglements (see Latimer and Lopez Gomez, 2019) – through which these views play out and these actions play off each other and mutually shape one another. At the very least, as Puig notes, one should be asking such questions as: 'who is doing the caring?', 'who is being harmed or excluded by this caring?' and 'what are the observer's (researcher's) own cares?' (Puig del la Bellacasa, 2011, p.91–92).

The foregoing comments are suggestive of a profoundly complex – one might even say topological and vertiginous – process of caring that is part of the research event. To practise care is, to repeat, to be caught up in a nexus of care, of compassion. For example, as noted earlier, to be engaged in care is to be aware that this is mutually emergent insofar as caring for others is paralleled by the care as exercised by those others (the participants). After all, insofar as they are invited by a participant to ask questions, to make observations – the researcher is being cared for. And the researcher is also cared for when their questions – however, seemingly alien, or tangential to the matters that most concern the participants – are treated respectfully and answered thoughtfully. To the degree that there is a circulation and an iterativity of care – a compassion – in the research event, there is also the prospect of mutual change in which the grounds of care might be reshaped. In other words, to care is also to be sensitive to the ways in which the research event unfolds, and the participants within that event, whether researchers or researched, co-become in the process of mutual caring – shared studying – (sometimes transforming the very character of the 'research' event). Having painted this picture, research events can be highly agonistic of course, but nevertheless still yield a co-becoming, even if that takes the form of a greater polarization (as was hinted at, in relation to certain interdisciplinary relations).

However, to do care is also to care about its reach, its function, its negative ramifications (where, say, care can translate as support for problematic sociopolitical positions). Care can thus be subject to a version of critique that is – in parallel to the account of care presented previously – 'multi-dimensional' (Puig, 2011). For Puig, in the context of care, critique in the traditional sense tends to be one-dimensional. Typically, it involves detachment in insofar as the critic distances themselves from the criticized, severing interconnecting links in order to show how the criticized are subject to conditions of which they are not aware (Latour, 2004b) but of which the critic is. Puig, by comparison, notes that as a matter of care, critique needs to be expanded to accommodate the multiplicity of relations that attach the seemingly antagonistic critic and critiqued. If one difference between the hater and lover of the SUV centres on the vehicle as it is variously enacted (especially gas-guzzling versus especially safe), there might still be points of interconnection that include the love of one's children, a sense of general environmental degradation, worries about urban traffic and pollution, a delight in the countryside, a recognition of the social pressures that underpin consumerism, an interest in art and so on and so forth. Or these interconnections need not be 'substantive'; they might be more 'affective' such as mutual curiosity or a common sense of humour. The point is that in the process of caring for care, one must also be critical of criticism, and, as a corollary, this multivalency of care and critique suggests an openness to the speculative, to emergent patterns of interconnection and prospective co-becoming.

As a coda to this caring reading of compassion, it is worth noting again that research participants are also entangled in multidimensional relations with the researcher. Participants are not just 'seeing' a 'researcher': they are seeing a polysemic actor whose identities – or rather, the relations that they bring with them into the research event – are not always uncomplicated. By way of a stark example, we can refer to interviews we conducted with scientists and technicians who were involved in animal experimentation (Michael and Birke, 1994a,b). These participants were confronted with me (a youngish male sociologist) and a colleague (an older female biologist) who were engaged in a project funded by a popular science magazine, and both a pro- and an anti-animal experimentation organization. Were we social scientists, natural scientists, academic researchers or journalists? Were we pro- or anti-animal experimentation? One can imagine that the participants were faced with a rather challenging array of relations: depending on which were emphasized, their interpretation of the questions were likely to change. Indeed, at the analytic phase, to consistently interpret their responses required that we 'stabilize' their understanding of the researcher, and thus the questions that were being posed. As we shall see in Chapter 7, keeping such multiple-relationalities open, and even proliferating them, allows for a more speculative – indeed, 'aesthetic' – analytic engagement with the data.

In this section, the aim has been to explore how the research event is marked by a version of compassion understood as a complex interplay of processes of care and critique that is mutually enacted by co-practitioners. This requires that closer attention be paid to the multidimensionality of all practitioners beyond 'researcher' and 'researched' – that they are more than that which seems immediately relevant to the research event. One implication is that this raises issues for institutionalized forms of research ethics as they play out in the concrete unfolding of the research event. But it also points towards the involuted temporalities entailed in the research event, and it is to this theme that we turn in the next section.

Composting

The notion of 'composting' is introduced as a tentative heuristic for addressing the complex temporal dynamics of the research event. In particular, it connotes a nexus of unfoldings that allow us to unravel aspects of the process of satisfaction that marks the research event's concrescence. To begin with, 'composting' implicates forms of death and decay – a decomposition. In an obvious way, a research event decomposes both at its 'end' and throughout its course, as practitioners come and go. However, this depiction of the research event at the 'completion' of which researchers and participants or interdisciplinary collaborators go their separate ways does not simply conclude. Those elements – practitioners – of the research event emerge from it, potentially having co-become, to enter into and influence subsequent events, or expand and reconfigure the present research event. In other words, composting connotes the continued movement (and becoming) of constituents beyond the research event and its 'satisfaction'.

That this suggests that those elements have 'retained' a certain cogency within and beyond the research event is hardly surprising. This is because the given research event co-exists with, and maps onto, other events (e.g. other research, domestic, corporeal, etc. events) in which practitioners are simultaneously co-becoming. In other words, practitioners are an event in themselves, which concresce multiple prehensions of which the research event is but 'one'. These multiple events – individual biographies, disciplinary traditions, institutional and sociopolitical histories as well as biological and physical processes – unfold within different timeframes (see Connolly, 2013). If composting connotes such layered temporalities, it also resonates with the idea of care discussed previously: namely, that a sensitivity to the multiplicity inherent to practitioners is key to a research event, even if that sensitivity is tinged with a care about caring that necessitates criticism. All this is simply another way of getting at the above-mentioned points made in relation to compromising among energy communities (where we noted that the Energy Babble project could be understood as a prehension in the event of attracting future funding for energy communities).

Relatedly, if composting points to a framing of the research event among a wider array of associations (and events), it can also be specified as a nexus of environmental–technological–human relationalities. Following Haraway (2015, 2016), such a nexus can be characterized in more or less hopeful ways. The research event can thus either contribute to big (arrogant) stories that narrate apocalyptic, global, inevitable changes (Anthropocene and the Capitalocene are mentioned by Haraway), or it can contribute to another narrative that decentres the human, but also, by paying attention to the heterogeneous microprocesses of composition can narrate – speculatively fabulate – alternative possibilities (Haraway calls this the Chthulucene). Composting the research event thus also means incorporating elements (including forms of engagement ranging from alternative modes of empirical attunement to explicit practices of speculative design, and different types of analysis) that open up potential ways of thinking and doing that can explore possible ways of living in, and shaping, the emerging patterns of loss and life that we face. In this respect, composting also signals a 'forging' of temporalities.

So far, we have dealt with the research event as if it 'leads to' composting. But of course, it is itself a moment of composting – it is, after all, the product of preceding events' 'decomposition'. That is to say, and here we draw on additional meanings of composting, the research event is also party to 'incubation' and 'fertilization'. These senses of composting have been applied to the techniques of writing: as Kortekallio (2017, n.p.) notes: 'Composting … is also a name for a particular method of process writing: you acquire materials, think them through, and leave them be for a while. Something will emerge'. In keeping with our notion of the research event, this is indicative of the process whereby multiple components mutually change to produce something new, but it also reminds us that we as researchers are not always aware of what components go into the research event or how they co-become at different 'rates'. In other words, the ingredients we add and marshal within a research event might well carry with them a range of unintended or unanticipated elements that co-become in more or less disjunctive temporalities.

In sum, whether connoting the 'internal' temporalities of prehensions as they co-become at different rates 'within' the research event, signalling the timelines of other events within which the research event is a prehension, or pointing to the more or less hopeful pre-propositions that a research event affords, the notion of composting serves as a reminder of the multiple temporalities in which the research process is entangled.

Concluding remarks

This chapter began with a consideration of the intertwined roles of disciplinarity and interdisciplinarity within the research event, before expanding the heterogeneity of knowledge and practice to encompass not only researchers but research participants. In other words, key here was the view that researchers of all sorts along with participants are practitioners – who bring to the research event a multitude of epistemic and practical capabilities. This muddying of researchers and participants allowed us to explore further the parameters of the research event. Drawing on the – hopefully – suggestive concepts of composition, comprehension, compromise, compassion and composting, we attempted further to think through the ways in which the research event incorporated affect, orientations to the future, a focus on heterogeneity and the concrete, the interdigitations of care and critique and multiple temporalities. Taken together, these trouble the apparent systematicity of research methodology and tease out the vertiginous array of interrelations and dynamics that comprise the research event. These notions comprise therefore, still more conceptual and practical prompts to lure our thinking towards – to encourage a sensibility towards – the potentialities entailed in the research event.

Of course, all the preceding discussions have done is, at base, to suggest ways of thinking about the relations that are conducted within the research event – primarily as a way of 'obtaining data', 'gathering material' or, more precisely, co-generating or co-enacting significations, affects, materials. These are subject to 'analysis' (which might well be happening at the same time as the co-enacting) – that is, they are the basis for the production of more significations, affects, materials that are sent into circulation among – become the prehensions of subsequent – (research) events. In the next chapter, we address in more detail what it is we might do with such significations, affects, materials – that is, how we go about the process of 'analysis' in a way that emphasizes the prospective and composes interesting pre-propositions.

7
THE EVENT OF ANALYSIS
Patterns, abstraction, expression

Introduction

Sitting around a large desk with designer and social science colleagues, we were confronted with a set of cultural probe returns (see Boucher et al., 2018), answers to a set of probe exercises that had been sent to a range of participants who were members of Energy Communities. My social scientific instincts were to seek patterns in these responses: what were common themes across the various texts, drawings, photos, etc. that we might collectively identify? But it soon became apparent that common themes as derived from these arrayed materials were not the aim. Rather, given that these materials were meant to feed into the design of a prototype (what would eventually turn out to be the Energy Babble), the purpose of the exercise was rather different, though initially I couldn't tell what that was. What I found particularly alien was the way that the designers drew connections between specific returns and other materials that were also strewn about the place: art magazines, design books, academic texts. They did not seem at all interested in the social scientific imperative to analyse systematically across a delineated corpus of materials: rather idiosyncrasy and 'interest' seemed more important. After a period of disorientation, I began to ask whether there is a value to this type of 'analysis' which was tracing out and privileging unique connections across and beyond these disparate texts and materials?

In this chapter, I turn to the analysis of empirical materials in ways that are prospective. That is to say, the research event also encompasses the processes of analysis, and the ways in which these are bound to numerous elements. These can include expectations about the 'proper' forms of analysis that are deemed valid and/ or valuable, relevant and/or reliable, and tacit knowledge as to what sort of writing (or other form of production) is currently considered useful, publishable or fashionable. More specifically, are there ways in which the intersection of empirically

DOI: 10.4324/9781351133555-7

collected materials with practices such as analysis, connection, application, comparison, abstraction and juxtaposition open up potentialities – that is, 'readings' that suggest unforeseen possibilities for the meanings and uses of data. How do such responses to data affect the relations between collaborators, or 'work' in relation to the shape of the research question, project or programme? What sort of pre-propositions become apparent in the process of doing analysis?

In what follows, I briefly outline some of the typical ways of thinking about what is usually spoken of as 'analysis' – specifically the analysis of qualitative materials. I will examine how we go about deriving patterns in a body of data, but also how we can deviate from this, to pursue synthesis, abduction and the idiosyncratic. As such, I suggest ways in which we can reconsider the treatment of empirical materials within the research event that grapples in a different way with their potentialities. Here, I also discuss the aesthetics of analysis – how empirical materials 'fit' (where, as before, fit can signify disharmony as well as harmony) with other elements that have entered into the research event. On this score, such notions as (heterogeneous) scholarship and abduction will be explored as heuristic means of examining 'fit' as a moment of potentiality. There will also be a consideration of the sorts of generalizing claims that can be made for an analysis. In other words, how does abstraction from one case to another become feasible, and what does that imply for the analytic process? I then go on to present some thoughts on the ways in which the process of writing and dissemination is also ingredient to the analytic research event. The chapter concludes with a discussion of how we account for the value of analysis – it is here where we address what it might mean for such a notion as 'validity' to feature within a research event oriented towards the prospective.

Pattern and analysis

It is commonplace, when faced with a plethora of interview transcripts, or visual materials, or notes, or some combination of all of these (and more), that the researcher enters a period of disorientation. In spite of a carefully crafted research question, in spite of a finely tuned understanding of the relevant literatures, in spite of a systematic process of data collection and organization (sometimes with the aid of digital systems such as NVivo and Atlas.ti), these materials confront one with a morass of meanings, of hermeneutically shifting side alleys and byways from which it oftentimes seems agonizingly arduous, if not quite impossible, to derive a map. To be a proficient social scientific researcher, one must bring to these materials some sort of order, to find the pattern among their seemingly confused interrelations. Of course, various techniques have been suggested for navigating through a corpus of data – cross-sectional analysis, non-cross sectional analysis, seeking out themes and refining codes, generating sensitizing concepts, iteratively scrutinizing concepts through guided sampling, use of outlier case studies and so on and so forth (a sample of relevant texts that guide the researcher through the analytic process might include: Mason, 2017; Silverman, 2006; Seale, 2012). For example, as Braun and Clarke (2006), among many, have noted, this process of identification and refinement is preceded by a series of decisions around epistemology, level of theme (surface or latent), analytic frame (inductive or theoretical) and the balancing or prioritization of the numerous issues addressed over the course of the research.

And yet, such a sequence of actions should not lull us into a sense of analytic security. Treated as a list of instructions, this belies the need for tacit knowledge – as Potter and Wetherell (1987) put it, doing qualitative analysis (in their case, discourse analysis) is like riding a bike; there are a range of tacit skills needed that are difficult fully to articulate, and which are grounded in ongoing practice.

Now, we are rarely confronted with a 'data set' out of the blue, so to speak. We have developed, especially if we are the ones collecting the data, a rough sense of ways in which they might be patterned. Indeed, the constant updating of analytic thinking in parallel with fieldwork is a mainstay of ethnographic practice (e.g. Atkinson et al., 2001). Nevertheless, the process of patterning data remains no easy matter.

Having made this general point, there is a key issue to raise here: what precisely does the derivation of a pattern yield for us? Not unusually, we assume that pattern *per se* is of value. No doubt that is fair enough – partially. After all, we derive insight into a phenomenon, perhaps even sketch connections between observed conditions and recorded actions. However, as Janis Jefferies (2012) has suggested, pattern can also be stultifying and destabilizing: to paraphrase, pattern can make sense but not meaning in that it can flatten the irregular, or mesmerically detract from the unexpected. That is to say, while an interpretative pattern might 'feel right' it can fail to come to grips with those aspects of the data that don't make sense but which might nevertheless situate the pattern in ways that are 'interestingly problematic'. For instance, when interviewing members of the public about their understanding of ionizing radiation, it was clear that they professed and warranted their seeming lack of knowledge in patterned ways (Michael, 1996), through a number of repeated 'discourses of ignorance'. However, when one participant claimed, in an assertively self-confident way, to know about ionizing radiation but got it seriously 'wrong' (at least when compared to accredited accounts), it was difficult to incorporate it into the analysis, or the broader framework of the time in which the public were regarded as in possession of folk knowledge that was counterposed to the accredited knowledge of scientific institutions. Indeed, it threw into relief the assumption that, by and large, the public was conceptually enacted in romantic terms as a lay local community, rather than a collective entangled in the dynamics of consumption and globalization (Michael, 1998) and, beyond that, immersed in and emergent from heterogeneous, and sometimes agonistic (ethno-epistemic – Irwin and Michael, 2003) assemblages which incorporated mixtures of various other actors (expert, legal, media, charity, etc.).

However, this does not take away from the point that pattern can itself be unexpected – it can emerge through an engagement that surprises and excites. When patterns begin to emerge out of a once seemingly chaotic data landscape, this can be one of the great joys of analysis. But this order need not necessarily fit with the pre-existing suppositions (whether empirical or theoretical) of the field.

On this score, we can turn to some recent thinking on abduction. Here, whether the data surprise the researcher or not, there are ways of recasting the material in ways which furnish new insights, and are generative of more interesting problems. For Barry (2013) abduction means resisting the temptation to demarcate the empirical field from which the data are derived, especially where that field is being delineated by particular political actors. However, according to Barry such fields are not pre-set, but rather are necessarily extendable, and part of the analytic task is to trace out empirically how such a field has come to be, its history and its connections to other issues or political situations. In contrast, for Timmermans and Tavory (2012), abduction comes to the fore when the analyst encounters a finding (or pattern of findings) that is unexpected or surprising in a way that does not resonate with existing or familiar theory. Here, abduction also entails a resituating of the data, less by expanding the empirical field than by a de-familiarization with data, or a re-visiting of the data under different circumstances to re-experience them afresh, render them more 'luminous'. In both cases, the meaning and relevance of the data is reconfigured. In accordance with their commitment to grounded theory, Timmermans and Tavory also insist that data analysis is entangled iteratively with theoretical exploration, but stress the need for familiarity with a wide diversity of theories such that different theoretical frameworks can be applied and 'tested' against the data. In both of these approaches, this expansion of the framing of the data (whether that be empirical, theoretical or even perceptual) the purpose is to delve into the data for the 'unusual', and for the possibility of crafting more interesting problems.

Of course, as Timmermans and Tavory note, the application of different theoretical (and indeed empirical) frames is always limited, not least by the analyst's own academic training as well as their own broader situated-ness (e.g. Haraway, 1995). However, for another author, a virtue can be made of these limitations. Billig (1988) contrasts methodology, with its emphasis on routinization and the removal of the individuality of the researcher, to what he calls 'traditional scholarship', with its privileging of the scholar's idiosyncrasy and quirkiness. The traditional 'scholar' is expected to have read in many languages and across many genres, and to pursue unusual connections across the data and draw atypical links between the data (or particular aspects of it) and other empirical and conceptual resources. The aim is to derive otherwise obscure or occluded meanings, to re-articulate anew the problem that the data illuminate. Additionally, it is assumed that the scholar is relatively unbothered by their own situatedness and its shaping of their analysis. This is because, they are fully aware that they are operating within an argumentational field in which they are held (and hold themselves) responsible, and in which their work will be subject to criticism (just as they will subject the work of others to criticism).

To revivify this figure of the scholar is partly to celebrate idiosyncrasy as providing a different perspective on data that adds to a process of argumentation, discussion, debate over that data and the phenomena on which the analyses are supposed to shed light (or, rather, enact). Needless to say, such idiosyncrasy, or 'individuality' is always likely to be present: after all, even the methodological proceduralism that,

Billig argues, routinizes research, cannot totally expunge individuality. And as the Sociology of Scientific Knowledge has taught us (e.g. Collins, 1985; Lawrence and Shapin, 1998), in 'hard' sciences too, the production of knowledge is subject to local exigencies, whether they be physical, corporeal, cultural or cognitive. The broader point is that 'idiosyncratic' analysis has value in opening up the research event such that the pre-propositions that emerge concern not just the topic at stake, but the relationalities with and within a field of argumentation, of contested endeavour.

In some ways, the efforts of the designers that are described in the opening paragraph of this chapter can be understood as a sort of heterogeneous, collective instantiation of Billig's version of scholarship. After all, the idiosyncrasy of the divergent resources (art magazines, academic works, design texts, rather than wide reading in different languages) is brought to bear on the collected material in order to generate ideas that can reframe the meaning of that material in new and unexpected ways that can yield inventive problems. One might even say that the probe materials are not only analysed (in the sense of being split apart and ordered) but also selectively synthesized with other materials, leading to novel pre-propositions that eventually came to be embedded in, and mediated through, the Energy Babble prototype. To the degree that design and the design studio can be understood as sites of synthesis (e.g. Wilkie and Michael, 2016), this is perhaps not surprising.

But there is another meaning of pattern that we need to address – as a model which can be copied. In the admixture of abduction and scholarship, we perhaps find a pattern/model on which to build new sets of practices better able to analyse/ synthesize, and through which to seek out the possible rather than the probable. And yet, there is a problem here. The researcher, the designer, the scholar, remain apart from their material – they are the subjects that work on the objects that are the data, who interpret, who abduct, who argue and so on. In the next section we look to a different account of pattern which troubles this subject/object divide and which leads us towards another consideration of the aesthetics of the analytic research event.

Pattern and aesthetics

Paul Stenner (2012) suggests that pattern is not simply concerned with ordering, but rather embodies the differences between order and disorder, the shifts between gathering and dispersal. Moreover, in the process of these dynamics, pattern should not be understood as a representation, but rather grasped as a relation and an interaction. To be sure, the individual certainly perceives particular orderings, but at base this entails a selectivity that allows them to engage practically with an otherwise overwhelming world. This selectivity is grounded in present needs and past experience. At the same time, the world in its activity impacts on the body of the perceiver, affecting the patterns that they can perceive. Pattern should, then, be treated as emergent within the event of the interaction of perceiver and world, or for present purposes within the research event in which the researcher engages (and emerges) with data. Put otherwise, the world in its various guises – this might be a flock of starlings in flight (in Stenner's case), a sculpture-in-process, or a data set-in-analysis that calls – indeed, demands – to be grasped in a particular way. Returning to Stengers and Latour's (2015) commentary on Etienne Souriau's *The Different Modes of Existence* (see Chapter 3), they suggest that for Souriau, a work in the making – a block of stone, say – asks, difficult Sphinx-like questions of the sculptor, it makes demands upon them to 'work it out'. This demand extends beyond art practice to all engagement in which the world 'demands' that we work it out, give it form. As such, the sculptor or the researcher does not simply subjectively impose form, but interacts with the material to let form emerge. This is more or less difficult, more or less 'skilled': it will be shaped by corporeal capacities and experience, or what Dewey (1934, p.60) might call 'apprenticeship'. In any case, here we begin to treat data 'aesthetically', though, as before, what is meant by aesthetic is less about 'art' and more about the process of 'conformation' or 'fit' (and 'mis-fit').

There are two broader points to elaborate here. First, this emergence of pattern within an event is suggestive of a sort of 'harmony' – an aesthetic fit between two classes of ingredient, broadly speaking the perceiver and the perceived (or the researcher and the data). However, as we saw in Chapter 3, for Whitehead, aesthetics applies to all events, it is central to the very process of concrescence, of becoming. This implies that prehensions as the items of experience (where experience is understood as the heterogeneous relations between heterogeneous elements) accommodate to one other within the event or actual occasion. This, of course, is a process of concrescence wherein prehensions come together in a 'satisfaction', that is, 'some kind of harmony in the same entity' (or event) to quote Connolly (2013, p.159) again. Stated crudely, the event is characterized by elements fitting together to produce a whole of sorts. Part of this process is the exclusion of certain elements, a selectivity, since not everything 'fits' with everything. In the case of the research event of analysis, data and researcher fit together through the harmony of certain aspects of each. But note, this fit need not be expected or typical: there is still room for the surprising, where experience resonates – where harmony emerges – between usually untapped aspects of the researcher and of the data to produce an unforeseeable pattern in which researcher and data co-become.

By way of illustration we can return to an example discussed in Chapter 3. There, in the study by Michael et al. (2007), an unexpected pattern emerged in which interviewed scientists resisted the (reputationally efficacious) temptation of deriding and impugning those colleagues who attached themselves to the subsequently discredited Lumelsky protocol (for the differentiation of insulin-producing cells). This was a surprise in the context of the focus in science studies on controversy, and on the agonistic process whereby scientists compete for reputation not least by disparaging their opponents (i.e. those scientists who take a different empirical or theoretical position – see, for example, Collins, 1985; Gilbert and Mulkay, 1984). But further, Michael et al. went on to propose that one possible reason for this 'forgiveness' was that the interviewed scientists might intuit that, unbeknownst to themselves, they too might currently be straddling a bandwagon, and that they too might one day be proven mistaken, foolish even. This 'but for the grace of god' discourse, as Michael et al. called it, arguably resonated with the authors' own sense of possibly being on a bandwagon (not least a conceptual one). In other words, the unexpected finding of 'forgiveness' (in the context of the prevailing agonistic frame in science studies) fit with a latent sense of the analysts' own position, leading to the unexpected suggestion of a 'but for the grace of god' discourse.

The second point is that the implied harmony involved in the emergence of pattern, of form, need not just entail 'ordering' (however unexpected that might be): it can also precipitate disorder, invite dispersal, opening up novel pre-propositions. A person's aesthetic engagement with an artistic object or event can be hugely affecting, difficult to articulate, suggestive of all sorts of possibilities because of a lack of pattern. Returning to Massumi's (2011) concept of 'semblance', this opening up of potentialities can emerge out of the mutual mis-fit, or disharmony, of elements. Conversely, as Massumi argues, sometimes the artistic work can fail to induce semblance, and indeed, through what he calls 'action-reaction circuits', potentialities might be diffused or deflected because the artistic work devolves into something more staid or dirigiste (e.g. agitprop). Alternatively, it is the observers or audience (or analyst, for that matter) who are too unresponsive, who 'accede too much to conventional wisdom or power' (Connolly, 2011, p.159) to be able to indulge the potentialities occasioned by the artwork, or, in the present case, to engage with the semblance evinced in an analytic pattern. In addition, we might add, that this accession can be recast in terms of other ingredients within the event. Thus, in the research analytic event, it need not be the researcher *per se* that is 'responsible' for the dissipation of semblamatic potentialities within the data, but a series of other elements such as collaborators and co-writers, expectations about the expectations of journals and referees, the imminent ending of contracts, the imperative to write end-of-award reports and so on and so forth.

In summary, pattern emerges in the concrescence of data and researcher (along with many other ingredients) that comprise the research analysis event. This is a process of aesthetic harmonization or satisfaction that can generate novelty and the unexpected, that can evoke potentiality. If this rests on some sort of 'fit' or 'consonance' between ingredients, there are also events characterized by a 'mis-fit', a lack of harmonization, which likewise open up a space of possibility, a semblance that is potentially productive.

Aesthetics, engagement, analysis

In this section, the role of aesthetics is expanded to encompass both the processes of empirical engagement and subsequent analysis. Drawing on a probe workshop with energy communities, we examine how the workshop event aimed at enabling 'possibilistic' data to emerge which could, in turn, be subjected to semblamatic analysis (see Michael et al., 2018). As we shall see, this was by no means straightforward, especially in light of the ingredients that entered the research event. Along the way, we also draw connections to previous discussion on the role of the idiotic in enacting the research event.

As was set out in Chapter 5, the probe workshop was a part of the larger ECDC research project which engaged with a range of UK 'energy communities' who were concerned with reducing their energy-demand. After initial ethnographic visits to the communities, the probe workshop featured as a way of gathering materials that would feed into the design, build and implementation of a prototype, that is, what became the 'Energy Babble'. This latter would be deployed to explore playfully participants' views on such relevant notions as energy, community, information and the future. Of the three probe exercises, I focus on the collective map exercise in which participants from different communities were asked to depict a common community. This was done on a large map populated with mainly minimal graphic features (e.g. blocks stacked into the shapes of buildings), participants used pens, post-it notes and stickers of various entities ranging from the highly relevant (e.g. cars, trees) or rather obscure (e.g. alien spaceships, bears). Participants were asked to draw on their diverse experiences, knowledge and practices as members of energy communities in order to collectively construct diagram of a hybrid, mutually encompassing community. As a probe exercise, both the sparseness in the layout of the base map, and the array of opaque stickers were meant to serve as prompts for opening up the meanings of the map and of 'community': they were ingredients that implied a misfit with other more straightforwardly accessible elements (e.g. images of electricity pylons and wind turbines), and thereby enabled the possibility of semblance.

At first sight, it is clear that the depictions of community the participants generated together were highly heterogeneous and not a little messy. Not unexpectedly, the maps were liberally dotted with energy-related stickers and drawings. Some were electricity technologies (e.g. pylons, turbines and solar panels), some were carbon-impacting elements (e.g. flowers, bees and beehives, community gardens), some were energy-related activities (e.g. recycling, car sharing, plane flight pathways). However, other signs, marks and stickers seemed to be of less relevance to the assumed characteristics of an 'energy community': the provided stickers of dinosaurs, space ships, cups of tea and spiders' webs were stuck here and there, almost but not quite at random; emotion terms such as 'shame' and 'pleasure' were written next to 'bad' and 'good' activities and spaces (e.g. gardens); some areas were drawn to signal particular types of collective activity (e.g. schools, marketplaces, art festivals). These 'less relevant' elements reminded us that the identities of 'energy communities' were not exhausted by energy – that the collective community was much more than this, involving other practices and endeavours. Indeed, it emphasized the sense that energy was always enmeshed with – mediated by and through – other activities. In other words, these 'mis-fitting' markings of the map signalled that the probe workshop event involved otherwise neglected prehensions and hinted at other prepropositions. This reading was redoubled in light of those parts of the collective maps that resisted easy interpretation: for instance, a monumental arch printed on the map had a rat (or a mouse) drawn onto it, and a post-it note illustrating 'a spring' was attached apparently haphazardly to the map. If we can attune ourselves to the semblamatic quality of these, what possibilities do such seeming obscurities open up? Or rather, put otherwise, if we bring an ingredient semblamatic sensibility to these products of the research event, what sort of potentialities emerge? Can the messiness and disconnectedness of the probe workshop portrayals of community be grasped – experienced – as indicative of the possibly chronic unpredictability of communities' composition, of their on-going processuality as they are made and remade?

But then, we must also be wary of such a reading: predictably, others might bring different ingredients to their engagement with this material (and the foregoing analysis of the material, such as it is). Do these portrayals of 'a collective energy community' also serve as part of a research event that reflects energy communities' extended position within the broad political field of energy demand reduction? As the 'population' that has been most studied by social scientists in the United Kingdom, these communities might well entertain a degree of scepticism (see Clark, 2008). Perhaps there is an element of irony at play in the engagement with the probe exercises in which such seemingly 'senseless' – idiotic? – additions to the map evoked the communities' political and economic situation as they competed with one another and researchers for scarce funding? It follows that while any semblamatic entanglement with empirical material might be 'satisfied' in a glimpse of potentiality, it can also yield analyses that are more typically 'standard' (the workshop failed methodologically because the participants didn't take it 'seriously') or 'critical' (the workshop generated material that reflected the structural circumstances in which the energy communities were obliged to operate). The even broader point is that each of these engagements with the probe workshop material bring different ingredients to bear within the research event, and each have something to offer (each other). The researcher that concresces in, and emerges from, the analytic event like the data, can take on various patterns.

Comparison and hybridity

Clearly, the emergence of patterns also entails comparison. Of the many additional points one can make about the 'derivation' of patterns in data (and the co-present patterning of self as researcher), here I will focus on how hybridity can affect the process of comparison in analytic patterning.

In finding a 'satisfaction' or concrescence in patterns, in the linking of different elements to abstract commonalities of 'meaning' – which as the following discussion suggests should be understood in terms of heterogeneous ordering (see, for example, Akrich and Latour, 1992) – there is a simultaneous process of exclusion. Parameters and criteria emerge which enable the grouping of some empirical materials (and the omission of others) and thus the emergence of analytic patterns. Deville et al. (2016), while acknowledging that these lines of comparison might be either found within the material itself (as part of indigenous practices of categorization), or be impressed upon the data set by the researchers themselves, or both, insist on the heterogeneity – the sociomateriality – at the heart of the doing of comparison. In this respect, they discuss 'comparators' as the 'the human and non-human entity that jointly produces comparison ... Humans combine their sensory and organisational apparatuses with those of tools and machines. Comparators are unique too, and vary between each project' (p.30). We can see echoes in this statement of the heterogeneous composition of the research (analytic) event as depicted above: how the material comes to resolve into particular patterns shaped by the complex iterative application of parameters is marked by all manner of elements, not least by the funding proposal that, through its specification of method and personnel, affects who (researchers, researched) and what (methods, materials) can play a part in the comparator.

As we might expect, this can be a more or less 'disciplined' process: for some approaches, this can be highly delineated (e.g. in the case of structured interview data or a single researcher), in other cases, the comparator is altogether more distributed and open (e.g. in the case of the designers' eclectic, speculative and collective engagement with the probe materials). However, we should not get too comfortable with this (disciplined) comparison between these two forms of comparison. After all, the particular comparative line drawn as 'more or less disciplined' can be contrasted with other comparators (e.g. policy-relevant or generative of inventive problems). If we seem to be approaching an infinite regress in which comparators inform the comparison of comparators, this is not necessarily a bad thing for it alerts us to the expansive processuality of comparison, patterning and analysis.

With this in mind, we can draw another comparison, this time with previous debates about the social constructed-ness of accounts, whether everyday and/or analytic. In the late 1980s, much effort was expended on mapping the convolutions that arose when one addressed the observation that social constructionist accounts were themselves socially constructed thereby potentially negating the very idea of social constructionism (e.g. Ashmore, 1989; Mulkay, 1985; Woolgar, 1988). Of the various criticisms of this extended exercise, I concentrate on those arguments that stressed the collective character of reflexivity – that rather than try to incorporate the construction of construction within a single analytic text, construction could be laid bare through the communal conversations and debates that embed any analysis. As Latour (1988) noted in response to these debates, the point of writing is always to make people believe you, even if what you want them to believe is that they should not believe you. This is echoed in another tradition, that of rhetoric: thus Billig insisted in his reflections on scholarship, that scholars' writings are always produced within a field of argumentation and that the expectation is that one will be critiqued, and that one will be counter-critiquing in response.

If we regard analytic accounts as the product of heterogeneous composition, rather than social construction, the point that comparison is exercised within and through a broader academic field still holds, only this time that field is constituted sociomaterially. The composition involved in comparison is therefore also a composition of a heterogeneous 'community' or rather a nexus of comparable or differentiated 'communities'. If various materials, affects, nonhumans, all play their part in the comparative emergence of an analysis, these are also instrumental in the crafting of relations with those who will take up that analysis, who will find it 'useful' or who will offer criticism (see below).

Above, the mention of 'disciplining' comparison implied the classification of data within a system of classes, categories, codes or themes that involved the more or less strict application of one or more comparators. Of course, such classification is typically iterative as the researcher moves between data and system of categories, in the process refining the latter (and the comparisons with other categories). However, it can also be 'meandering' and 'additive', as it were. Arguably, we saw this in the practices of the designers who recruited other 'extraneous' materials into the engagement with the probe returns, yielding something rather more idiosyncratic than a pattern of comparisons (codes, etc.). Instead, those returns opened up possibilities for thinking about the prototype. The value of the 'analysis' thus lay more in the novel potential connections that were traced out across the combination of probe returns and other materials, and therefore in the novel relations that were suggested for embodiment within the prototype and extended to the users of the prototype. The contrast being drawn here (sic) is between a grid of categories within which data can be distributed, and a meandering trajectory that traces its way across and through the corpus of data and additional materials, pre-propositionally drawing out connections and relationalities. If this echoes the famous distinction between strategy and tactics formulated by de Certeau (1984), it also does not exclude the mixing of these processes: after all, a novel grid might be traced in the process of meandering.

Another way of being idiosyncratic with data that opens up the process of comparison in analysis might be derived from reconfiguring the 'unit of analysis'. In Chapter 4, there was a discussion of the disastrous interview episode in which the interview was parasited (productively disrupted) by the 'misbehaviour' of the participant, her dog and her cat. There, it was suggested that this disruption implicated other sorts of orderings in play in which hybrids – combinations of, for example, pit bull, person and cat – were instrumental in the unfolding of the research event. Here, notions such as hybrid (e.g. Latour, 1993), monster (Law, 1991) and co(a) gent (Michael, 2000b) can be recruited as means for creatively concocting (also see Woodward, 2020) the heterogeneous 'actors' at work in the research event. In the case of the disastrous interview, the hybrid pitpercat (as the entity comprised of pit(bull) + per(son) + cat) was usefully deployed to grasp the (lack of) data. At base, the pitpercat (which is a rather obvious combination) along with other hybrids were introduced to suggest a way of re-patterning the 'observations' (and affects) from the disastrous interview episode so that it took on the status of research event and furnished insights into the complex and unexpected ways in which institutions could be enacted (see Michael, 2004b).

However, this could be expanded for more exploratory and speculative analyses. How is potentiality afforded when disparate components 'within' a research event are combined in unusual ways? As a brief illustration, we can return to the probe workshop. With one exercise, our aim was to explore how members of the energy communities, in the context of their homes, came to experience energy and to be emotionally affected by their various forms of energy use. We provided several diagrams (projections, plans, cross-sections) of domestic settings and asked participants to indicate their energy-related experiences in relation to the various parts of the household with their associated everyday practices. This was facilitated by the provision of rubber stamps impressed with a particular pattern (wave, line and dot) and different coloured ink-pads. Along with pens for writing and drawing, the stamps could provide depictions of their activities (e.g. cooking, eating, relaxing) and any linked emotions (e.g. stress, relief). In considering, these portrayals in which humans, spaces, practices and emotions were combined in various ways, we could develop hybrid units of analysis (as noted above). In one case, the preparation and eating of meal with friends entailed a trajectory of killing chickens, cooking, eating with friends and relaxing. Along with this, signalled by the differently coloured stamps were different levels of stress – red for stressed, blue for relieved. Each of these moments could be seen as suggesting hybrids that serially encompassed, for illustration, killing and chickens, cooking, utensils and ingredients, eating, friends and crockery, relaxing and armchairs. However, one might also argue that we can analytically enact a combination of emotions (as related to everyday domestic practices through the stamps) and emissions (as related to energy demand reduction and everyday practices). Perhaps a term such as 'emossions' might prove useful as a unit of analysis that lures our thinking towards the co-becoming in their specificity of emotion, energy and emissions. In which case, what does this open up for our engagement with, and inventive problem-making for, the inter-relations of everyday practices, affect, mundane artefacts and energy use? Can such, more or less forced, linguistic hybridity point towards novel pre-propositions that complicate and enhance our grasp of the relation between emotions and energy use?

To complicate matters further, we might ask if these hybrid units of analysis can be further expanded? The probe workshop was held in Geffrye Museum (now renamed the Museum of the Home) in Hackney, East London. Selected as a venue because it was comparatively accessible to participants and did not possess the typical University connotations, the museum specializes in the British domestic interior and its transformation over time. This history is portrayed through a series of rooms ('living rooms' – though this is historically specific) that 'are based on real London homes and span 1630 to 1990. Their owners would have had enough money to decorate and live comfortably'.[1] In the specificities of the particular probe workshop exercise, how do we think the museum as an ingredient to the research event? To the extent that the museum marks the 'evolution' of the home, what does it add to the data that we are engaging with? Does it contribute a temporal dimension to the hybrid unit of analysis such as 'emossions', for example?

In proposing this technique (or tactic), the purpose is not simply to add another 'idiosyncratic' dimension to the process of analysis, but to enable engagements with the data which might otherwise remain untapped, 'othered'. Of course, not all such hybrid units of analysis will turn out to have 'value', but then, as will be suggested later, 'value' is itself a fluid and contested measure.

Cases and abstraction

In attempting a semblamatic analysis as proposed in the foregoing, in conducting a more or less inventive process of comparison and hybridization, we are also doing something akin to abstraction. After all, hybrids and comparators are abstracted from a corpus of materials or data that have both 'yielded' and 'accommodated' them, then been applied beyond that corpus to other materials or data. At the same time, we are effectively also dealing with 'cases': by this I mean that in the process of analysis, we are operating with a 'case' in which data in one way or another cohere (empirically, methodologically, analytically) and from which ostensibly we abstract some sort of general principle or insight or pattern or category that might apply to, or be used for comparison with, other 'such' cases. As such, data collected from a series of events – ethnographic visits, interviews, focus groups – can be treated as separate cases that are mined for what is shared among them: they are compared, ordered or patterned according to how they exemplify that which is apparently held in common. Or, alternatively, they can be regarded together as a case in which these data or materials cohere in some way and can thus be compared with other like, heterogeneously composed, cases.

This suggests that what counts as a case is not straightforward as many have noted (e.g. Berlant, 2007), not least when the term 'case' can presuppose a common category, indicated in the phrase 'a case of', or serve as a 'limit case' against which a category can be fashioned. Further, if cases are attached, as above, to different methods, their comparability and combination can be problematic (Abbott, 2001b). For present purposes, we prefer to grasp cases as research events whose empirical borders can be expanded or contracted to encompass anything from a 'whole' study (as in A case study) to a limited empirical engagement (as in a single interview). Here, there are no easy distinctions by which to identify cases: a case study can have n = 1, after all (see, for example, Flyvbjerg, 2006; also, Burawoy, 1998; Stake, 2000). For present purposes, then, I take cases minimally to signify research events of whatever size that are ostensibly comparable, that is, from which it is seems possible 'to abstract' a common element or category. Or rather, I want to suggest that the process of abstraction is itself an event partly shaped by the common presence in the cases of what Whitehead calls 'eternal objects' which, as I use this concept, indicate the sharing across case events of a particular sort of 'abstract' element or elements.

Now, in Lapworth's (2015) reading of Whitehead, abstraction amounts to a material process which precipitates thought that sensitizes us – lures us – towards novel possibilities and affective potentialities. Moreover, abstractions need to be subject to experiment lest they become reified and divert thought and feeling from immanent prospects – certainly they need to be treated with care (Rosengarten and Savransky, 2019). However, while retaining this idea of abstraction that in the case of working with cases translates as an affective openness to an array of 'data' as sociomaterials, I also want to suggest that it might be fruitful to engage with cases as commonly shaped by potentialities. By this I mean that, abstractions 'from' cases should remain suggestive of potentialities, thus keeping the analysis, and the comparison across cases, open. That is to say, while we might 'detect' or propose commonalities across cases, these are not 'final' or static (see Michael, 2019). In order to unpick this in more detail, we can detour through Whitehead's conceptualization of 'eternal objects'.

According to Whitehead (1978; see also Halewood and Michael, 2008), an eternal object enters, or 'ingresses', into an event or actual occasion thereby affecting its potentiality. Thus one type of eternal object – redness – can enter into the eventuation of, say, a chair as a particular red chair. Crucially, the redness of the chair is peculiar to that eventuation (see also Chapter 6 on primary and secondary qualities): the eternal object of redness does not specify the actualized redness of the chair. Rather, Debaise (2017) tells us, the potentiality of redness is not exhausted in any given case (or event) because eternal objects 'exist entirely through their ingressions, without ever being entirely adequate to or identifiable with them … (nevertheless) they are fully engaged in existence (yet) … indifferent or neutral to it'. As such they can be 'simultaneously incarnated in several entities without altering their nature, without changing or modifying in relation to their actualizations' (p.99).

If eternal objects can enter into a range of events, how precisely they manifest will be specific to each event, even as they nevertheless retain a certain 'cogency', even if they are 'pure possibilities' (Debaise, 2017, p.94). This specific specificity, as it were, reflects the non-idealized status of the eternal object – all it can introduce into an event is a potentiality that is actualized as a concrete particularity. In sum, the eternal object is a purely abstract potential that manifests in specific ways in specific events, while remaining unaffected and thus able to enter into multiple actualizations. As Michael (2019) suggests, this is reminiscent of DeLanda's (2002) account of the attractor which is similarly 'never actualized' (p.29) and stands as a 'locus' towards which entities or events unfold yet never 'reach'. That is to say, as entities or events become 'they approach an attractor indefinitely close but never reach it' (p.29). As for the eternal object, attractors are 'nevertheless real and have definite effects on actual entities' (p.29). Within the unfolding of an event there will be many eternal objects and attractors, that will make their presence felt.

It will not come as a surprise that eternal objects, abstractions and attractors as portrayed here do not necessarily sit easily with one another (at least philosophically). However, as a nexus of prompts, together they alert us to: the sociomaterial processes of the world that lure us towards certain potentialities (abstractions); the unfolding of (research) events as affected by ingredient potentials (eternal objects); and the unfolding events towards states that are never actualized (attractor). We can tentatively and heuristically propose the hybrid term 'abstractor' as a way of capturing these various dimensions.

By way of circumspect illustration, let us consider an analysis of the cases in which the nanotechnology VANTAblack becomes embroiled with particular versions of the 'public' (see Michael, 2018b, 2019). VANTAblack is a forest or carpet of carbon nanotubes (with a diameter of around 20 nm) and a length of between 14 μm and 50 μm. It takes around a billion nanotubes to comprise a surface area of 1 cm^2. Light entering this substance bounces between nanotubes such that its energy is absorbed. Given the dimensions of the nanotubes and their distribution, only a tiny fraction of the light entering can escape. The upshot of this is that a coating of VANTAblack makes the surface look uncannily black and flat: because so little light can escape – that is, be reflected – there is almost no indication of facets, edges or undulations in a surface. A prime example of this is that where on a crumpled sheet of aluminium foil there us coating of VANTAblack that portion looks completely featureless – a black hole, as it is sometimes described, in the midst of the usual shiny peaks and troughs of foil.

In exploring VANTAblack, the researcher is confronted with a number of discrete cases. When I engaged with this topic a few years ago, these cases included variously: initially a radio report about a controversy in the art world over who had rights to VANTAblack's artistic use; the website of the developers of VANTAblack, namely Surrey NanoSystems; linked examples of the science communication of VANTAblack (an item on the BBC TV's then popular One Show and a large display of VANTAblack in the 'Technology Now' section of London's Science Museum); and an advertising campaign for deodorant Lynx Black (where a canister had been coated with VANTAblack and exhibited in an art gallery and promoted on YouTube). Concomitant with three key enactments of VANTAblack (artistic controversy, science communication, deodorant campaign) there seemed to be three divergent portrayals of the public. These can be roughly summarized as: artistic-elite (the public were elite cultural observers of a dispute over what sort of artist – or artists – could best aesthetically exploit VANTAblack); epistemic-promissory (the public were interested in the specifics of the technology, the knowledge it embodied and its potential applications); consumer-social (a specific consumer public were attracted to the mystique that attached to both VANTAblack and Lynx Black, which in turn mediated peer identification).

In each of these cases, we might say that certain abstractors (let us call them, respectively, artistic-elite, epistemic-promissory and consumer-social) are in operation drawing our analysis in their respective directions. But there is another abstractor that draws these together, that renders commonality and comparability across the cases. This is evidenced in the developer's website but is also present in all the cases. VANTAblack is possessed of ostensibly objective properties that, in light of the sensitivity of human eye and the structure of the human visual system, is eerily blank, utterly featureless. This, let us call it, 'objective-perceptual' abstractor draws together all three cases. It would indeed appear to underpin the enactment of VANTAblack as an artistic resource to disorient and expand the consciousness of the audience, as a technical capacity with specific optical functions, and as an affective, mysterious, quality that can connect with particular sense of peer identity.

And yet, it behoves us to exercise care and caution in relation to an account in which the three abstractors (artistic-elite, epistemic-promissory and consumer-social) are 'subordinated' to the objective-perceptual abstractor. Given their definition, these three abstractors also make themselves felt in other events – we can expect them to feature in respectively, other debates over the merits of particular artistic practices, other arguments over scientific and technological popularization, other studies of the commercial circulation of affect in the production of peer identity. Here, the objective-perceptual abstractor becomes 'subordinate' to each of these other abstractors in that it might be ingredient to their manifestation as concrete specificities in other sorts of cases.

The practical point of all this is that the abstractor can, hopefully, usefully serve as a partial means of modulating the process abstraction from and across cases. It alerts us, for example, to the affective dimensions of abstraction (why have these categories come to be attractive?), to the 'incompletion' of abstractions that can never be fully actualized (what work has to be done to crystallize or demarcate abstractors?), and to the ways in which the many abstractors that ingress into any given case can draw many different links to a plethora of other cases (why do we follow these abstractors and draw these commonalities across cases?).

In this section, I have attempted a quasi-Whiteheadian perspective on abstraction as it features in the process of drawing links across cases. As such, I have tentatively proposed that it can be understood in terms of the derivation of abstractors within and across cases. If the idea and practice of the abstractor can 'lure' thinking towards critical and careful reflection on the contingencies (incompletion, affect), it can also 'lure' more speculative thought, not least towards the possible novel links to – that is, the pre-propositions with – other cases (and thus other lines of analysis).

The event of 'expression'

If the preceding sections have tried to grapple with various aspects of the event of analysis, in many ways these have enacted analysis as an almost a-material process. To be sure, bodies and affects are present (the Whiteheadian notion of abstraction indexes this, as does the discussion of aesthetics). However, what has been left out of the reckoning is the possibility that analyses can also be entangled with the concrete prospects of 'dissemination'. By this I mean that the practice of analysis is also mediated by a panoply of corporeal, cultural and institutional entanglements with the ways in which analysis is 'displayed' – concretized as particular sociomaterials that can be put into circulation (see Latour, 1987). The 'expression' of the work is, in other words, central to the work. Put otherwise, one might point to a nexus or knot of not easily differentiable ingredients within the analytic research event that involves such elements as, for example, the practices and materials of 'writing' (text, drawings, maps, etc.), the concrete tactics entailed in local forms of self-presentation (to collaborators, supervisors, auditors, peers), the strategic considerations of dissemination (choosing an 'audience' and a 'genre', adopting a journal's 'house style', committing to contributing a chapter in someone else's edited collection). In what follows, I touch on some of these ingredients (though practically these are not easily differentiated – things are much blurrier). First, I address the issue of 'representing practices' in the broadest sense in order to suggest ways in which these might interestingly (ideally) open up the analytic event. Second, I discuss how the complex and variegated dynamics of collaborative writing might be woven into analysis.

Third, I consider how the prospect of dissemination can serve in 'expanding' and complexifying the analytic event.

Some thoughts on writing as analysis

It is not uncommon to speak of 'writing as analysis' in ethnographic research. That is to say, the process of writing concretizes thoughts that are as yet unformed or immanent. As the saying goes, for some, thoughts are at the end of the researcher's pen, or more likely between fingertip and keyboard. For my part, I find that when I reach a particularly difficult part in an analysis I have to resort to pen and paper – I have to work out the 'solution', that is the idea, by writing longhand. Of course, there is no such thing as 'writing in itself' – we write within particular institutional assemblages, within particular genres, with particular readers (and co-authors) in mind, etc. Moreover, writing occurs throughout the research event – note-taking, annotation, scraps of ideas, think pieces, presentations, papers in progress, etc.

If we take writing as an agglomeration of practices, we can ask about the extent to which writing as a process and a product can explore the prospective in the object of study, that is, enables us to ask more interesting and inventive questions. Practically, we can open up the analysis by experimenting with the ways in which text is 'composed'. For instance, particular constraints can be imposed (for example, writing within 'unusual' word number constraints – e.g. Berlant and Stewart, 2019), drawing on 'atypical' genres such as detective stories or plays (e.g. Austrin and Farnsworth, 2005; Ashmore, 1989; Latour, 1996), or contrasting and connecting textual fragments (Wilkie and Michael, 2017). In all these cases there is a prospect of prompting the emergence of a not-as-yet thought, of pushing the analysis in unexpected directions. Leaving aside the possibility that 'opening up' the possible becomes an ossified procedure that maps onto a community of opening-up practice, opening up *per se* does not necessarily open up something 'valuable' (see later discussion on 'value'). As Wilkie and Michael (2017) note, a procedure such as brainstorming (in which post-it notes are deployed to mix up and link texts) can serve as much to exclude that which is 'difficult', that is, that cannot be readily assimilated into the emerging consensual analysis. As a corollary, we can also note that even the most traditional modes of writing can open up to the potential, can be generative of inventive problems. An invitation into the unfolding and the speculative can be as thematically polished as the most realist narrative.

Some thoughts on writing as collaboration

Lest the foregoing implies a single author, we should remember that writing can also be collaborative, and as such bring with it its own range of possibilities and problems. We have already touched on the vagaries of interdisciplinary collaboration, and some of the issues discussed there apply no less to the process of co-writing, even where there are ostensibly shared disciplinary and institutional commitments. For example, the perspective colleagues might have on the data, on the relevant theory, on the matter with methods might vary only slightly but can nevertheless lead to all manner of tensions. I recall at one research meeting in which the senior academic on a project presented a very interesting and subtle analysis of the data, while their junior colleague audibly huffed and tutted at the narrative travesty done to the ethnographic material: the complexity of research participants' contributions had, according to the junior researcher, been expunged in the process of delivering what for them was too neat an analytic account. This incident again evokes the idea of the value/validity of research. Here, there is a contrast in values: between something like the value of being 'true to the data' versus something like the value of being 'true to the politics of the field'. This example also points to the way in which writing orients to different assemblages and requires more or less careful negotiation. For instance, in working with one particular colleague, we were interested in addressing divergent constituencies: they were more focused on policy-related readership, while I was more concerned with a public-focused audience. Our de facto response was to divide up our labour and to write for different journals and into our respective areas of interest. By contrast, in another collaboration, there was a tacit consensus that while we were writing towards different audiences, these would be reached through the same publications. In this case, where each author was quite happy to engage and work with the other's critical comments, the writing simply went through a number of iterations, with the first named author taking responsibility for the final submitted version. Finally, different writing projects can entail deference where a particular colleague is regarded as the 'lead author' because of expertise or reputation or stylistic or analytic 'flair'. In this case, one's ideas may be dropped or adapted, not least for the sake of the prospect of publication.

Of course, what is missing from this account is that the collaborative event of writing entails a plethora of sociomaterial ingredients which reflect all manner of disparities of resource – in time, in energy, in experience, in connections, in capacity. These elements, along with the data, affect what is written (or more broadly what is disseminated – see next section). And yet, if data can surprise, trigger an unexpected analytic trajectory, be interestingly abducted, so too can these other ingredients. There is nothing in such events that does not allow for the more senior practitioner to nurture the more junior scholar, to encourage the development of a half-thought and to remain open to criticism. Drawing on a previous discussion, compassion can also characterize the collaborative writing process. As a young aspiring 'critical social psychologist' I co-wrote a paper with a much more senior, depressingly and inspiringly polymathic, academic who showed me nothing but kindness and tolerance, in spite of (or possibly because of), in retrospect, my amateurish ravings. His gentle practice of rigorous criticism and joyful creativity in which I was always treated as an equal left its mark on me: a model that I've tried to emulate, though doubtless not always successfully.

In these days of mentorship programmes, and supervisory training, and writing retreats, the foregoing with its emphasis on the multiple dynamics of collaborative writing, might seem quaint. If collaborative writing can't quite be codified, it can be enabled and enhanced – en-skilled, as it were. These en-skilling systems can contribute yet more ingredients that feed into the event of writing, and at the very least serve as useful provocations especially when set in relation to the ever-present pressures to publish to a particular standard, at a particular tempo, for a particular level of impact.

Some thoughts on disseminating and engaging

The foregoing has assumed, by and large, that academic writing is the main medium of dissemination. Of course, this is far from the case as social scientists have long been concerned that their work is read and used by a readership beyond academia. Thus, policy reports, position papers, journalistic pieces, advisory briefings, blogs have become a key part of much social scientific practice. To be sure, this depends on a range of factors that include funder expectations, workload allocation, subject area and institutional preference as well as the researchers' own aims and aspirations. Needless to say, there are techniques for writing into these genres but, for present purposes, I want simply to note that the prospect of such writing also leads to particular forms of, for want of a better term, translation. And with translation come forms of 'betrayal': to draw on Serres' (1982b) figure of Hermes, the unreliable messenger of the gods, to convey the message to a different audience is also to adapt it and, in various ways, to 'betray' the 'original meaning'. However, this is not quite right in that the meaning and value of data, as I've argued above, emerges from the ingredients that enter into the process of analysis and writing. Indeed, such meaning can change over time as data are revisiting at a later moment: with all the new elements that are brought to bear subsequently, the yield might be a very different analysis. As a corollary, as the research event unfolds, and new prehensions come to be relevant – and that includes the desire to reach various audiences, or the aim to have impact on particular constituencies – not only is the interpretation, analysis and 'opening up' of data affected, but so too is what can count as data in the first place.

Put otherwise, researcher(s) adopt divergent practices and relationalities (one might almost say 'identities') in which they simultaneously address themselves to different constituencies: they can be at once researchers who want, on the one hand, to be what was called 'true to the data' and 'true to those participants', and on the other 'true to stakeholders' and their attendant worlds. Oftentimes, there is no tension between these, but sometimes there is, especially where the complexity of the data that could be accommodated by an academic publication, comes to be reduced for the sake of a practical recommendation or intervention or institutional circumstance. A negative personal example of this comes in a piece of research we did with a government body where we showed how three different versions of science were in operation within that organization. Though we argued that this multiplicity was a good thing, when we shared the draft paper with the head of the organization, who was adamant that there was only one – traditional – version of

142 The event of analysis

science present, we were obliged to halt publication. Under the then prevailing political circumstances, the rejection of the paper was not altogether surprising, and we could have written the paper in a way that placed the emphasis on the traditional (objectivist) version of science. It wasn't until several years later – and after the political conditions had changed – that we were able to publish the piece in a rather obscure outlet. The simple point is that, as researchers, we are caught in complex and variegated assemblages that can eventuate analytic or interpretive variety: that is to say, as the research event enfolds a multiplicity of entanglements, the data open up to variable meanings, some of which are not necessarily welcome or comfortable. Having noted this, in a different project on scientists' views of the animal experimentation controversy, we were concerned that the articles we published in a popular science magazine would generate even more controversy across the antagonistic constituencies, would precipitate attacks on us and our account – surprisingly, we seemed to satisfy everyone.

Of course, there are other forms of dissemination – for instance, texts and photographs (e.g. Holm, 2008; Robinson, 2011) or cartoons (e.g. Bartlett, 2012) – that can make the potentiality of data available to audiences, though these can also be concerned with more 'straightforward' dissemination. One 'class' of dissemination which seems particularly promising in terms enabling this openness to data includes exhibition, curation and installation (though this might not always work as, as we saw in our discussion of the idiot in Chapter 4, an installation can 'trigger' reactions that close down or divert meanings – though this might, in the end, prove productive). In any case, where data and other materials are creatively and collaboratively arranged, across diverse media, they can have affective impacts that are generative of openness, possibility, potentiality in meaning. As Puwar and Sharma (2012) put it:

> Curating sociology therefore should not be reduced to a set of research techniques or methods. Rather, it is a methodological commitment to collaborative knowledge production for creative public intervention and engagement. Notably, methodologies from other disciplines are imputed, poached and mutated with sociological issues and concerns.
>
> *p.43*

In the process, a 'public' is as much constituted as recruited or invited, not least when

> A public cannot be assumed to either be on the side of the sociologist or be interested in what academics have to say. This is indeed a fraught field of intervention. Curating sociology is careful not to idealize the public sphere or the constituency of the 'public', however this amorphous collectivity is defined ... The manner in which publics are constituted and mobilized through creative practices is contingent on a range factors, including the modes of dialogic collaboration forged by research projects.
>
> *p.45*

Put in present terms, the engagement with the 'public' involves an event in which that 'public' co-becomes, not least with the researcher and the research. For Puwar and Sharma, their installation event 'Noise of the Past' served both as a form of doing and disseminating research simultaneously. The Noise of the Past was a multidisciplinary endeavour that juxtaposed site, vision and sound in ways that raised issues about the ways in which British national remembrance could be related to the representations of multicultural belonging. What is opened up here was the prospect of, at the very least, more culturally inclusive forms of remembrance. If this was 'disseminated', it also led to a collection of responses – a doing of research, evidenced in Puwar and Sharma's use of quotes from visitors to the Noise of the Past.

This openness and potentiality of interpretation that exhibitions can enable can be also be found in Latour and Wiebel's (2002) Iconoclash exhibition. Directly counterposed to iconoclasm, Iconoclash juxtaposed an array of artistic, religious and scientific imagery not so much to generate criticism through one (say the scientific) of another (say religious) artefact. Rather the aim was to encourage the visitor to engage with the contingency and constructedness or composition of all artefacts: how they were each grounded in a panoply assumptions, practices, discourses, etc.

There are a number of points to raise about curatorial events of dissemination. The most obvious is that such events can, for a range or reasons, be exclusionary (even if they are posted online) – as is well known, such events do not necessarily appeal to everyone, or even to the majority of the group with whom one most wishes to engage. Prior connections with relevant communities are important in helping to make these events 'approachable'. But these events also serve to highlight the blurriness of the research event's boundaries. As Puwar and Sharma demonstrate, moments of dissemination are also moments of research – data can be gathered on people's responses. Furthermore, such events can resonate in low key ways – people take away with them particular impressions, affects, semi-articulated insights that become the objects of research at a later date (as well as comprising diffuse, circuitous impacts of research). In comparison to the way that dissemination 'does' research, the doing of research is also a moment of dissemination. Engaging with participants is also a way of disseminating: turning full-circle, the recruitment of participants also entails modes of dissemination if not of findings, then of diffuse expectations of findings (which can likewise generate complex patterns of inclusion and exclusion, see Michael, 2015).

The point of this short ramble through dissemination practices as ingredient to analysis (and I can only claim to have scratched the surface – I have not even mentioned the public engagement and impact professionals that have become part of the academic landscape and thus also able to affect the research event) is to raise again the matter of the flexible borders of the research event. In this respect, research can emerge out of the 'prospects' ('necessity', even) of dissemination too, even if this seems counter to the typical 'value' and 'validity' of social scientific research. It is to these concerns that the final section turns.

Conclusion: on value and validity

The question of validity is a mainstay of many traditional methods books – how can we be sure that what we are measuring reflects what is in the world? Do our analytic categories – discourses, observations, processes – accurately represent what they claim to be representing? How can we check on this claim? Perhaps we can triangulate across different types of data – interviews, participant observations, textual materials, surveys? But then are these of the same status – can they really be compared (Silverman, 2006)? How do we establish their comparability? According to, for example, Silverman (2006), different methods can be grounded in disparate theoretical backgrounds and draw on divergent contexts of application: this means that the data they generate are by no means straightforwardly comparable. Or perhaps we can check our accounts with our research participants – can they reassure us that we are on the right track? And yet, whether they agree with, or dispute, our account, is this an actual check or simply more data as people's responses are as much concerned with performing in relation the present social situation of 'checking' as with assessing the academic account or analysis (e.g. Potter and Wetherell, 1987). As Silverman (2006) has suggested, perhaps we should not be seeking to validate our analysis through coherence across different methods or timeframes, but actually see the differences as an opportunity to explore the research question and the data further (also see Mason's (2011) 'facet methodology', for an elaboration of the use of difference in the research process).

However, the question of validity raises a number of interesting issues when related to the idea of the research event. As noted at the outset, to do research is partly to enact – to constitute – the stuff that one is studying. Research is performative, and while a sometime part of that performance is to claim validity (that one has more or less accurately depicted the world) in some guise or other, the performance is geared to a number of other elements too. For instance, as Mulkay (1979) showed long ago in his critique of Merton's (1973/1942) CUDOS norms in science, what is most valued in science is what is useful (not whether scientists' practice adheres to certain scientific norms). The obvious question that follows is what is 'useful', of value, in relation to the research event?

The first thing to note is that value can be understood as what 'fits' within an extended research event that includes the community of 'relevant' scholars. If one's research (findings, account, analysis) 'contributes' – becomes a prehension – within subsequent research events, then it has a value. What is at stake is how that 'fit' and 'contribution' happens in relation to the other elements that comprise that subsequent research event. As such, to be of value is not just a matter of some sort of 'calculative performance' – after all, given that the researcher also emerges from the research event, one might ask 'who' (or indeed 'what') is doing the performance? Rather, a research event becomes ingredient to subsequent research events because it is relevant to them. But this relevance (which will include difference and thus exclusion), can depend on many factors. After all, as with scientists, social scientists can find themselves on a bandwagon (Michael et al., 2005) – attached, say, to one of series of turns – the linguistic turn, the materialist turn, the affective turn which will be supplanted in due course. In any case, to be part of a turn is to be part of a larger research event in which one's research can be taken to have more value than work which is not part of that turn. And if value is associated with a particular turn, this might well in time become degraded in value, with the pivoting of another turn. Social scientists are well aware of the turnover of turns: as with scientists who suspect they are on a bandwagon that might in due course be overturned, social scientists might find themselves turning to other turns and recalibrating the value of prior research events.

Having said this, the valuation of research is something that is not readily predictable. Research events in this larger guise can take some unexpected directions. A long time ago, I was part of an interdisciplinary research team on a project I thought was essentially flawed, not only in terms of design, data collection and analysis, but also in terms of the 'turn' to which it owed allegiance. Despite a few well-placed publications, my general impression was that the project was a failure. However, what I did not appreciate – as a relative neophyte researcher – was the way the project fitted within a broader research event that extended beyond a research programme to encompass a range of political, policy and institutional actors. Within this emerging event the project was deemed highly innovatory, a huge success.

The moral of this anecdote is that whatever one thinks of the value of one's research, it is routinely overtaken by events. Or rather, research and researcher are emergent within these larger events, and valued in ways that do not always resonate with the researcher's own original valuation of their work. Another moral is that if an abiding value of the research event as discussed in this volume is that it is marked by openness, emergence, potentiality and so on, that value is itself subject to valuation. For instance, openness, emergence and potentiality do not necessarily yield anything valuable – their value partly lies in facilitating reflection on how research is eventuated: How has this research question come to the fore? How has this set of observations come to be privileged or ignored? How has analysis proceeded in this direction? But, to reiterate, does such questioning – and the linked pursuit of inventive problems – also reflect broader processes: is the present seeking out of the 'inventive' (allied as that is to the 'creative') an outcome of what Thrift (2005) has called 'knowing capitalism' in which the pursuit of 'inventiveness' and 'creativity' have become a managerial adaptation to the chronic crises that confront late capitalism?

Note

1 See www.museumofthehome.org.uk/whats-on/galleries-and-gardens/rooms-through-time/.

8
CONCLUDING ... BUT NOT ENDING

Concluding ...

I could have begun this concluding chapter with an anecdote about how, in the process of writing this book, I went through a series of major personal and professional difficulties. For once, I'll spare the reader the gory details, but these more or less extended events were all part and parcel of a definitely prolonged process of composition. While I can't say precisely how these 'life experiences' shaped the volume, I can say that the result is a text that is more disjointed than I would have liked, more convoluted than I was expecting, and more perambulatory than I initially proposed. Having said that, dissatisfaction with one's own writings is a chronic feature of academic life, and a fitting affect for a book concerned with openness and potentiality. Hopefully, it is nevertheless of some use to some readers.

Accordingly, the concluding remarks that follow are really an inevitably and resolutely partial reflection on the ostensible shortcomings of the book, not as a way of excusing them, but as way of seeing how they might be fruitfully developed, of pointing towards inventive problems and their related avenues of research practice.

As mentioned in Chapter 1, the book eschews a range of traits that typify a text devoted to the discussion of social methodology. To reiterate, there has been an attempt to avoid the usual hierarchical divisions between ontology, epistemology, theory, methodology and method, and discrete methods. Even where these terms are presented, they are neither especially well-detailed nor exemplified for ease of application. Moreover, several standard issues with the specific practices and processes of qualitative research are neglected or else 'mangled' (Pickering, 1995) with other concerns. Thus, for instance, matters of validity and ethics are read through such notions as, respectively, value and usefulness, and care and compassion. And sampling and reliability are, more tangentially and tacitly referenced through, respectively, cases and the pliability of the research event, and scholarship and

DOI: 10.4324/9781351133555-8

idiosyncrasy. The purpose of this, and the array of terms that have been collected and promoted – attunement, disconcertment, idiot, parasite, hybrid categories, heterogeneous scholarship, compromise, fit and so on – is to encourage a different sensibility to the doing of social research that engages with the possibilities and potentialities made present through the research event. Needless to say, this sensibility applies no less to these terms and the very notion of research event.

Also as mentioned previously, the sorts of empirical elements that have been featured in the various discussions given earlier have been of a rather limited kind. While I have very lightly touched on such issues as, for instance, global climate change, gender inequalities, postcolonialism, digital surveillance, these have been treated as elements or ingredients that ingress into the research event rather than affecting the very framing that the 'research event' brings with it. In all these cases (and this point applies no less to other 'broader' or 'macro' sociomaterial conditions), the aim is to engage with these conditions – how these ingress into, and are concresced within, the research event – in terms of their specificity. As the references to the fallacy of misplaced concreteness, primary and secondary qualities, and the abstractor, indicate, there is a hesitation in taking these as conditions as givens, as partly explanatory of how an actor manifests in the unfolding of a research event. Rather, they have been approached through the particularities of the research event, whether that be through the shaping of research questions, attunement and disconcertment in empirical engagement or the process of analysis and abstraction.

One negative implication is that this might appear to trivialize the political and ethical dimensions of sociology and the social sciences more generally. Reinforcing this appearance is the reticence about the impact of contemporary conditions such the COVID-19 pandemic, the systemic recourse to online and digital modes of communication, or the increasing prominence of digital research methods engaging with digitized social processes (though see, for example, the account of the Energy Babble). Of course, all these can be grasped through the framing of the research event with its focus on specificity and the speculative. Thus, in relation to COVID-19, we can ask how the research into accounts about COVID-19's emergence and spread might be opened up through an attunement to more topological models of zoonosis (Hinchliffe et al., 2012). Or we might explore how popular visualizations of the units of safe distancing can open up questions about the changing character of expertise and trust (Michael, 2020). Or we might open up questions about Twitter's role in the formulation and enactment of the pandemic and vaccination by interjecting an idiotic 'bot' (see Wilkie et al., 2015).

Now, the terminology of 'opening up' has played a pivotal role in this volume. In relation to the present discussion, opening up also equates with a sensibility towards the composedness of these broad or macro-social conditions (class, gender, etc.): they too are concresced and eventuated in various ways (e.g. official statistics, theoretical traditions, political histories). If they comprise prehensions within the research event, 'opening up' thus means being open to their prior status as events concresced out of other prehensions, including the work of social theory (e.g. Latour, 2003). While we as researchers in a particular field might have neither the skill nor the inclination to open up these conditions, we can nevertheless recognize that they are themselves composed (as well as made manifest in a more or less distinctive specificity).

These issues can be approached in another way, through a tentative contrast between 'Writing Up' and 'Writing Down'. If writing up implies a tidying of the research process (including a tidy accounting of its untidiness) often in a preset format such as that of a thesis or academic journal paper, writing down connotes being in the midst of grubby detail that resists tidiness (and simplified pattern). In some ways, we are always writing down: a data set is liable to escape its analysis as it becomes concresced with other prehensions (e.g. encounters new theoretical resources or merges with new empirical insights – see, for example, the discussion of anecdotalization given earlier), and its grubby details can become 'luminous' once more (to draw on Timmermans and Tavory, 2012, again). Relatedly, the event of writing up is itself composed of various elements: the not-so-diffuse formal and informal pressures to 'finish' and publish; the responsibility to colleagues who have asked for a contribution to a collection; the plain exhaustion that overcomes one in the midst of the research process. In this respect, writing up is a punctuation in a research process that is, in principle, a work-in-progress. But, of course, even the written-up work is converted into a 'work-in-progress' as it enters the field of argumentation associated with a community of peers.

In light of this, perhaps the use of the extended sociomaterial conditions (and categories and concerns) to order data might be usefully thought in terms of an oscillation between writing up (and 'closing down') and writing down (and 'opening up'). However, this is not quite right. After all, data's encounter with new theory (and macro categories) can open up interesting questions, and grubby detail can mire an analysis, so that the potentiality of an empirical event becomes difficult to articulate. This point simply serves to intimate that we should be wary of indulging the fallacy of misplaced concreteness when it comes to the present analysis too, and to the various concepts that have been suggested. It will not have gone unnoticed that despite the insistence on the concrete and the specific throughout this book, much of the discussion has tended towards the abstract. If I were sufficiently cynical, I would claim this has been deliberate – a means of modulating the abstraction of, of not over-concretizing, the 'concrete'. Still, I'm happy to accept this happy accident insofar as it exemplifies the caution and care that needs to be exercised in writing up and writing down, and, indeed, in the application of caution and care (sic).

This general point applies no less to the notions of potentiality and opening up that have been used so liberally over the course of this book. Potentiality and opening up are not necessarily 'a good thing' on several levels. We have already mentioned that they might be reflective of a neoliberal management reaction to the crises of late capitalism. That is to say, the use of these terms might be tacitly drawing on an imaginary (and related practices) that sees 'creativity' (and cognate qualities such as potentiality) as a good thing in that it opens up the range of responses to 'insufficient productivity' and to the need for more novel commodities and services.

Relatedly, the present volume, insofar as it shifts emphasis from findings and facts, to inventive problems, potentiality, and pre-propositions, will, for some, be another instantiation of a post-truth 'malaise' in which, as Kelly and McGoey (2018, p.6) put it 'The social and political failures of neoliberalism ... have profound epistemic reverberations: post-truth is managerialism come home to roost'.

Now, Science and Technology Studies – especially in its constructionist and compositionist guises (that have been so central to the current volume) – has long been embroiled in debates over its political value (e.g. Scott et al., 1990). Even where scholars have been sympathetic to the present perspective, they have noted its evident naivete in the world of 'real politics' (e.g. Blok, 2011). Yet, in keeping with the critical ethos of evoking how things might be other than they are, the present approach does this but in small diffuse steps, as a sort of invitation to attune to the unexpected ways an event (including the event of how that event is defined and demarcated) might unfold, to explore what pre-propositions might be afforded. Ultimately, as with any other form of politics that draws on social science's methodological and theoretical practices, there are no guarantees of successful intervention. Even care and compassion exercised within a research event can be read as patronization and lead to polarization among co-practitioners ...

So where does this leave us? Well, within a research event (as manifested in this book), this 'dissatisfaction' is also an opening up to potentiality, to the exploration of pre-propositions ...

... But not ending

Research methods text books rightly set out how one might practically go about the various phases of doing social research. I have done this at various points, suggesting practical orientations hopefully without being too insistent on their great value or utility: they are merely heuristics, suggestions to be built on, or adapted, or to prompt alternatives. Had I been braver or more able, I would have written a more 'idiotic' text ... one that is designed to make the reader hesitate, in Stengers' beautiful phrase Stengers (2005a), to demand 'that we slow down, that we don't consider ourselves authorized to believe we possess the meaning of what we know' (p.995). In line with this, I was hoping to round the book off, not with methodological instructions of course, but with choice aphorisms in the cautiously inspirational manner of Adorno (1951/1978). These would serve as a lure towards a reconsideration of how we authorize our belief that we possess the meaning of what and how we know. As it turns out, I could only manage a short list of 'idiotic slogans' that ideally feed into the continued pre-propositionality of this text:

- Your concepts are always begging to be betrayed ...
- There are only heuristics, including this one ...
- The mess of method needs the clutter of thought ...
- In attuning, be disconcerted, and vice versa ...
- Always you are someone and something else's event ...

REFERENCES

Abbott, A. (2001a). Time Matters: On Theory and Method. Chicago, IL: Chicago University Press.
Abbott, A. (2001b). The Chaos of Disciplines. Chicago, IL: Chicago University Press.
Adam, B. and Groves, C. (2007). Future Matters: Action, Knowledge, Ethics. Leiden; Boston, MA: Brill.
Adams, D. and Lloyd, J. (1983). The Meaning of Liff. London: Pan and Faber & Faber.
Adams, V., Murphy, M. and Clarke, A.E. (2009). Anticipation: Technoscience, Life, Affect, Temporality. Subjectivity, 28(1), 246–265.
Adams, C. and Thompson, T.L. (2016). Researching in a Posthuman World: Interviews with Digital Objects. Basingstoke: Palgrave MacMillan.
Adkins, L. and Lury, C. (2009). Special Issue: What is the Empirical?. European Journal of Social Theory, 12(1), 5–187.
Adorno, T. (1951/1978). Minima Moralia. London: Verso.
Agee, J. (2009). Developing Qualitative Research Questions: A Reflective Process. International Journal of Qualitative Studies in Education, 22(4), 431–447.
Akrich, M. and Latour, B. (1992). A Summary of a Convenient Vocabulary for the Semiotics of Human and Nonhuman Assemblies. In Bijker, W.E. and Law, J. (eds.). Shaping Technology/Building Society (pp. 259–263). Cambridge, MA: MIT Press.
Anderson, B. (2010). Preemption, Precaution, Preparedness: Anticipatory Action and Future Geographies. Progress in Human Geography, 34, 777–798.
Anderson, B. (2014). Encountering Affect: Capacities, Apparatuses, Conditions. Farnham: Ashgate.
Ardevol, E., Pink, S. and Lanzeni, D. (eds.) (2016). Designing Digital Materialities: Knowing, Intervention and Making. London: Bloomsbury.
Asdal, K. and Moser, I. (2012). Experiments in Context and Contexting. Science, Technology, & Human Values, 37(4), 291–306.
Ashmore, M. (1989). The Reflexive Thesis: Wrighting Sociology of Scientific Knowledge. Chicago, IL: Chicago University Press.
Atkinson, P., Coffey, A., Delamont, S., Lofland, J. and Lofland L. (eds.) (2001). Handbook of Ethnography. London: Sage.

Austrin, T. and Farnsworth, J. (2005). Hybrid Genres: Fieldwork, Detection and the Method of Bruno Latour. Qualitative Research, 5(2), 147–165.
Back, L. and Puwar, N. (eds.) (2012). Live Methods. Malden, MA; Oxford; Carlton: Wiley-Blackwell.
Bailey, C.A. (2017). A Guide to Qualitative Field Research. New York, NY: Sage.
Barad, K. (2007). Meeting the Universe Halfway. Durham, NC: Duke University Press.
Bargal, D. (2006). Personal and Intellectual Influences Leading to Lewin's Paradigm of Action Research: Towards the 60th Anniversary of Lewin's 'Action Research and Minority Problems' (1946). Action Research, 4, 367–388.
Barnwell, A. (2016). Creative Paranoia: Affect and Social Method. Emotion, Space and Society, 20, 10–17.
Barry, A. (2013). Material Politics: Disputes Along the Pipeline. West Sussex: Wiley-Blackwell.
Barry, A. and Born, G. (eds.) (2013a). Interdisciplinarity: Reconfigurations of the Social and Natural Sciences. London; New York, NY: Routledge.
Barry, A. and Born, G. (2013b). Introduction. In Barry, A. and Born, G. (eds.). Interdisciplinarity: Reconfigurations of the Social and Natural Sciences (pp. 1–56). London: Routledge.
Barry, A., Born, G. and Weszkalnys, G. (2008). Logics of Interdisciplinarity. Economy and Society, 37(1), 20–49.
Bartlett, R. (2012). Playing with Meaning: Using Cartoons to Disseminate Research Findings. Qualitative Research, 13(2), 214–227.
Bates, C. and Rhys-Taylor, A. (eds.) (2017). Walking through Social Research. London: Routledge.
Bauman, Z. (1976). Socialism: The Active Utopia. London: George Allen and Unwin.
Beaver, J., Kerridge, T. and Pennington, S. (eds.) (2009). Material Beliefs. London: Goldsmiths, University of London.
Beckman, F. (2009). The Idiocy of the Event: Between Antonin Artaud, Kathy Acker and Gilles Deleuze. Deleuze Studies, 3(1), 54–72.
Bennett, J. (2010). Vibrant Matter. Durham, NC: Duke University Press.
Berlant, L. (2007). On the Case. Critical Inquiry, 33, 663–672.
Berlant, L. and Stewart, K. (2019). The Hundreds. Durham, NC: Duke University Press.
Billig, M. (1988). Methodology and Scholarship in Understanding Ideological Explanation. In Antaki, C. (ed.). Analysing Everyday Explanation (pp. 199–215). London: Sage.
Binder, T., Brandt, E., Ehn, P. and Halse, J. (2015). Democratic Design Experiments: Between Parliament and Laboratory. CoDesign, 11(3–4), 152–165.
Blackman, L. and Venn, C. (2010). Affect. Body and Society, 16(1), 7–28.
Blok, A. (2011). War of the Whales: Post-Sovereign Science and Agonistic Cosmopolitics in Japanese-Global Whaling Assemblages. Science, Technology & Human Values, 36, 55–81.
Blume, S. (1990). 'Interdisciplinarity in the Social Sciences' SPSG Concept Paper No. 10. Amsterdam: University of Amsterdam.
Bochner, A.P. and Ellis, C. (2003). An Introduction to the Arts and Narrative Research: Art as Inquiry. Qualitative Inquiry, 9(4), 506–514.
Boehner, K., Gaver, W. and Boucher, A. (2012). Probes. In Lury, C. and Wakeford, N. (eds.). Inventive Methods: The Happening of the Social (pp. 185–201). London; New York, NY: Routledge.
Boettger, O. (1998). From Information Technology to Organising Information: An Interdisciplinary Study. Unpublished PhD Thesis. Centre for Social Theory and Technology, Keele University.

Borup, M., Brown, N., Konrad, K. and Van Lente, H. (2006). The Sociology of Expectations in Science and Technology. Technology Analysis & Strategic Management, 18(3–4), 285–298.

Boucher, A., Gaver, W., Kerridge, T., Michael, M., Ovalle, L., Plummer-Fernandez, M. and Wilkie, A. (2018). Energy Babble: Entangling Design and STS. Manchester: Mattering Press.

Bourdieu, P. (1977). Outline of a Theory of Practice Cambridge. Cambridge: Cambridge University Press.

Bourdieu, P. (1984). Distinction: A Social Critique of the Judgement of Taste. London: Routledge.

Bowker, G.C. and Star, S.L. (1999). Sorting Things Out: Classification and Its Consequences. Cambridge, MA: The MIT Press.

Braidotti, R. (2013). The Posthuman. Cambridge: Polity Press.

Braun, V. and Clarke, V. (2006). Using Thematic Analysis in Psychology. Qualitative Research in Psychology, 3(2), 77–101.

British Sociological Association (2017). Statement of Ethical Practice. www.britsoc.co.uk/media/24310/bsa_statement_of_ethical_practice.pdf.

Brosnan, C. and Michael, M. (2014). Enacting the 'Neuro' in Practice: Translational Research, Adhesion, and the Promise of Porosity. Social Studies of Science, 44(5), 680–700.

Brown, N. (2003). Hope Against Hype: Accountability in Biopasts, Presents and Futures. Science Studies, 16(2), 3–21.

Brown, N. and Michael, M. (2003). A Sociology of Expectations: Retrospecting Prospects and Prospecting Retrospects. Technology Analysis and Strategic Management, 15(1), 3–18.

Brown, S.D., Kanyeredzi, A., McGrath, L., Reavey, P. and Tucker, I. (2019). Affect Theory and the Concept of Atmosphere. Distinktion: Journal of Social Theory, 20(1), 5–24.

Burawoy, M. (1998). The Extended Case Method. Sociological Theory, 16, 4–33.

Callard, F. and Fitzgerald, D. (2015). Rethinking Interdisciplinarity Across the Social Sciences and Neurosciences. Basingstoke: Palgrave Macmillan.

Callon, M., Lascoumbes, P. and Barthe, Y. (2001). Acting in an Uncertain World: An Essay on Technical Democracy. Cambridge, MA: The MIT Press.

Calvert, J. (2018). Wedging. In Lury, C., et al. (eds.). Routledge Handbook of Interdisciplinary Methodology (pp. 352–354). Abingdon: Routledge.

Carter, S.M. and Little, M. (2007). Justifying Knowledge, Justifying Method, Taking Action: Epistemologies, Methodologies, and Methods in Qualitative Research. Qualitative Health Research, 17(10), 1316–1328.

Chang, H. (2008). Autoethnography as Method. Walnut Creek, CA: Left Coast Press.

Clark, T. (2008). We're Over-Researched Here! 'Exploring Accounts of Research Fatigue Within Qualitative Research Engagements. Sociology, 42(5), 953–970.

Clough, P.T. and Halley, J. (eds.) (2007). The Affective Turn: Theorizing the Social. Durham, NC: Duke University.

Cockburn, C. and Ormerod, S. (1993). Gender and Technology in the Making. London: Sage.

Coleman, R. (2020). Glitterworlds: The Future Politics of a Ubiquitous Thing. London: Goldsmiths Press.

Coleman, R. and Tutton, R. (2017). Special Issue: Austerity Futures. The Sociological Review, 65(3), 440–543.

Collins, H.M. (1985). Changing Order. London: Sage.

Collins, H. and Evans, R. (2002). The Third Wave of Science Studies: Studies of Expertise and Experience. Social Studies of Science, 32, 235–296.

Connolly, W.E. (2011). A World of Becoming. Durham, NC: Duke University Press.

Connolly, W.E. (2013). The Fragility of Things. Durham: Duke University Press.

Cook, P.S., Kendall, G., Michael, M. and Brown, N. (2011). The Textures of Globalization: Biopolitics and the Closure of Xenotourism. New Genetics and Society, 30, 101–114.

Cooper, C.B., Dickinson, J., Phillips, T. and Bonney, R. (2007). Citizen Science as a Tool for Conservation in Residential Ecosystems. Ecology and Society, 12(2), 11. [Online] URL: www.ecologyandsociety.org/vol12/iss2/art11/.

Crain, R., Cooper, C. and Dickinson, J.L. (2014). Citizen Science: A Tool for Integrating Studies of Human and Natural Systems. Annual Review of Environment and Resources, 39, 641–665.

Czarniawska, B. (2004). On Time, Space, and Action Nets. Organization, 11(6), 773–791.

Czarniawska, B. (2008). A Theory of Organizing. Cheltenham: Edward Elgar.

Czarniawska, B. and Hernes, T. (eds.) (2005). Actor-Network Theory and Organizing. Malmo/Copenhagen: Liber/CBS.

Davies, G., Greenhough, B., Hobson-West, P. and Kirk, R.G.W. (2018). Science, Culture, and Care in Laboratory Animal Research: Interdisciplinary Perspectives on the History and Future of the 3Rs. Science, Technology, & Human Values, 43(4), 603–621.

Davies, S.R. (2018). Characterizing Hacking: Mundane Engagement in US Hacker and Makerspaces. Science, Technology and Human Values, 43(2), 171–197.

Dean, M. (1999). Governmentality: Power and Rule in Modern Society. London: Sage.

Debaise, D. (2017). Speculative Empiricism: Revisiting Whitehead. Edinburgh: Edinburgh University Press.

De Certeau, M. (1984). The Practice of Everyday Life. Berkeley: University of California Press.

Delamont, S. (2007). Arguments against Auto-Ethnography. Qualitative Researcher, 4, 2–4.

Delaney, K.J. (2007). Methodological Dilemmas and Opportunities in Interviewing Organizational Elites. Sociology Compass, 1(1), 208–222.

DeLanda, M. (2002). Intensive Science and Virtual Philosophy. London: Continuum.

Deleuze, G. (1990). The Logic of Sense. New York, NY: Columbia University Press.

Deleuze, G. (2004). Difference and Repetition. London: Continuum.

Deleuze, G. and Guattari, F. (1988). A Thousand Plateaus: Capitalism and Schizophrenia. London: Athlone Press.

Deleuze, G. and Guattari, F. (1994). What is Philosophy? London: Verso.

Despret, V. (2016). What Would Animals Say if We Asked the Right Questions? Minneapolis, MN: Minnesota University Press.

Deville, J., Guggenheim, M. and Hrdličkova, Z. (2016). Introduction: The Practices and Infrastructures of Comparison. In Deville, J., Guggenheim M. and Hrdličkova, Z. (eds.). Practising Comparison: Logics, Relations, Collaborations (pp. 17–41). Manchester: Mattering Press.

Dewey, J. (1934). Art as Experience. New York, NY: Perigee Books.

Dickinson, J.L., Zuckerberg, B. and Bonter, D.N. (2010). Citizen Science as an Ecological Research Tool: Challenges and Benefits. Annual Review of Ecology, Evolution, and Systematics, 41, 149–172.

D'Onofrio, A. (2017). Reaching for the Horizon. In Salazar, J.F., Pink, S., Irving, A. and Sjoberg, J. (eds.). Anthropologies and Futures: Researching Emerging and Uncertain Worlds (pp. 189–207). London: Bloomsbury.

Dunne, A. (2005). Hertzian Tales: Electronic Products, Aesthetic Experience, and Critical Design. Cambridge, MA: MIT Press.

Dunne, A. and Raby, F. (2001). Design Noir: The Secret Life of Electronic Objects. London/Basel: August/Birkhauser.

Dunne, A. and Raby, F. (2013). Speculative Everything: Design, Fiction and Social Dreaming. Cambridge, MA: MIT Press.
Economic and Social Research Council (2021). Research Ethics. https://esrc.ukri.org/funding/guidance-for-applicants/research-ethics/.
Ehn, P. (1988). Work-Oriented Design of Computer Artefacts. Stockholm: Arbetslivscentrum.
Elias, N. (1994/1939). The Civilizing Process. Oxford: Blackwell.
Elliott, J. (2005). Using Narrative in Social Research: Qualitative and Quantitative Approaches. London: Sage.
Ellis, C., Adams, T.E. and Bochner, A.P. (2011). Autoethnography: An Overview. Forum: Qualitative Social Research, 12(1). http://nbn-resolving.de/urn:nbn:de:0114-fqs1101108.
Farias, I. and Wilkie, A. (eds.) (2016). Studio Studies Operations, Topologies & Displacements. London: Routledge and CRESC.
Featherstone, M. (1991). Consumer Culture and Postmodernism. London: Sage.
Featherstone, M. (1992). The Heroic Life and Everyday Life. Theory, Culture and Society, 9, 159–182.
Felski, R. (1999–2000). The Invention of Everyday Life. Transformation, 39, 13–31.
Felt, U. and Fochler, M. (2010). Machineries for Making Publics: Inscribing and Describing Publics in Public Engagement. Minerva, 48(3), 219–238.
Fineman, J. (1989). The History of the Anecdote: Fiction and Fiction. In Veeser, H.A. (ed.). The New Historicism. New York, NY: Routledge.
Flyvbjerg, B. (2006). Five Misunderstandings about Case-Study Research. Qualitative Inquiry, 12(2), 219–245.
Fontana, A. and Frey, J. (1994). Interviewing: The Art of Science. In Denzin, N. (ed.). The Handbook of Qualitative Research (pp. 361–376). Thousand Oaks, CA: Sage.
Forster, A. (2003). Report into the ESRC's Promotion of Successful Interdisciplinary Research – Report for the ESRC. Bristol: University of Bristol.
Foucault, M. (1979). Discipline and Punish. Harmondsworth: Penguin.
Fraser, M. (2006). Event. Theory, Culture & Society, 23(2–3), 129–132.
Fraser, M. (2010). Facts, Ethics and Event. In Bruun Jensen, C. and Rödje, K. (eds.). Deleuzian Intersections in Science, Technology and Anthropology (pp. 57–82). New York, NY: Berghahn Press.
Frickel, S., Albert, M. and Prainsack, B. (2017). Introduction: Investigating Interdisciplinarities. In Frickel, S., Albert, M., and Prainsack, B. (eds.). Investigating Interdisciplinary Collaborations (pp. 5–24). New Brunswick: Rutgers University Press.
Fukushima, M. (2018). Scaling. Compromising. In Lury, C., et al. (eds.). Routledge Handbook of Interdisciplinary Methodology (pp. 343–346). Abingdon: Routledge.
Gabrys, J. and Yusoff, K. (2012). Arts, Sciences and Climate Change: Practices and Politics at the Threshold. Science as Culture, 21(1), 1–24.
Gallagher, M. and Prior, J. (2017). Listening Walks: A Method of Multiplicity. In Bates, C. and Rhys-Taylor, A. (eds). Walking through Social Research (pp.162–177). Abingdon: Routledge.
Gan, E., Tsing, A., Swanson, H. and Bubandt, N. (2017). Introduction: Haunted Landscapes of the Anthropocene. In Tsing, A., Swanson, H., Gan E. and Bubandt, N. (eds.). Arts of Living on a Damaged Planet (pp. 1–15). Minneapolis, MN: Minnesota University Press.
Garfinkel, H. (1967). Studies in Ethnomethodology. Cambridge: Polity Press.
Garforth, L. and Kerr, A. (2011). Interdisciplinarity and the Social Sciences: Capital, Institutions and Autonomy. The British Journal of Sociology, 62(4), 657–676.
Gaver, W., Boucher, A., Bowers, J. and Law, A. (2007). Electronic Furniture for the Curious Home: Assessing Ludic Designs in the Field. International Journal of Human-Computer Interaction, 22(1–2), 119–152.

Gaver, W., Boucher, A., Law, A., Pennington, S., Bowers, J., Beaver, J., Humble, J., Kerridge, T., Villar, N. and Wilkie, A. (2008). Threshold Devices: Looking Out from The Home. In Proceeding of the 26th Annual SIGCHI Conference on Human Factors in Computing Systems, Florence, Italy (pp. 1429–1438). New York, NY: ACM Press.

Gaver, W.W., Bowers, J., Boucher, A., Gellerson, H., Pennington, S., Schmidt, A., Steed, A., Villars, N. and Walker, B. (2004). The Drift Table: Designing for Ludic Engagement, CHI'04 Extended Abstracts on Human Factors in Computing Systems (pp. 885–900). New York, NY: ACM Press.

Gaver, W., Bowers, J., Kerridge, T., Boucher, A. and Jarvis, N. (2009). Anatomy of a Failure: How We Knew When Our Design Went Wrong, and What We Learned from It. In CHI '09: Proceedings of the SIGCHI Conference on Human Factors in Computing Systems, April 2009 (pp. 2213–2222).

Gaver, W., Wright, P., Boucher, A., Bowers, J. Blythe, M., Jarvis, N., Cameron, D., Kerridge, T., Wilkie, A. and Phillips, R. (2011). The Photostroller: Supporting Diverse Care Home Residents in Engaging with the World. In CHI'11: Proceedings of the SIGCHI Conference on Human Factors in Computing Systems, May 2011 (pp. 1757–1766).

Geuss, R. (1981). The Idea of a Critical Theory. Cambridge: Cambridge University Press.

Gibson, J.J. (1966). The Senses Considered as Perceptual Systems. Boston, MA: Houghton Mifflin.

Gibson, J.J. (1979). The Ecological Approach to Visual Perception. Boston, MA: Houghton Mifflin.

Gilbert, G.N. and Mulkay, M. (1984). Opening Pandora's Box: A Sociological Analysis of Scientists' Discourse. Cambridge: Cambridge University Press.

Goffman, E. (1959). The Presentation of Self in Everyday Life. Harmondsworth: Penguin.

Greenwood, D.J. and Levin, M. (2007). Introduction to Action Research (2nd ed.). Thousand Oaks, CA: Sage.

Gregg, M. and Seigworth, G.J. (eds.) (2010). The Affect Theory Reader. Durham, NC: Duke University Press.

Halewood, M. (2011). A Culture of Thought. A.N. Whitehead and Social Theory. London: Anthem Press.

Halewood, M. and Michael, M. (2008). Being a Sociologist and Becoming a Whiteheadian: Concrescing Methodological Tactics. Theory, Culture and Society, 25(4), 31–56.

Haraway, D. (1991). Simians, Cyborgs and Nature. London: Free Association Books.

Haraway, D. (1992). Ecce Homo, Ain't (Arn't) I a Woman, and Inappropriate/d Others: The Human in a Post-Humanist Landscape. In Butler, J. and Scott, J. (eds.). Feminists Theorize the Political (pp. 86–100). New York, NY: Routledge.

Haraway, D. (1995). Situated Knowledges: The Science Question in Feminism and the Privilege of Partial Perspective. In Feenberg, A. and Hannay, A. (eds.). Technology and the Politics of Knowledge (pp. 175–194). Bloomington, IN; Indianapolis, IN: Indiana University Press.

Haraway, D. (2015). Anthropocene, Capitalocene, Plantationocene, Chthulucene: Making Kin. Environmental Humanities, 6(1), 159–165.

Haraway, D. (2016). Staying with the Trouble: Making Kin in the Chthulucene. Durham, NC: Duke University Press.

Harre, R. (ed.) (1986). The Social Construction of Emotions. Oxford: Blackwell.

Hawkins, G. (2011). Packaging Water: Plastic Bottles as Market and Public Devices. Economy and Society, 40(4), 534–552.

Held, D. (1980). Introduction to Critical Theory. London: Hutchinson.

Heritage, J. (1984). Garfinkel and Ethnomethodology. Cambridge: Polity Press.

Highmore, B. (2002). Everyday Life and Cultural Theory: An Introduction. London: Routledge.

Hinchliffe, S. (2007). Geographies of Nature. London: Sage.

Hinchliffe, S., Allen, J., Lavau, S., Bingham, N. and Carter, S. (2012). Biosecurity and the Topologies of Infected Life: From Borderlines to Borderlands. Transactions of the Institute of British Geographers, 38(4), 531–543.

Hjorth, L. and Richardson, I. (2020). Playing. In Jungnickel, K. (ed.). Transmissions: Critical Tactics for Making and Communicating Research (pp. 89–107). Cambridge, MA: MIT Press.

Holm, G. (2008). Photography as a Performance. Forum: Qualitative Social Research, 9(2). www.qualitative-research.net/index.php/fqs/article/view/394/857.

Holton, G. (1992). How to Think about the 'Anti-Science' Phenomenon. Public Understanding of Science, 1, 103–128.

Horigan, S. (1988). Nature and Culture in Western Discourses. London: Routledge and Kegan Paul.

Horst, M. (2008). In Search of Dialogue: Staging Science Communication in Consensus Conferences. In Cheng, D., et al. (eds.). Communicating Science in Social Contexts (pp. 259–274). Berlin: Springer.

Horst, M. and Michael, M. (2011). On the Shoulders of Idiots: Rethinking Science Communication as 'Event'. Science as Culture, 20, 283–306.

Hyvarinen, M. (2016). Narrative and Sociology. Narrative Works: Issues, Investigations, & Interventions, 6(1), 38–62.

Irwin, A. (1995). Citizen Science. London: Routledge.

Irwin, A. and Michael, M. (2003). Science, Social Theory and Public Knowledge. Buckingham: Open University Press.

Jefferies, J. (2012). Pattern, Patterning. In Lury, C. and Wakeford, N. (eds.). Inventive Methods: The Happening of the Social (pp. 125–135). London: Routledge.

Jerak-Zuiderent, S. (2015). Keeping Open by Re-Imagining Laughter and Fear. The Sociological Review, 63(4), 897–921.

Johnson, J.M. (2002). In-Depth Interviewing. In Gubrium, J.F. and Holstein, J.A. (eds.). Handbook of Interview Research: Context and Method (pp. 103–119). Thousand Oaks, CA: Sage.

Jungnickel, K. (ed.) (2020). Transmissions: Critical Tactics for Making and Communicating Research. Cambridge, MA: MIT Press.

Jungnickel, K. and Hjorth, L. (2014). Methodological Entanglements in the Field: Methods, Transitions and Transmissions. Visual Studies, 29(2), 136–145.

Keat, R., Whiteley, N. and Abercrombie, N. (eds.) (1994). The Authority of the Consumer. London: Routledge.

Kelly, A.H. and McGoey, L. (2018). Facts, Power and Global Evidence: A New Empire of Truth. Economy and Society, 47(1), 1–26.

Kelty, C.M. (2018). Hacking the Social. In Marres, N., Guggenheim, M. and Wilkie A. (eds.). Inventing the Social (pp. 287–297). Manchester: Mattering Press.

Klein, J. (2010). A Taxonomy of Interdisciplinarity. In Frodeman, R., Klein, J. and Mitcham, C. (eds.). The Oxford Handbook of Interdisciplinarity (pp. 15–30). Oxford: Oxford University Press.

Kortekallio, K. (2017). Becoming Compost. In Paper Presented at 7th Biennial Congress of the European Network for Comparative Literary Studies (ENCLS), University of Helsinki 23.–25.8.2017. https://storageorgan.wordpress.com/2017/08/25/becoming-compost/.

Lange, A.-C. (2012). Inclusive Differentiation: A Study of Artistic Techniques and Devices of Innovation. Doctoral Thesis. Goldsmiths, University of London.

Lapworth, A. (2015). Beyond Bifurcation: Thinking the Abstractions of Art-Science after A.N. Whitehead. Transformations: Journal of Media & Culture, 26(5). DOI: 10.3351/ppp.0005.0003.0001. www.transformationsjournal.org/wp-content/uploads/2016/12/Lapworth_Transformations26.pdf.

Lash, S. and Lury, C. (2007). Global Culture Industry: The Mediation of Things. Cambridge: Polity.
Last, A. (2014). Who's the Pest? Imagining Human–Insect Futures Beyond Antagonism. Science as Culture, 23(1), 98–107.
Latimer, J. and López Gómez, D. (2019). Intimate Entanglements: Affects, More-Than-Human Intimacies and the Politics of Relations in Science and Technology. The Sociological Review, 67(2), 247–263.
Latour, B. (1987). Science in Action: How to Follow Engineers in Society. Milton Keynes: Open University Press.
Latour, B. (1988). The Politics of Explanation – An Alternative. In Woolgar, S. (ed.). Knowledge and Reflexivity: New Frontiers in the Sociology of Knowledge (pp. 155–176). London: Sage.
Latour, B. (1993). We Have Never Been Modern. Hemel Hempstead: Harvester Wheatsheaf.
Latour, B. (1996). Aramis, or the Love of Technology. Cambridge, MA: Harvard University Press.
Latour, B. (1999). Pandora's Hope: Essays on the Reality of Science Studies. Cambridge, MA: Harvard University Press.
Latour, B. (2003). Is Re-Modernization Occurring – And If So, How to Prove It? A Commentary on Ulrich Beck. Theory, Culture & Society, 20(2), 35-48.
Latour, B. (2004a). Politics of Nature. Cambridge, MA: Harvard University Press.
Latour, B. (2004b). Why Has Critique Run Out of Steam? From Matters of Fact to Matters of Concern. Critical Inquiry, 30(2), 225-248.
Latour, B. (2005). Reassembling the Social. Oxford: Oxford University Press.
Latour, B. (2010a). On the Modern Cult of the Factish Gods. Durham, NC: Duke University Press.
Latour, B. (2010b). Steps toward the Writing of a Compositionist Manifesto. New Literary History, 41, 471–490.
Latour, B. (2011). From Multiculturalism to Multinaturalism: What Rules of Method for the New Socio-Scientific Experiments? Nature and Culture, 6(1), 1-17.
Latour, B. and Wiebel, O. (eds.) (2002). Making Things Public: Atmospheres of Democracy. Cambridge, MA: MIT Press.
Law, J. (1991). Introduction: Monsters, Machines and Sociotechnical Relations. In Law, J. (ed.). A Sociology of Monsters. London: Routledge.
Law, J. (1994). Organizing Modernity. Oxford: Blackwell.
Law, J. (2004). After Method: Mess in Social Science Research. London: Routledge.
Law, J. (2011). Collateral Realities. In Dominguez Rubio, F. and Baert, P. (eds.). The Politics of Knowledge (pp. 156–178). London: Routledge.
Law, J. and Lin, W-Y. (2010). Cultivating Disconcertment. The Sociological Review, 58(S2), 135–153.
Lawrence, C. and Shapin, S. (eds.) (1998). Science Incarnate: Historical Embodiments of Natural Knowledge. Chicago, IL: University of Chicago Press.
Leavy, P. (2015). Method Meets Art: Art-Based Research Practice. Guildford: Guildford Press.
Le Dantec, C. and DiSalvo, C. (2013). Infrastructuring and the Formation of Publics in Participatory Design. Social Studies of Science, 42(2), 241–264.
Lefebvre, H. (1947). Critique of Everyday Life. London: Verso.
Lemaine, G., Macleod, R., Mulkay, M. and Weingart, P. (eds.) (1976). Perspectives on the Emergence of Scientific Disciplines. Berlin: De Gruyter Mouton.
Levitas, R. (2013). Utopia as Method: The Imaginary Reconstitution of Society. Basingstoke: Palgrave.
Lewin, K. (1946). Action Research and Minority Problems. In Lewin, G.W. (ed.). Resolving Social Conflicts (pp. 201–216). New York, NY: Harper & Row.

References

Lezaun, J. and Soneryd, L. (2007). Consulting Citizens: Technologies of Elicitation and the Mobility of Publics. Public Understanding of Science, 16, 279–297.

Lindstrom, K. and Stahl, A. (2020). Living With. In Jungnickel, K. (ed.). Transmissions: Critical Tactics for Making and Communicating Research (pp.131–151). Cambridge, MA: MIT Press.

Livesey, G. (2007). Deleuze, Whitehead, the Event, and the Contemporary City. In Paper Presented at the "Event and Decision: Ontology and Politics in Badiou, Deleuze and Whitehead" Conference, Claremont Graduate University, Claremont, CA, December 6–8.

Lorimer, H. (2005). Cultural Geography: The Busyness of Being 'More-Than-Representational'. Progress in Human Geography, 29(1), 83–94.

Lupton, D. and Michael, M. (2017). 'Depends on Who's Got the Data': Public Understanding of Personal Digital Dataveillance. Surveillance and Society, 15(2), 254–268.

Lury, C. (1996). Consumer Culture. Cambridge: Polity.

Lury, C. (2018). Introduction: Activating the Present of Interdisciplinary Methods. In Lury, C., et al. (eds.). Routledge Handbook of Interdisciplinary Research Methods (pp. 1–25). Abingdon: Routledge.

Lury, C., Clough, P., Chung, U., Fensham, R., Lammes, S., Last, A., Michael, M. and Uprichard, E. (eds.) (2018). Routledge Handbook of Interdisciplinary Methodology. London: Routledge.

Lury, C., Parisi, L. and Terranova, T. (2012). Introduction: The Becoming Topological of Culture. Theory, Culture & Society, 29, 3–35.

Lury, C. and Wakeford, N. (eds.) (2012). Inventive Methods: The Happening of the Social. London: Routledge.

Lyotard, J.-F. (1984). The Postmodern Condition: A Report on Knowledge. Manchester: Manchester University Press.

Mann, A.M., Mol, A., Satalkar, P., Savirani, A., Selim, N., Sur, M. and Yates-Doerr, E. (2011). Mixing Methods, Tasting Fingers: Notes on an Ethnographic Experiment. HAU: Journal of Ethnographic Theory, 1(1), 221–243.

Mason, J. (2011). Facet Methodology: The Case for an Inventive Research Orientation. Methodological Innovations Online, 6(3), 75–92. DOI: 10.4256/mio.2011.008.

Mason, J. (2017). Qualitative Researching (3rd ed.). London: Sage.

Mason, J. and Davies, K. (2009). Coming to Our Senses? A Critical Approach to Sensory Methodology. Qualitative Research, 9(5), 587–603.

Massumi, B. (2002). Parables of the Virtual. Durham, NC: Duke University Press.

Massumi, B. (2011). Semblance and Event. Cambridge, MA; London: MIT Press.

Mauss, M. (1973 [1935]). Techniques of the Body. Economy and Society, 2(1), 70–87.

May, T. (2011). Social Research: Issues, Methods and Process (4th ed.). Maidenhead: Open University Press/McGraw-Hill.

McLeish, T. and McLeish, V. (2016). Evaluating Interdisciplinary Research: The Elephant in the Peer-Reviewers' Room. Palgrave Communications, 2, 16055. DOI: 10.1057/palcomms.2016.55.

Merton, R.K. (1973/1942). The Sociology of Science: Theoretical and Empirical Investigations. Chicago, IL: University of Chicago Press.

Michael, M. (1996). Ignoring Science: Discourses of Ignorance in the Public Understanding of Science. In Irwin, A and Wynne, B (eds.). Misunderstanding Science? The Public Reconstruction of Science and Technology (pp. 105–125). Cambridge: Cambridge University Press.

Michael, M. (1997). Inoculating Gadgets against Ridicule. Science as Culture, 6(2), 167–193.

Michael, M. (1998). Between Citizen and Consumer: Multiplying the Meanings of the Public Understanding of Science. Public Understanding of Science, 7, 313–327.

Michael, M. (2000a). These Boots Are Made for Walking …: Mundane Technology, the Body and Human-Environment Relations. Body and Society, 6(3–4), 107–126.

Michael, M. (2000b). Reconnecting Culture, Technology and Nature: From Society to Heterogeneity. London: Routledge.

Michael, M. (2001). Technoscientific Bespoking: Animals, Publics and the New Genetics. New Genetics and Society, 20(3), 205–224.

Michael, M. (2002). Comprehension, Apprehension, and Prehension: Heterogeneity and the Public Understanding of Science. Science, Technology and Human Values, 27(3), 357–370.

Michael, M. (2004a). On Making Data Social: Heterogeneity in Sociological Practice. Qualitative Research, 4(1), 5–23.

Michael, M. (2004b). Roadkill: Between Humans, Nonhuman Animals, and Technologies. Society and Animals, 12(4), 277–298.

Michael, M. (2006). Technoscience and Everyday Life. Maidenhead: Open University Press/McGraw-Hill.

Michael, M. (2010). Sticking Plasters and Standardization. In Higgins, V. and Larner, W. (eds.). Calculating the Social: Standards and the Re-Configuration of Governing. Basingstoke: Palgrave.

Michael, M. (2011). Affecting the Technoscientific Body: Stem Cells, Wheeled-Luggage and Emotion. Tecnoscienza: Italian Journal of Science and Technology Studies, 2(1), 53–63.

Michael, M. (2012a). "What Are We Busy Doing?": Engaging the Idiot. Science, Technology and Human Values, 37(5), 528–554.

Michael, M. (2012b). Toward an Idiotic Methodology: De-Signing the Object of Sociology. The Sociological Review, 60(S1), 166–183.Michael, M. (2015). Ignorance and the Epistemic Choreography of Method. In Gross, M. and McGoey, L. (eds.). Routledge International Handbook of Ignorance Studies (pp. 84–91). London: Routledge.

Michael, M. (2016a). Neoliberalism and the Ontological Turn: Conflicts and Collusions. Science as Culture, 25(3), 361–366.

Michael, M. (2016b). Notes toward a Speculative Methodology of Everyday Life. Qualitative Research, 16(6), 646–660.

Michael, M. (2016c). Speculative Design and Digital Materialities: Idiocy, Threat and Com-Promise. In Ardevol, E., Pink, S. and Lanzeni, D. (eds.). Designing Digital Materialities: Knowing, Intervention and Making (pp. 99–113). London: Bloomsbury.

Michael, M. (2017a). Destroying iPhones: Feral Science and the Antithetical Citizen. Public Understanding of Science, 27(6), 731–744.

Michael, M. (2017b). Actor-Network Theory: Trials, Trails and Translations. London: Sage.

Michael, M. (2017c). Walking, Falling, Telling: The Anecdote and the Mis-Step as a 'Research Event'. In Bates, C. and Rhys-Taylor, A. (eds.). Walking through Social Research. London: Routledge.

Michael, M. (2018a). Valuing and Validating: On the 'Success' of Interdisciplinary Research. In Lury, C., et al. (eds.). Routledge Handbook of Interdisciplinary Methodology (pp. 269–278). Abingdon: Routledge.

Michael, M. (2018b). On 'Aesthetic Publics': The Case of VANTAblack. Science, Technology and Human Values, 43(6), 1098–1121.

Michael, M. (2018c). Compromising. In Lury, C., et al. (eds.). Routledge Handbook of Interdisciplinary Methodology (pp. 279–283). Abingdon: Routledge.

Michael, M. (2019). Toward the Abstractors: Modes of Care and Lineages of Becoming. Distinktion: Journal of Social Theory, 20(3), 328–341.

Michael, M. (2020). The Unit of Measurement. www.indexofevidence.org/unit-of-evidence.

Michael, M. and Birke, L. (1994a). Animal Experimentation: Enrolling the Core Set. Social Studies of Science, 24(1), 81–95. ISSN 0306 3127.

Michael, M. and Birke, L. (1994b). Accounting for Animal Experiments: Credibility and Disreputable 'Others'. Science, Technology and Human Values, 19(2), 189–204. ISSN 0162 2439.

Michael, M. and Carter, S. (2001). The Facts about Fictions and Vice Versa: Public Understanding of Human Genetics. Science as Culture, 10(1), 5–32.

Michael, M. and Lupton, D. (2016). Toward a Manifesto for the Public Understanding of Big Data. Public Understanding of Science, 25(1), 104–116.

Michael, M. and Rosengarten, M. (2012). HIV, Globalization and Topology: Of Prepositions and Propositions. Theory, Culture and Society, 29(45), 93–115.

Michael, M. and Rosengarten, M. (2013). Innovation and Biomedicine: Ethics, Evidence and Expectation in HIV. Basingstoke: Palgrave.

Michael, M., Wainwright, S. and Williams, C. (2005). Temporality and Prudence: On Stem Cells as 'Phronesic Things'. Configurations, 13(3), 373–394.

Michael, M., Wainwright, S., Williams, C., Farsides, B. and Cribb, A. (2007). From Core Set to Assemblage: On the Dynamics of Exclusion and Inclusion in the Failure to Derive Beta Cells from Embryonic Stem Cells. Science Studies, 20(1), 5–25.

Michael, M., Wilkie, A. and Ovalle, L. (2018). Aesthetics and Affect: Engaging Energy Communities. Science as Culture, 27(4), 439–463.

Miles Todd III, W. (2004). Introduction. In Fyodor Dostoyevsky, The Idiot (pp. xi–xxxiv). London: Penguin.

Miller, D. (2009). The Comfort of Things. Cambridge: Polity.

Mol, A. (2002). The Body Multiple: Ontology in Medical Practice. Durham, NC: Duke University Press.

Mol, A. (2008). The Logic of Care: Health and the Problem of Patient Choice. Abingdon: Routledge.

Mol, A. and Law, J. (1994). Regions, Networks and Fluids: Anaemia and Social Topology. Social Studies of Science, 24(4), 641–671.

Morris, M. (2006). Identity Anecdotes: Translation and Media Culture. London: Sage.

Mouffe, C. (2005). On the Political. London; New York, NY: Routledge.

Mulkay, M. (1979). Science and the Sociology of Knowledge. London: Allen and Unwin.

Mulkay, M. (1985). The Word and the World. London: George Allen and Unwin.

Mulkay, M. (1997). The Embryo Research Debate: The Science and Politics of Reproduction. Cambridge: Cambridge University Press.

Myers, G. (1989). The Pragmatics of Politeness in Scientific Articles. Applied Linguistics, 10, 1–35.

Nowotny, H., Scott, P. and Gibbons, M. (2001). Re-Thinking Science: Knowledge and the Public in an Age of Uncertainty. Cambridge: Polity Press.

Nyong'o, T. (2019). Afro-Fabulations: The Queer Drama of Black Life. New York, NY: University Press.

O'Connell, J. (1993). Metrology: The Creation of Universality by the Circulation of Particulars. Social Studies of Science, 23, 129–173.

Papanek, V. (1984). Design for the Real World (2nd ed.). London: Thames and Hudson.

Phillips, J. (2006). Agencement/Assemblage. Theory, Culture and Society, 23, 108–109.

Pickering, A. (1995). The Mangle of Practice: Time, Agency and Science. Chicago, IL: University of Chicago Press.

Pink, S. (2012). Situating Everyday Life: Practices and Places. London: Sage.

Pink, S. (2015). Doing Sensory Ethnography. London: Sage.

Pippan, T. and Czarniawska, B. (2010). How to Construct an Actor-Network: Management Accounting from Idea to Practice. Critical Perspectives on Accounting, 21, 243–251.
Potter, J. and Wetherell, M. (1987). Discourse and Social Psychology. London: Sage.
Prainsack, B. (2014). Understanding Participation: The 'Citizen Science' of Genetics. In Prainsack, B., Schicktanz, S. and Werner-Felmayer, G. (eds.). Genetics as Social Practice (pp. 147–164). Farnham: Ashgate.
Puig de la Bellacasa, M. (2011). Matters of Care in Technoscience: Assembling Neglected Things. Social Studies of Science, 41(1), 85–106.
Puig de la Bellacasa, M. (2012). "Nothing Comes Without Its World": Thinking with Care. The Sociological Review, 60(2), 197–216.
Puig de la Bellacasa, M. (2017). Matters of Care: Speculative Ethics in More than Human Worlds. Minneapolis, MN: University of Minnesota Press.
Puwar, N. and Sharma, S. (2012). Curating Sociology. The Sociological Review, 60(S1), 40–63.
Raven, P.G. and Stripple, J. (2021). Touring the Carbon Ruins: Towards an Ethics of Speculative Decarbonisation. Global Discourse, 11(1–2), 221–240.
Reason, P. and Bradbury, H. (eds.) (2001). Handbook of Action Research. London: Sage.
Redclift, M. (2004). Chewing Gum: The Fortunes of Taste. London: Routledge.
Reissman, C.K. (2008). Narrative Methods for the Human Sciences. Thousand Oaks, CA: Sage.
Robinson, A. (2011). Giving Voice and Taking Pictures: Participatory Documentary and Visual Research. People, Place & Policy Online, 5(3), 115–134.
Rosengarten, M. and Savransky, M. (2019). A Careful Biomedicine? Generalization and Abstraction in RCTs. Critical Public Health, 29(2), 181–191. DOI: 10.1080/09581596.2018.1431387.
Royal Society of London (1985). The Public Understanding of Science. London: The Royal Society.
Ruppert, E., Law, J. and Savage, M. (2013). Special Issue: The Social Life of Methods. Theory, Culture and Society, 30(4), 3–177.
Salazar, J.F., Pink, S., Irving, A. and Sjoberg, J. (eds.) (2017). Anthropologies and Futures: Researching Emerging and Uncertain Worlds. London: Bloomsbury.
Savransky, M. (2016). The Adventure of Relevance: An Ethics of Social Inquiry. London: Palgrave Macmillan.
Savransky, M. (2021). Problems All the Way Down. Theory, Culture & Society, 38(2), 3–23.
Schatzki, T., Knorr-Cetina, K. and von Savigny, E. (eds.) (2001). The Practice Turn in Contemporary Theory. London: Routledge.
Scott, P., Richards, E. and Martin, B. (1990). Captives of Controversy: The Myth of the Neutral Science Researcher in Contemporary Scientific Controversies. Science, Technology and Human Values, 15, 474–494.
Seale, C. (ed.) (2012). Researching Society and Culture (3rd ed.). London: Sage.
Serres, M. (1982a). The Parasite. Baltimore, MD: Johns Hopkins University Press.
Serres, M. (1982b). Hermes: Literature, Science, Philosophy. Baltimore, MD: Johns Hopkins University Press.
Serres, M. (1995a). Genesis. Ann Arbor, MI: Michigan University Press.
Serres, M. (1995b). Angels: A Modern Myth. Paris: Flammarion.
Serres, M. and Latour, B. (1995). Conversations on Science, Culture and Time. Ann Arbor, MI: Michigan University Press.
Shaviro, S. (2007). Deleuze's Encounter with Whitehead. www.shaviro.com/Othertexts/DeleuzeWhitehead.pdf (accessed 23 November 2015).
Shaviro, S. (2014). The Universe of Things. Minneapolis, MN: Minnesota University Press.

Shove, E. (2002). Comfort, Cleanliness and Convenience. Oxford: Berg.
Shove, E., Pantzar, M. and Watson, M. (2012). The Dynamics of Social Practice. London: Sage.
Shove, E. and Wouters, P. (2005). Interactive Agenda Setting in the Social Sciences – Interdisciplinarity. Workshop Discussion Paper. Interdisciplinary Fields and Fashions: Making New Agendas. https://core.ac.uk/download/pdf/18543024.pdf.
Silverman, D. (2006). Interpreting Qualitative Data: Methods for Analysing Talk, Text and Interaction (3rd ed.). London: Sage.
Stake, R. (2000). Qualitative Case-Studies. In Denzin, N.K. and Lincoln, Y.S. (eds.). The Sage Handbook of Qualitative Research (3rd ed.) (pp. 443–467). London; New York, NY: Sage.
Stengers, I. (2000). The Invention of Modern Science. Translated by Smith, D.W. Minneapolis, MN: University of Minnesota Press.
Stengers, I. (2005a). The Cosmopolitical Proposal. In Latour, B. and Webel, P. (eds.). Making Things Public (pp. 994–1003). Cambridge, MA: MIT Press.
Stengers, I. (2005b). Introductory Notes on an Ecology of Practices. Cultural Studies Review, 11, 183–196.
Stengers, I. (2010). Cosmopolitics I. Minneapolis, MN: University of Minnesota Press.
Stengers, I. and Latour, B. (2015). The Sphinx of the Work. In Souriau, E. The Different Modes of Existence (pp. 11–90). Minneapolis, MN: Univocal.
Stenner, P. (2012). Pattern. In Lury, C. and Wakeford, N. (eds.). Inventive Methods: The Happening of the Social (pp. 136–146). London: Routledge.
Stephens, N. (2007). Collecting Data from Elites and Ultra Elites: Telephone and Face-to-Face Interviews with Macroeconomists. Qualitative Research, 7(2), 203–216.
Stewart, K. (2007). Ordinary Affects. Durham; London: Duke University Press.
Stewart, K. (2011). Atmospheric Attunements. Environment and Planning D, 29(3), 445–453.
Stirling, A. (2008). "Opening Up" and "Closing Down": Power, Participation, and Pluralism in the Social Appraisal of Technology. Science Technology Human Values, 33, 262–294.
Thompson, I., Stott, N. and Kerridge, T. (n.d.). Biojewellery: Designing Rings with Bioengineered Bone Tissue. https://research.gold.ac.uk/id/eprint/2317/2/biojewellery-booklet.pdf.
Thompson Klein, J. (2000). A Conceptual Vocabulary of Interdisciplinary Science. In Weingart, P. and Stehr, N. (eds.). Practising Interdisciplinarity (pp. 3–24). Toronto: University of Toronto Press.
Thrift, N. (2005). Knowing Capitalism. London: Sage.
Thrift, N. (2008). Non-Representational Theory. London: Routledge.
Timmermans, S. and Tavory, I. (2012). Theory Construction in Qualitative Research: From Grounded Theory to Abductive Analysis. Sociological Theory, 30(3), 167–186.
Toomey, A.H., Markusson, N., Adams, E. and Brockett, B. (2015). Inter- and Trans-Disciplinary Research: A Critical Perspective. Lancaster: Environment Centre. https://sustainabledevelopment.un.org/content/documents/612558-Inter-%20and%20Transdisciplinary%20Research%20-%20A%20Critical%20Perspective.pdf.
Tsing, A. (2014). Blasted Landscapes (and the Gentle Arts of Mushroom Picking). In Kirksey, E. (ed.). The Multispecies Salon (pp. 87–110). Durham, NC: Duke University Press.
Tsing, A. (2015). Mushroom at the End of the World: On the Possibility of Life in Capitalist Ruins. Princeton, NJ: Princeton University Press.
Vannini, P. (ed.) (2015). Non-Representational Methodologies: Re-Envisioning Research. London: Routledge.
Verran, H. (1999). Staying True to the Laughter in Nigerian Classrooms. In Law, J. and Hassard, J. (eds.). Actor Network Theory and After (pp. 136–155). Oxford; Keele: Blackwell; The Sociological Review.

Verran, H. (2001). Science and an African Logic. Chicago, IL: University of Chicago Press.

Wainwright, S., Williams, C., Michael, M., Cribb, A. and Farsides, B. (2006). From Bench to Bedside? Biomedical Scientists' Expectations of Stem Cell Science as a Future Therapy for Diabetes. Social Science & Medicine, 63, 2052–2064.

Wajcman, J. (1995). Feminist Theories of Technology. In Jasanoff, S., Markle, G.E., Peterson, J.C. and Pinch, T. (eds.). Handbook of Science and Technology Studies (pp. 189–204). Thousand Oaks, CA: Sage.

Watson, A. (2016). Directions for Public Sociology: Novel Writing as a Creative Approach. Cultural Sociology, 10(4), 431–447.

Watson, A. (2021). Writing Sociological Fiction. Qualitative Research. Inline First. DOI: 10.1177/1468794120985677.

Watts, G. (2008). Getting the Best from Research Funding. British Medical Journal, 336(7636), 120–122. www.ncbi.nlm.nih.gov/pmc/articles/PMC2206262/.

Weingart, P. (2000). Interdisciplinarity: The Paradoxical Discourse. In Weingart, P. and Stehr, N. (eds.). Practising Interdisciplinarity (pp. 25–45). Toronto: University of Toronto Press.

Weingart, P. and Stehr, N. (eds.) (2000). Practising Interdisciplinarity. Toronto: University of Toronto Press.

Wetherell, M. (2012). Affect and Emotion: A New Social Science Understanding. London: Sage.

Whitehead, A.N. (1933). Adventures of Ideas. Cambridge: Cambridge University Press.

Whitehead, A.N. (1978). Process and Reality. An Essay in Cosmology (Gifford Lectures of 1927–8). New York, NY: The Free Press.

Whitley, R. (2000). The Intellectual and Social Organization of the Sciences (2nd ed.). Oxford: Oxford University Press.

Wilkie, A. and Michael, M. (2016). The Design Studio as a Centre of Synthesis. In Farias, I. and Wilkie, A. (eds.). Studio Studies (pp. 25–39). London: Routledge and CRESC.

Wilkie, A. and Michael, M. (2017). Doing Speculation to Curtail Speculation. In Wilkie, A., Savransky, M. and Rosengarten, M. (eds.). Speculative Research: The Lure of Possible Futures (pp. 84–97). London: Routledge and CRESC.

Wilkie, A. and Michael, M. (2018). Designing and Doing: Enacting Energy-and-Community. In Marres, N., Guggenheim, M., and Wilkie, A. (eds.). Inventing the Social (pp. 125–147). Manchester: Mattering Press.

Wilkie, A., Michael, M. and Plummer-Fernandez, M. (2015). Speculative Method and Twitter: Bots, Energy and Three Conceptual Characters. The Sociological Review, 63(1), 79–101.

Wilkie, A., Savransky, M. and Rosengarten, M. (eds.) (2017). Speculative Research: The Lure of Possible Futures. London: Routledge and CRESC.

Woodward, S. (2020). Material Methods: Researching and Thinking with Things. London: Sage.

Woolgar, S. (ed.) (1988). Knowledge and Reflexivity: New Frontiers in the Sociology of Knowledge. London: Sage.

Woolgar, S. and Neyland, D. (2013). Mundane Governance: Ontology and Accountability. Oxford: Oxford University Press.

Woolley, J.P., McGowan, M.L., Teare, H.J.A., et al. (2016). Citizen Science or Scientific Citizenship? Disentangling the Uses of Public Engagement Rhetoric in National Research Initiatives. BMC Medical Ethics, 17, 33. DOI: 10.1186/s12910-016-0117-1.

Wynne, B. (2003). Seasick on the Third Wave? Subverting the Hegemony of Propositionalism. Social Studies of Science, 33, 401–418.

INDEX

abstraction 135–138
action nets 35
Action Research 92
actor-network theory (ANT) 2, 35, 40, 63
Adams, D. 77
Adorno, T. 48, 149
aesthetics 10; attuning to 53–55; engagement, analysis and 129–131; pattern and 127–129
affect 36; anecdote and 40–46; attunement and 46–53
affective turn 34
analysis: aesthetics, engagement and 129–131; cases and abstraction in 135–138; comparison and hybridity in 131–134; event of expression 138–143; introduction to 123–124; pattern and 124–127; value and validity in 144–145; writing as 139–143
Anderson, B. 41, 46
anecdote 1–2, 6, 33, 146; affect and 40–46; and anecdotalization 37–40; auto-ethnography and 38–39
art of noticing 50
attunement: to aesthetics 53–55; affect and 46–53
auto-ethnography 38–39

Barry, A. 103, 126
Bauman, Z. 82
Beckman, F. 68–69
becoming, process of 9–10, 12
Bennett, J. 48

Billig, M. 126–127
Binder, T. 91
'blasted landscapes' 83
Bochner, A. P. 81
Boehner, K. 93
Born, G. 103
Braun, V. 124–125
Brosnan, C. 113
Brown, G. 20

Callard, F. 103–104, 106
Callon, M. 22
Camille Stories 85–86
Carter, S. 71
cases and abstraction 135–138
Chang, H. 38
Chthulucene 83, 84–85
Clarke, V. 124–125
Coleman, R. 83
collaboration, writing as 139–141
collateral realities 62
comparison and hybridity 131–134
compassion 116–120
complexity: revealing 64–66; seeking 66–68
composition 107–112
composting 120–122
comprehension 109–112
compromise 112–116
Connolly, W. 7, 9, 10, 25, 128
cosmopolitics 108–109
COVID-19 pandemic 147
critical design 91
Czarniawska, B. 35–36

Davies, K. 51
Debaise, D. 136
de Certeau, M. 133
Delamont, S. 39
Deleuze, G. 7, 11, 41, 68–69
Despret, V. 70
Deville, J. 131
Dewey, J. 128
Different Modes of Existence, The 54, 128
DiSalvo, C. 91
disciplinarity and interdisciplinarity 112–116, 122; compassion and 116–120; composition of 107–109; composting and 120–122; comprehension and 109–112; compromise and 112–116; interrelations between practitioners and 106–122; introduction to 101–102; research event and 102–106
'disciplinary idiot' 90
disconcertment, productive 76–78; doing 59–62; encountering the idiot and 72–74; the idiot and 68–76; introduction to 57–59; the parasite and 62–68; proactive idiot and 76; revealing complexity 64–66; seeking complexity 66–68; seeking out the idiot and 74–76
dissemination and engagement 141–143
Dunne, A. 95

Elias, N. 44
Ellis, C. 38–39, 81
'emossions' 134
emotion 40–41
Energy Babble 96–97, 115, 130
Energy-demand Reduction: Co- Designing Communities and Practice (ECDC) 94–97, 115, 130
engagement and dissemination 141–143
en-skilling systems 141
eternal objects 136
event(s), conceptualization of 8–10
everyday life 24–25
excluded third 63–64
experts 110–111
expression, event of 138–143

fabulation: circulating 84–86; detecting 83–84; interjecting 86–87; speculative 81–87
Fitzgerald, D. 103–104, 106
Five Obstructions, The 23
Fraser, M. 12, 54
funding, research 20–24

Gallagher, M. 50
Gaver, W. 95
generative critique 61
Gibson, J. J. 50, 52
glitter-bombing 83–84
Glitterworlds 83
Goffman, I. 44
Greenpeace 33
Guattari, F. 11, 41, 69

Halewood, M. 110
Haraway, D. 7–8, 31, 80, 83–85
Hawkins, G. 46
Hernes, T. 35
heuristic(s) 3, 5, 6–7, 9, 11, 58, 149; abstractor 136; composting 120–122; noticing and asking 26–27; posing and querying 29–31; remembering and reflecting 27–29; teasing 61
Holton, G. 20
Home Health Monitor 98
Horst, M. 72–73
hybridity and comparison 131–134
hypervigilance 48
Hyvärinen, M. 81, 83

iconoclasm 143
idiot, the 68–72; encountering 72–74; as proactive 76; seeking out 74–76; threat, promise and 97–99
Idiot, The 69
iPhones 26, 74–76

Jefferies, J. 125
Jerak-Zuiderent, S. 59–61
Jungnickel, K. 86

Kelly, A. H. 149
Kerridge, T. 88
Kortekallio, K. 121

Landscape of Expectations 72–73, 76, 82
Lapworth, A. 135
Latour, B. 7, 45, 54, 113, 128, 142; on composition 107–108; critique of critique 60; on factish 37; on matters of concern 118; on the point of writing 132
Law, J. 7, 11–13, 19, 52, 61–62
Le Dantec, C. 91
Lefebvre, H. 49
Levi-Strauss, C. 8
Levitas, R. 82–83
Lezaun, J. 68
LGBTQ* issues 83–84

Index

Lin, W.-Y. 61–62
Listening Walks 50–51
'little problems' 77–78
Lloyd, J. 77
logic of care 117
logic of choice 117
Lumelsky protocol event 41–42
Lupton, D. 95
Lury, C. 106
Lyotard, J.-F. 20

Mason, J. 51
Massumi, B. 38, 81, 93, 129
May, T. 3
McGoey, L. 149
McKechnie, R. 33
Meaning of Liff, The 77
mental models 19
mentorship programmes 140–141
Merton, R. K. 144
method assemblage 11–12, 19
Michael, M. 72–73, 95, 96–97, 139; on feral science 75; on focus groups 71; on 'little problems' 78; on Lumelsky protocol 41–42, 128–129
Mills Todd III, W. 69
Mol, A. 117
Morris, M. 37
Mulkay, M. 144
multisensory engagement 51

nanotechnologies 136–137
Neuroscope 88–89
Neyland, D. 68
noticing and asking 26–27
Nyong'o, T. 83

otherness 12

parasite, the 62–68; revealing complexity 64–66; seeking complexity 66–68
Parasite, The 64
participatory design 86–87, 90–91
pattern: aesthetics and 127–129; analysis and 124–127; comparison and hybridity of 131–134
philosophy of prepositions 10–11
Pink, S. 51
Pippan, T. 35
posing and querying 29–31
Potter, J. 125
prehensions 53–54, 109–112
preposition, philosophy of 10–11
pre-propositions 5, 25, 34, 55, 81

Prior, J. 50
probes 93–94, 130
prototypes 95, 98
Public Engagement with Science and Technology (PEST) 88–90
Public Understanding of Science (PUS) 18, 33, 71
Puig de la Bellacasa, M. 7, 60, 118, 119
Puwar, N. 142

quasi-objects 63

Raby, F. 95
remembering and reflecting 27–29
research: affective dimension of 2; COVID-19 pandemic and 147; different methodologies of 3–4, 146–147; funding and support for 20–24; introduction to three strands in 18–20; noticing and asking in 26–27; posing and querying in 29–31; process philosophers and social science scholars on 7; remembering and reflecting in 27–29; sensibility, sub-topicality and everyday life 24–31; sub-topical 25–32
research event: anecdote/anecdotalization and 37–40; attunement and affect and 46–53; compassion and 116–120; composition of 107–109; composting and 120–122; comprehension and 109–112; compromise and 112–116; conceptualization of the event and 8–10; disciplinarity and 102–106; fit and 33–35, 55; heterogeneous 7–8; heuristic functions of 5–7, 149; implications of thinking in terms of 11–13; introduction to 1–4; method assemblage and 11–12, 19; otherness and 12; speculation and 12–13; telling stories in/about the organization and 35–36
responsibilization 67–68
rhetoric 132
rolling luggage 67

Savransky, M. 12
science and technology studies (STS) 20, 23, 29, 34, 88–90, 106, 149
semblance 81, 95, 130–131
sensibility 6, 24–26, 50–52
Serres, M. 7, 10–11, 45, 58, 63–64, 141
Sharma, S. 142
Shove, E. 50, 104
Silverman, D. 144
Social Research: Issues, Methods and Process 3

Sociology of Scientific Knowledge 127
Soneryd, L. 68
Souriau, E. 54, 128
speculation 12–13, 99–100; introduction to 79–81; threat, promise and the idiot 97–99
speculative design 87–97; encountering 88–90; partial others and 90–92; as social science method 92–97
speculative fabulation 81–87
Staying with the Trouble 84
Stengers, I. 7, 13, 54, 68, 128, 149; on cosmopolitics 107–109; on the idiot 58–59, 69
Stenner, P. 127
Stewart, K. 7, 47–48
storytelling 35–36; *see also* anecdote
sub-topicality 25–26, 31–32; noticing and asking in 26–27; posing and querying in 29–31; remembering and reflecting in 27–29

tacit knowledge 125
Tavory, I. 126
teasing 61
temporality 45
Thatcher, M. 21
threshold devices 95
Thrift, N. 145

Timmermans, S. 126
Tsing, A. 31, 83

utopia 82–83

validity 144–145
VANTAblack 136–137
Velcro 66–67
Verran, H. 60, 61
von Trier, L. 23

Walking through Social Research 28
Watson, A. 84
Wetherell, M. 41, 125
'What is Philosophy' 69
Whitehead, A. N. 128; abstraction and 135–136; on compositionism 108; on fallacy of misplaced concreteness 65, 110; on prehensions 53–54; research event and 6–11
Wiebel, O. 142
Wilkie, A. 96–97, 139
Woolgar, S. 68
Wouters, P. 104
writing: as analysis 139; as collaboration 139–141; disseminating and engaging through 141–143

YouTube 26, 74

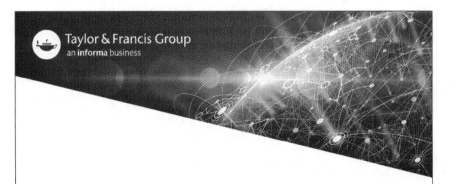

Printed in the United States
by Baker & Taylor Publisher Services